Teaching English

Working with Emergent Language

Ideas and activities for developing your reactive skills in class

Richard Chinn and
Danny Norrington-Davies

Pavilion elt

Working with Emergent Language: Ideas and activities for developing your reactive skills in class

Published by:
Pavilion Publishing and Media Ltd
Blue Sky Offices
25 Cecil Pashley Way
Shoreham by Sea, West Sussex
BN43 5FF

Tel: 01273 434 943
Email: info@pavpub.com
Web: www.pavpub.com

Published 2023

A catalogue record for this book is available from the British Library.

Print: 978-1-80388-128-7
Epub: 978-1-80388-130-0
PDF: 978-1-80388-129-4
Kindle: 978-1-80388-131-7

Pavilion is the leading training and development provider and publisher in the health, social care and allied fields, providing a range of innovative training solutions underpinned by sound research and professional values. We aim to put our customers first, through excellent customer service and value.

Authors: Richard Chinn and Danny Norrington-Davies
Development editor: Penny Hands
Glossary author: Kirsten Holt, Pavilion Publishing and Media Ltd
Content/copy editor: Kirsten Holt, Pavilion Publishing and Media Ltd
Production editor: Hannah Hobbs, Pavilion Publishing and Media Ltd
Publishing head: Kirsten Holt, Pavilion Publishing and Media Ltd
Cover design: Tony Pitt, Pavilion Publishing and Media Ltd
Page layout and typesetting: Tony Pitt, Pavilion Publishing and Media Ltd
Printer: CMP Digital Print Solutions

Working with Emergent Language: Ideas and activities for developing your reactive skills in class

Also available from Pavilion ELT at Pavilion Publishing and Media

A Comprehensive Language Coaching Handbook	ISBN 978-1-80388-035-8
An Introduction to Evidence-Based Teaching in the English Language Classroom	ISBN 978-1-913414-89-4
A Practical Introduction to Teacher Training in ELT	ISBN 978-1-910366-99-8
Become an Online English Teacher	ISBN 978-1-910366-77-6
Best Practices for Blended Learning	ISBN 978-1-911028-84-0
Integrating Authentic Listening into the Language Classroom	ISBN 978-1-914010-45-3
Learning While Teaching	ISBN 978-1-914010-37-8
Live Online Teaching	ISBN 978-1-914010-41-5
Putting the Human Centre Stage	ISBN 978-1-912755-28-8
Structuring Fun for Young Learners in the ELT Classroom	ISBN 978-1-913414-53-5
Structuring Fun for Young Language Learners Online	ISBN 978-1-913414-85-6
Teaching and Learning English in the Early Years	ISBN 978-1-80388-039-6
Teaching English One to One 2nd Edition	ISBN 978-1-912755-66-0
Teaching English with Drama	ISBN 978-1-80388-216-1
Teaching Grammar: From Rules to Reasons	ISBN 978-1-911028-22-2
The Creative Teacher's Compendium	ISBN 978-1-913414-52-8
Understanding Teenagers in the ELT Classroom	ISBN 978-1-912755-00-4
Understanding Teenage Language Learners Online	ISBN 978-1-914010-33-0
ETpedia	ISBN 978-1-910366-13-4
ETpedia Business English	ISBN 978-1-911028-20-8
ETpedia Exams	ISBN 978-1-911028-80-2
ETpedia Grammar	ISBN 978-1-912755-02-8
ETpedia Management	ISBN 978-1-912755-27-1
ETpedia Materials Writing	ISBN 978-1-911028-62-8
ETpedia Teacher Training	ISBN 978-1-913414-16-0
ETpedia Technology	ISBN 978-1-911028-58-1
ETpedia Teenagers	ISBN 978-1-911028-44-4
ETpedia Vocabulary	ISBN 978-1-912755-26-4
ETpedia Young Learners	ISBN 978-1-911028-21-5
Successful International Communication	ISBN 978-1-912755-13-4
Langwich Scool	ISBN 978-1-80388-004-4
Teaching English to Health and Social Care Workers	ISBN 978-1-911028-07-9

For full details of all our books, events and our new-look *Modern English Teacher* magazines, go to: **https://www.pavpub.com/pavilion-elt.**
Visit: **www.modernenglishteacher.com**

About the authors

Richard Chinn is an experienced teacher and teacher educator based in the UK. He works at International House London, where he trains teachers on initial and in-service teacher development courses; he is also a teaching associate at King's College London, where he works on MA and BA courses. He has taught and trained teachers in a number of countries in Europe, Africa, Asia, Central and South America, and the Middle East. He regularly presents at conferences, and delivers workshops to teachers and trainers. His main professional interests are in classroom interaction, teacher education and teacher development.

Danny Norrington-Davies is a teacher and teacher educator at International House London. He has taught and worked with teachers in Europe, Asia, Africa, the Middle East and South America, and he regularly presents at conferences. Along with emergent language, his interests in ELT are creativity, classroom interaction, grammar teaching and materials development. His first book, *Teaching Grammar: From Rules to Reasons*, was published by Pavilion Publishing and Media in 2016.

Contents

Acknowledgements

Along with all the learners who allowed us to record their lessons so we could collect data on our teaching, we would like to thank the following for their contributions to the book: Holly Bailey, Jack Barron, Nick Bilbrough, Andrea Borsato, Jack Brighthouse, Giada Brisotto, Joshua Cannon, Chia Suan Chong, Linda Commisso, Melanie Cooke, Fenella Dale, Mamadou Kally Diallo, Khassoum Diop, Başak Erol, Steve Ferrara, Richard Gallen, Anastasiia Gavriushina, Yiota Gkiaouri, Luiz Gutierrez, Nick Hamilton, Katy Kelly, Sam Launay, Tim Matschak, Yaye Binetou Mbaye, Rodrigo Moreno, Will Morrow, Katherine Moynihan, Mansour Sy Ndiaye, Irina Nosova, Kadir Özoy, Alex Pinnell, Alex Quinn, Vicky Saumell, Gemma Smith, Zoe Helen Solomon, and Anne Timson.

We would like to thank the teachers and trainers we have worked with over the years who have had an impact on our development, especially those at International House London. We would particularly like to thank Melissa Lamb for all her ideas and inspiration, Maureen McGarvey for being a great mentor, and Sheila Thorn, Ben Beaumont, Chris Tang, Martin Dewey, Ursula Wingate and Marie Willoughby for their support and ideas. Most of all, we would like to thank Nick Andon for being an inspirational mentor, colleague, supervisor, and friend, and for getting the research started in the first place. We could not have written this book without him.

We especially want to thank Kirsten Holt and everyone at Pavilion for this opportunity and all their help over the course of writing the book. We would also like to say a huge thank you to Penny Hands for being such an insightful and supportive editor in helping us shape the book.

From Richard: I'd like to dedicate this book to my parents and Jimmy for their endless support and encouragement.

From Danny: Thank you, Gemma, as always, for everything. I'd like to dedicate this book to my parents for all their love and support over the years.

Introduction

> ***emergent language (n)*** *unplanned language that is needed or produced by learners during meaning-focused interactions. This language is then explored through reformulation, clarification and support from the teacher.*

We did not set out to be teachers who predominantly work with emergent language. It is not something we were trained to do, nor was there a specific moment in our careers when we both decided that this was an approach to teaching that we thought we should take. There was not one moment in class that provided an instant spark, nor did we draw solely on the teachings of a specific expert or methodologist in the path we took.

So how did it happen? We believe that, like language learning itself, our ability to work with emergent language and our belief in the importance of doing so developed over time, as did other aspects of our teaching. Our beliefs and skills did not develop in isolation either. There were multiple factors and influences that helped us along the way, including interactions with teachers, both new and experienced, echoing Freeman's (2016) suggestion that teacher learning and development is a social process, and that teachers are made over time through experience, input, feedback, and support.

What have been the key factors to writing this book? The first is our experience in the classroom. By regularly working with emergent language, we have seen first-hand those rewarding learning moments when learners respond to on-the-spot feedback by incorporating a new word or phrase in their speaking, notice gaps and reformulate their output, or make that lovely 'aaah' sound when they suddenly understand the meaning of a word or phrase. We have also observed learners becoming more confident about interacting in English through the support and scaffolding that a focus on emergent language can give them. Videoing our lessons and transcribing what we see has also been important in helping us become more aware of how we work, how learners react and respond to emergent language moments, and what we still need to learn and develop in our practice. We have also been happy that learners have told us how much they have enjoyed and learnt from this way of working.

Our experiences as teacher trainers have also been important. Regular discussions with teachers-in-training have shown us that many are unsure about whether they have the skills to work with emergent language, and when or why they should do so. We are regularly told about the difficulties teachers have encountered when trying to work with learner output, or the lack of support or input they have had in this area. In fact, we have learnt over time that many teachers have different perceptions of what emergent language is, which is perhaps down to the curious fact that little has been written on teachers' views about working with emergent language or how they should do so. Observing both new and experienced teachers has also been especially vital, as it has shown us that everyone can work with learner output, even if they don't believe that they can. They often just need a little nudge.

We have gained so many ideas through conversations with colleagues at International House London and King's College London, as well as teachers and teacher educators all over the world. Though we said above that we have not drawn on the teachings of a specific writer or methodologist, we have been greatly influenced by the work of Scott Thornbury and Luke Meddings and the idea of 'teaching unplugged', which gave a name to what we were doing and helped us better understand the principles underpinning it. We have also drawn inspiration from Jane and Dave Willis and their models of Task-Based Language Teaching (TBLT), as well as Mike Long's concept of Focus on Form. Steve Walsh's work on **Classroom Interactional Competence** has also been influential, as have his ideas on how to research classroom interaction. We were also fortunate to participate in a research project run by Dr Nick Andon at King's College London that enabled us to explore and question our own teaching, as well as giving us a greater understanding of how teachers can and do work with emergent language. In fact, Nick has been, and continues to be, an influential mentor to both of us.

So, is the ability to work with emergent language just a skill that a teacher develops over time? We believe that that is a part of it, but through this book we hope to convince more teachers to give it a go earlier in their careers. We also hope that the input and tasks found in the book will help to speed up the process of developing teachers' skills in this area. We would also like this book to provide evidence, support, and ideas for those who believe that they can't work with emergent language, either because they lack the skills or because they are unsure why they should do it. The stories and examples of successful teaching, learning and reflective professional development in this book have mostly come from teachers we have worked with and classes we have observed, and for many of the teachers, it was their first steps in working with emergent language that provided the examples. We intend that these stories should provide not just ideas but inspiration, too.

This publication is a resource for teachers wishing to develop their interactional skills and the way they work with, and respond to, learner output in the classroom, whether they choose to make it a significant part of their teaching or simply wish to make more time for brief emergent language moments in their classes. It is also aimed at teacher educators looking for ideas and techniques they can use to develop teachers in this area.

How the book is organised

The book provides both theoretical and practical ideas, backed up with findings from our reading, action research, teaching, and teacher training.

Part 1 of the book is largely theoretical and includes the following chapters:

- **What is emergent language?** (pages 7–12), which provides a definition of emergent language and give examples of how teachers in different contexts work with it in their classes.
- **Why work with emergent language?** (pages 13–28) then describes the rationale for working with emergent language by discussing how it not only leads to language development but also increases learner motivation and agency.
- **Creating the right conditions** (pages 29–52) looks at how teachers can create the conditions for generating emergent language in classes.
- **How to work with emergent language** (pages 53–74) draws on our research and evidence from the literature to look at the different ways in which experienced teachers typically respond to learner output and work with emergent language.
- **Exploring emergent language in lessons** (pages 75–102) closes this section by looking at how teachers might choose what emergent language to focus on, and how they might then deal with aspects of meaning, use, form and phonology in feedback. We will also briefly explore how you can review and recycle emergent language.

Part 2 is more practical, providing ideas, tips and tasks to help teachers develop their emergent language skills, either by themselves, with a peer or with a mentor. It includes ideas for teacher educators looking for ways of developing the teachers they work with, as well as explore how teachers in different contexts might work with emergent language.

- **Teacher development and emergent language** (pages 105–128) looks at how teachers can develop their skills in general by doing awareness-raising tasks, collecting evidence about their teaching practices, reflecting on what they do in class, and monitoring and tracking their own development.
- **Development tasks, ideas and commentaries** (pages 129–196) provides teachers, teachers-in-training and teacher trainers with a series of tasks designed to develop techniques and skills for working with emergent language. Each task is accompanied by a commentary, where we look at what practising teachers have gained and noticed from doing the tasks, and the advice they have for other teachers.
- **Emergent language in different teaching contexts** (pages 197–216) draws on the experience of different teachers to offer further tips for working with emergent language in different contexts. It also aims to dispel the notion often raised in discussions that teachers whose first language is not English are less well equipped for working with emergent language than those who have English as an L1. We firmly believe that this is not the case.

The **Appendix** provides definitions of key terminology and lists the references in full. Throughout this book you will find certain words have been highlighted in bold (usually in their first instance of appearing in the main body of the book) to signal that they can be found in the **Glossary** at the back of the book (pages 217–230), where you will find them explained in easy-to-digest terms. We have also included a list of titles that complement this book in the **Useful reading from Pavilion ELT** (page 231). Lastly, the appendix contains a **Bibliography** (pages 232–237), which lists the references we cited, along with the sources we consulted during the writing stages of this book. We hope these pages prove useful.

Let us begin by looking in detail at what is meant by **emergent language**.

Part 1:
In theory

1. What is emergent language?

This chapter focuses on what we mean by emergent language, and examples of teachers working with emergent language in class. Before we jump in, let us look at the two types of language that might feature in a lesson: target language and emergent language. Both are important, the former often being a part of lesson planning, the latter being spontaneously provided to learners at the point of need, so let us establish the key terms from the start:

- **emergent language** unplanned language that is needed or produced by learners during meaning-focused interactions. This language is then explored through reformulation, clarification and support from the teacher.
- **target language** pre-selected language points that are introduced and practised during a lesson. Target language is often included in lesson aims or learning outcomes. For example, 'by the end of the lesson the learners will be able to use the present perfect simple to talk about life experiences'. In this aim, the target language is *present perfect simple*.

Target language versus emergent language

Target language often takes precedence in classrooms as many teachers follow a language-focused syllabus. It also dominates on many teacher-preparation and development courses, where teaching points with specific language aims are given to teachers-in-training as the basis of the lessons they are assessed on. Emergent language, however, is something that is often treated as incidental or less important and is not commonly covered in methodology books for teachers. This has led to many teachers being unclear or in disagreement about the precise meaning of the term, making it harder for them to learn how to work with it.

Some examples of teachers working with emergent language

To better understand what is meant by emergent language, let us look at some classroom situations showing teachers working with it. As you read, think about this question: *Do you ever work with language in the same way as the teachers below?*

Classroom situation 1: Samir

Samir teaches a class of 16-year-olds in southern France. During a lead-in, the learners are brainstorming things people typically do at the weekend. They offer ideas, which Samir listens to and writes on the board (for instance, *go to the cinema, meet friends*). He also asks follow-up questions to explore the learners' ideas.

Samir also works with examples that are less well formed, unclear or could be expressed in another way. For example, when one learner says *do jobs in the house*, Samir introduces the collocation *do household* chores. When another learner suggests *make homework**, Samir indicates there this could be reformulated, and elicits *do homework*. Once they have finished brainstorming, Samir moves on to a listening text about weekends.

Classroom situation 2: Eddi

Eddi works with a small group of adult learners studying in the UK. The learners have read a short newspaper article about a round-the-world coach trip and answered comprehension questions to check their understanding of the text. Eddi then asks them to talk to each other about whether they would like to go on this trip. Eddi listens, and then gives feedback, responding to the learners' ideas and opinions. During this stage, Eddi also deals with any misunderstandings, and reformulates learner language. For example, when a learner says they wouldn't go on the trip because *it's too stress**, Eddi writes this on the board and elicits *too stressful*. They then elicit other adjectives that fit this pattern, for example, *It's too long/expensive* or *The bus is too crowded/uncomfortable*.

Classroom situation 3: Nora

Nora teaches a class of teenagers in Algeria who are preparing for a speaking exam. In one section of the exam, the learners will take part in an interview with the examiner, who will ask them to describe their likes and dislikes. Nora observes the learners as they practise using appropriate phrases to express likes and dislikes. While she is observing, she notices that they are struggling with the use of the adverb *too*, saying things like *I like playing football too much** or *I like spending too much time with my friends**. Nora decides that this would be a useful language point to explore, so she takes time in a follow-up lesson to explore the use of *too*, contrasting it with phrases like *a lot* and *very much*.

Classroom situation 4: Antoine

Antoine teaches English at a secondary school in Senegal. During a conversation class, the learners are talking about famous and important Senegalese people. One learner is telling the class about someone they admire, and asks how to say *Il est mon modèle* in English. Antione gives the learners the phrase *He is my role model.* To check everyone understands, Antoine then asks other learners to name their role model.

Classroom situation 5: Lin

Lin teaches on pre-sessional courses in China for learners preparing to go to university. As part of the programme, the learners give short presentations on a chosen subject. During rehearsals, Lin notes down how well the learners have met the assessment criteria by commenting on organisation, clarity, range of language and task achievement. Lin also notes down examples of useful language that have come up (to share with the rest of the group), as well as examples of unclear language. These notes are then given to the learners after the class to help them with their presentations.

Classroom situation 6: Natalia

Natalia teaches in-company one-to-one classes in Katowice, Poland. These classes are skills focused with an emphasis on speaking, and there are no specific language aims. During a class, a learner is describing what her company does and how it plans to expand. Natalia listens and asks follow-up questions. She does not focus on the learner's use of English or correct errors unless there is something she does not understand. She also records the interaction. The learner listens to the recording to try and identify any areas or issues that they would like to look at in future classes. In other words, Natalia's strategy is to work with language that the learner wants to focus on rather than choosing it herself.

Classroom situation 7: Kadir

Kadir works with learners who are learning English as part of a university programme in Turkey. The course follows a largely grammatical syllabus, and every lesson has a language-focused aim. Following input on the use of the present perfect to talk about situations that started in the past and continue in the present, the learners do a controlled practice activity in which they make sentences about themselves. As Kadir monitors, he notices that a learner has written *I have practised football* since I was a child*. Though the learner has used the target language effectively, Kadir decides to prompt the learner to use the collocation *play football* instead of *practise football*. After the learner reformulates, Kadir continues to monitor.

Classroom situation 8: Pablo

Pablo teaches Italian to adult learners taking evening classes in London, UK. During the lessons, he focuses on skills and language development. In class, the learners are reading a short newspaper article about a criminal case. After the learners have read the text and answered questions, one learner asks *Cosa significa 'colpevole'?* (*What does 'colpevole' mean?*). Once Pablo has explained the meaning, he goes into more detail about how the word is typically used by introducing the phrase *colpevole di omicidio/frode/furto* (= *guilty of murder/fraud/theft*). Then the class moves on to a speaking activity.

If you answered 'yes' to any of the scenarios above, you are including a focus on emergent language in your classes. But what is emergent language, and how is it different from target language?

Emergent language is unplanned

In Kadir's lesson, we see that he has planned to introduce and give his learners practice using the present perfect simple. This is the target language as it is the language that he has planned to teach. Emergent language, on the other hand, describes any language items that arise naturally during interaction in the lesson. These items may be ignored if you want to focus only on the target language or lesson aim. However, you may also choose to focus on emergent language items if you believe they are useful, interesting or learnable – and there is time in the lesson to do so. Alternatively, any emergent language you notice can become the target language of a future lesson. In this sense, you are using the learners' output to diagnose what they need. You can see this in Nora's lesson (pages 8–9), where she notices issues the learners are having with the adverb *too*, and chooses to cover this in a future class.

Emergent language arises from interaction

Emergent language arises naturally and spontaneously in a lesson. It can stem from learner-focused stages or student–student interactions, as we see in Nora and Lin's lessons. Emergent language can also stem from open-class stages and interaction between the teacher and the learner, as in Samir's, Eddi's and Antoine's classes. The third source of emergent language in a class is that which comes from interaction between learners and materials. This can be seen in Pablo's lesson, where a learner notices a word that they do not understand and asks the teacher to explain it.

Emergent language is not all about errors

Emergent language includes errors, as we see in Samir's lesson, where he takes time to deal with the error *make homework**. We also see Nora and Eddi working with errors in their classes. Note, though, that emergent language also refers to instances in which the learners *have* used an appropriate form, but the teacher believes that there is an alternative, more useful or more common way of expressing it. We see this in Samir's lesson, where he reformulates *do jobs in the house* as *do household chores*. What the learner originally said is accurate and comprehensible. However, Samir believes that *do household chores* would be preferable, so he takes time in the lesson to teach it.

In fact, emergent language work does not necessarily involve a focus on grammatical or lexical forms at all. From a sociocultural perspective, teachers can explore what made an interaction successful by looking at communication strategies like **turn-taking**, **paraphrasing**, or **clarification requests**. In other words, emergent language work can focus on pragmatic as well as linguistic properties.

Emergent language work can be initiated by learners

Emergent language work is not only initiated by teachers. It can also be prompted by questions or problems raised by learners about an aspect of language. We see this in Antoine's lesson, where a learner asks how to say a specific phrase in English (*He is my role model*). We also see it in Pablo's lesson, where a learner notices a word in a text that they want the teacher to explain. This means that the onus is not always on you to judge what is useful or interesting, and the learner has agency to make choices about the language they want to learn and use, even if it is something they have noticed outside class.

Emergent language work relies on in-class decisions

As emergent language work is unplanned, any decision about which items to focus on, when to focus on them, and how to do so, is made during the class. This makes emergent language work unpredictable and more difficult than working with target language, which you can prepare for before the class. We will look at how you can deal with such unpredictability and make decisions in **Exploring emergent language in lessons** (pages 75–102).

Conclusion

In summary, emergent language is unplanned language use that arises during meaning-focused stages, produced, or needed by learners as they interact. This language is then explored through clarification and support from you. But why is working with emergent language considered such an important part of the language learning process? This question will be explored in the next chapter.

Professional development

Questions for reflection

- Look at the eight lesson fragments described above. Which are most similar to your teaching context? How does your context influence the way you work with target and emergent language?
- Before moving on to **Why work with emergent language?** (pages 13–28), think about how working with emergent language might benefit learners and facilitate language acquisition.

Things to try

- Arrange to observe a colleague's lesson. Make notes on what language they record and how. Did they home in on any examples of emergent language as you saw in the classroom situations (pages 8–10)?

2. Why work with emergent language?

This chapter focuses on teaching approaches that generate emergent language opportunities and the factors that support working with emergent language in the classroom.

Here are some key terms that are useful to understand from the start:

- **affordance** is an opportunity that arises in class for focusing on emergent language.
- **agency** is the sense of control and feeling of ownership that a learner has over their learning (Larsen-Freeman et al., 2021).
- **focus on form** is the incidental switch from meaning to provide learners with language they need to express their message.
- **focus on forms** is the emphasis on specific items of pre-selected, discrete items of language.
- **scaffolding** is the language support that a more knowledgeable other provides a learner during interaction.
- **zone of proximal development (ZPD)** is the gap between what a learner can do without assistance and what they are capable of with guidance or collaboration with others.

Where does emergent language fit into second language development?

Emergent language is a natural part of language learning. Focusing on emergent language reflects a more organic way of acquiring a language, underpinned by the belief that it is not a linear process whereby linguistic items are introduced and learnt one after another in a set pattern. Instead, language is learnt through interaction with others and the world around us. During these interactions, we notice gaps in our knowledge or language items or strategies we need, and by noticing these things we add them to our repertoire and gradually acquire them. In this way, acquiring a second language (L2) is similar to how we learn our mother tongue. Below are three stories that demonstrate how we might learn an aspect of language by encountering it at the point of need or noticing it in day-to-day interaction.

Language learning story 1: Michael

I spoke a bit of Spanish and could get by in conversation. I was on holiday with friends at my family home in Spain and there was a fault with the electrics. I called my dad, who gave me the number of an electrician, but the electrician only spoke Spanish. During the conversation, he instructed me to go downstairs to the '*caja de fusibles*'. I didn't understand at first, but after going back and forth I realised he was talking about the 'fuse box'. I don't think I'd have ever learnt that word if I hadn't been in this situation, but I've never forgotten it. It really stuck.

Language learning story 2: Zhaida

I remember when I first came to live in London, I couldn't speak much English, and I found it really hard to say what I wanted. I knew what I wanted to say in Turkish but didn't have the words in English. I had a friend who was very good at English and his partner was English, so we would all talk together. Sometimes, when we were talking together, my friend would have to help me. I would tell him what I wanted to say in Turkish, we would have a quick discussion, then he would help me say the phrase or sentence in English. That way I could speak to his English-speaking partner and say what I wanted to say. Through this I learnt how to say lots of new things. I couldn't always use the new phrases straight away on my own, but I did get better over time.

Language learning story 3: Yanis

My first language is Greek, and I thought my English was pretty good, but when I was with some English speakers I got really confused as they kept saying 'though'. I had thought this meant 'although', but that didn't seem to fit in with what they were saying. After listening for a while, I realised it was something they were doing to emphasise what they were saying, like: 'That's not what I mean, though'! I hadn't noticed this before, but after that, I noticed people doing it all the time. That helped me get it.

All three stories are examples of how the situation we are in can create the opportunity for new language to become available to a learner. This new language is emergent language. Anyone who has spent time learning a language will be able to think of examples like these. In the first language learning story, Michael required a piece of new language that was necessary to solve a problem. By learning the item at the point of need, this made it more salient and memorable. In Zhaida's story, we see how a more knowledgeable other supported a less linguistically able person to express their meaning effectively. In Yanis's story, we see how new items or communicative strategies can be noticed from observing language in action around us. **Emergent language moments** can occur in the same way in the language classroom – in other words, in moments of learner need – in occasions when learners seek support, and in the language the learners notice around them. These moments where language emerges in a lesson provide what Allwright (2005) calls **learning opportunities**.

However, in classroom situations, opportunities for working with emergent language are often missed. This can be due to syllabus and assessment requirements, where there is a focus on specific language forms or skills-related competencies. As a result, teachers often don't have time to work with what emerges as they focus on meeting syllabus and test requirements. Obviously, the amount of autonomy and flexibility teachers have with the syllabus varies from context to context. Nevertheless, limited time to respond to, and work with, emergent language is a common concern of teachers we have spoken to.

Before we discuss the ideas and research findings that support the inclusion of emergent language work in class, let us explore the approaches to instructed language learning that created space for interaction and advocated a focus on emergent language.

Which approaches create space for emergent language?

This section will focus on three important approaches to instructed language learning which generate emergent language. First, let us focus on the more general approach of Communicative Language Teaching (CLT), then Task-Based Language Learning and Teaching (TBLT), and finally on Teaching Unplugged (Dogme ELT).

Communicative Language Teaching

The 1960s saw a growing movement for language teaching to focus on meaningful use of language, rather than using translation or rote learning of discrete items. In the 1970s, this approach became widely known as Communicative Language Teaching (CLT). CLT recognised that the prime purpose of language was creating meaning (East, 2021), and therefore that the teaching of language should focus on helping language learners understand and convey a genuine message. At the same time, the Common European Framework of Reference was devised, which focused on what people 'do' with language as well as what they know. This led to a greater focus on functional language as a means to enable language learners to interact and operate in an additional language in everyday life.

In its stronger form, CLT encouraged learners to experiment with making meaning and getting their message across. Because learners were encouraged to interact and convey genuine messages, CLT provided fertile ground for emergent language work: it created opportunities for learners to notice gaps in their performance, seek guidance from others and notice how language was being used by those around them. This communicative view of language learning in the classroom mirrors the incidental way in which learners pick up aspects of the language in everyday life, as we saw in the stories above. However, there was little mention of emergent language in methodology books at the time, and teachers were not given much guidance on how they might work with it in their classes beyond exploring error correction techniques.

CLT implemented an eclectic mix of procedures and techniques borrowed from other approaches and methods. In its purest form, its focus on meaning opened up the opportunity for emergent language. However, the reality was, and still is, that there was often an emphasis on teaching target language and discrete-item grammar. This has often come in the form of the popular Presentation–Practice–Production (PPP) procedure, whereby the teacher introduces a structure by way of a situation, then moves on to controlled, followed by less controlled, practice of the structure that has been introduced. The lesson finishes with some error correction of the target language. This approach to lesson design was commonly, and sometimes still is, employed and advocated on teacher training courses. The influence of the PPP procedure and the prevalence of a grammar syllabus is present in many current ELT coursebooks. While PPP can provide priming of new language for learners, if followed strictly, it reduces the opportunities for language to emerge during lessons, as the focus is on the correct use of the target language.

Task-Based Language Teaching

CLT paved the way for other meaning-focused classroom ideas. One such idea is that of Task-Based Language Teaching (TBLT), which became popular from the 1980s onwards. TBLT embodies the belief that language is learnt through the creation of a need to communicate (East, 2021). In TBLT, learners perform tasks with communicative outcomes in which language is the vehicle for communication rather than being the destination, as was the case with the PPP procedure – in other words, completing a task is the objective and language is supplied when required or in feedback. As an approach to learning, TBLT therefore creates a role for language to be supplied as and when the learners need it. In **Creating the right conditions** (pages 29–52), you will discover how tasks can create conditions for emergent language.

Teaching Unplugged and Dogme ELT

The term 'emergent language' seems to have come more widely into use in the ELT community around the early 2000s, when Dogme ELT (later known as 'Teaching Unplugged') was first widely discussed. Dogme ELT was a movement in language teaching which sought to remove a prescriptive syllabus of linguistic entities and replace it with interaction and a focus on emergent language. This approach sees learning as a social and dialogic process, where language 'emerges' rather than being 'input' in the traditional sense. The proponents of Dogme, Scott Thornbury and Luke Meddings, see language learning as an organic process that occurs when the conditions are right (Meddings & Thornbury, 2009), as we see in our stories above. These conditions are dependent on a humanistic stance to teaching, where the focus is on the learner and their feelings, experiences and voice, rather than their linguistic knowledge and competence.

Dogme ELT sees emergent language as language that arises in a lesson when learners are engaging meaningfully, with the teacher helping them by drawing their attention to language to aid the communication (see Thornbury, 2005). In this way, learning can be seen as dialogic. Rather than purely transmitting knowledge to the learner, the teacher supports them in constructing their message and gaining control over new linguistic forms to convey their intended meaning. This process is called **scaffolding**. A conversation in which meaning is co-constructed between teacher and learner is demonstrated in the dialogic exchange in Extract 2.1, where a learner is describing an ancient city in his home country, Syria.

Learner:	It's an ancient city and when you walk around … you can … [mimes breathing in deeply] the history is in the air.
Teacher:	It sounds amazing. Perhaps you can say *you can smell the history*. [Writes on the board] Is that what you mean?
Learner:	Yes, you can smell history in the air.
Teacher:	Yes, I like that. That's a nice phrase [adds ***in the air*** on the board].

Extract 2.1: Language input at the point of need

In this open-class exchange, the learner tells the group about a city in their country. The teacher responds to the message and reformulates the utterance to help the learner say what they want to say. The learner, who already understands the metaphor of *smell the history*, picks up on the reformulation and extends the metaphor. Listening to this, the teacher realises that the learner's extension is interesting and worth sharing with the class, so they write it on the board. The teacher can go on to explore this metaphor further by checking if the other learners understand what it means and how they might use it in other ways. This is an example of how language is 'created' in class. A learner expresses a meaning, and the role of their teacher is to listen to the learner and help when needed. This process is known as **scaffolding**, which we will look at in more detail later in this chapter (see pages 23–25).

The broad umbrella of CLT and meaning-focused approaches such as TBLT and Dogme have enabled teachers to create the right conditions for **emergent language** in class. However, the term emergent language is uncommon in the academic literature on classroom interaction, despite the fact that it has become a popular topic in ELT blogs, practical articles for teachers and conference talks. There is also little mention of the term itself in books and teacher development materials that provide a strong rationale for its use. The following section therefore presents an argument for why you should create space for emergent language in lessons. The reasons are not given in order of importance, and there is naturally some overlap in the ideas, but all factors feed into a rationale for working with emergent language.

Why focus on emergent language?

1. Emergent language helps learners at the point of need, and language input at the point of need aids acquisition

As we saw in Michael's story (on page 14), the phrase he learnt at the moment he needed it was quickly assimilated into his language repertoire. The idea underpinning this is that language provided at the point of need is more durable and memorable than that provided by a teacher from a pre-designed syllabus. One concept that supports helping learners at their point of need is Michael Long's idea of Focus on Form (FonF) (Long, 1991). Long made the distinction between Focus on Forms, which involves teaching learners discrete items of language one by one, and FonF, which is unplanned language input, provided when the learners need it. FonF happens when the learners are focused on expressing their meaning and their teacher instigates a brief shift to useful language to help them complete their idea. The input can come in the form of a correction or the provision of useful words or phrases (see **Ten intervention techniques**, pages 54–67, for a full discussion). FonF highlights the importance of responding to learners' emerging linguistic needs, which Long argues is key in language acquisition.

The notion of FonF runs counter to the idea of introducing a set of specific language items one after another. Instead, Long sees both the negotiation of meaning and helping learners when language is relevant to their communicative needs as prerequisites for language acquisition.

2. Working with emergent language meets the developmental needs of different learners

Long's notion of FonF also put forward the idea that each learner has an 'internal syllabus', and that space is needed in class to respond to this. He claimed that working with language-related problems or queries through corrective or interactional feedback respects this internal syllabus as it allows for the development of form–function mapping through the use of language during communicative tasks (Long, 2014).

The notion that language learners have a kind of internal syllabus suggests that some learners will be ready or able to learn a specific language item before others. This suggests that teaching a specific language form to a group of learners, as is the case with syllabuses based on discrete grammatical items, will mean that some of those learners will not be developmentally ready for it. This could result in the learners being unable to acquire the form at that specific moment. Many theorists, such as Rutherford (1987), Larsen-Freeman (2003) and van Lier (2004), believe that language teaching must move beyond atomistic rules, and instead focus on the learner's developmental needs. As van Lier suggests, it must focus on '… raising the learners' awareness of what they are trying to say and how they are saying it, and coming up with more efficacious ways of saying that thing' (2004:90).

Of course, learners will always produce errors or miscommunicate something while trying to use more complicated forms before they are ready, but working with emergent language and pushing learners to say what they want to say respects the idea that each learner is following a different developmental trajectory. Regardless of the complexity of what a learner is trying to say, noticing gaps in their performance has also been seen to aid acquisition, as you will see in point 3.

3. Working with emergent language promotes noticing

By drawing attention to language through intervention, you encourage the learners to **notice** new language. Schmidt (1990) hypothesised that noticing new language was a prerequisite for acquisition. By focusing on emergent language, an opportunity for new language to be noticed is created through teacher intervention, reformulation or discussion. The language comes from the learners' interaction, and emergent language work can help fill the gap in their current stage of language proficiency.

Ellis (2016) supports the concept of noticing, suggesting that when learners become aware of a gap in their existing L2 performance which prevents them from expressing what they want, they are sensitised to attend to any input containing the forms they need. Much of the input learners receive on their performance comes in the form of **corrective feedback**. Several meta-analyses suggest that corrective feedback has a sizable positive effect on L2 learning (for instance, Li, 2010; Lyster & Saito, 2010). The positive effects of intervention may be due to the process of noticing, the awareness of the gap, the fact that the intervention has come at the point of need, or a combination of all three. Regardless of the cause, this suggests strong support for the fact that working with emergent language in the form of teacher intervention has an impact on language development.

Of course, intervention is not the only way to enhance the noticing of language. Swain (1985) asserts that learners need to actually produce language in order to be able to notice the gap in their current language knowledge. By producing language, learners are able to see the limits of what they are able to do, and they are more ready to receive input on this as a result.

This was complemented by Long's claim (Long, 1981, revised in 1996) that interaction is integral in triggering the processes involved in language acquisition. Long drew attention to the way in which interaction often creates a need for the 'negotiation of meaning' when there is a breakdown in communication. Exploring communicative breakdowns in feedback and encouraging learners to reflect on how they negotiated their way out of them can provide useful and relevant input.

4. Language learning happens through the contexts we are situated in

Another view that supports working with emergent language is van Lier's belief that opportunities for learning arise incidentally and unexpectedly as we interact with the world around us. Van Lier, who uses the term **emergence** to describe this phenomenon (2004), saw language and language learning from an ecological perspective, arguing that as in the natural world, there are numerous complex systems that influence each other. This echoes Diane Larsen-Freeman's view that language learning is not simply a linear progression, but rather the interaction of countless complex dynamic systems (Larsen-Freeman, 1996).

In other words, it is the interaction of individual systems that lead to the emergence of language, instead of there being a central organising system that governs the way language is acquired. Van Lier made the point that not only is learning a language emergent because it is not only about learning rules, but it is also about getting a feel for how language is used and what you can do with it. He provides the analogy of children learning to play football; rather than learn about the rules, they learn to play by watching and taking part, and the rules are picked up in the playing of the game, as is the skill itself. Involved in this development is playing the game, but also the moves of the fellow participants and their responses to each move. In the same vein, language develops through language use, with learners observing how language works and receiving feedback from those they communicate with. In this way, language is an emergent phenomenon. Van Lier (2014) points out that specific situations provide opportunities for new language to be noticed. Where Allwright (2005) refers to these situations as learning opportunities, van Lier calls them **affordances**.

Social situations create affordances, and the classroom is a social environment that can provide our learners with rich learning opportunities. These affordances lead to language development. As van Lier puts it, 'emergence is the reorganisation of simple elements into a more complex system' (2004:81) – in other words, integrating small new language items into the learner's wider knowledge through experience of language in context. Allowing space for emergent language in class can accommodate this type of language development. In Michael's story above, we see that the problem with the electrics and the need to fix it **affords** the opportunity for new language to be noticed; the same can be said for Zhaida's need for language to express what she wants to say. For Yanis, on the other hand, the situation of listening to expert users of the language **affords** the opportunity for him to notice something new. The same principles are true for the classroom, where the following scenarios create affordances for emergent language:

- opportunities to take part in meaningful interaction
- opportunities to observe interaction
- opportunities for noticing in texts

You can also create affordances by providing learners with feedback on performance, either during interaction or after learners have completed communicative tasks. Research has shown that this is often done in the form of corrective feedback (for example, Lyster & Ranta, 1997; VanPatten & Williams, 2015) or in response to communicative breakdowns. However, feedback also comes in the way someone responds to a message. For example, if a teacher, or other learner, responds as the speaker expects or hopes, this suggests that the message has been conveyed successfully, thereby providing more data for the developing language system. This mirrors first language acquisition, where parents' responses and involvement in dialogue sustain interaction with a child and provide data for language development (Rost, 1990). In terms of language used by L2 speakers, you can also give feedback to learners by providing input on any of the following areas:

- giving alternative ways of producing the same meanings
- sharing language they heard in an interaction that they judge to be new, interesting or useful to share
- responding to learners' questions about an aspect of language

This will be explored in more detail in **How to work with emergent language** (pages 53–74).

Much as you pick up the rules of a game by playing it, van Lier saw language learning as something you pick up as you go along when affordances arise. This idea is situated in what is a wider influential idea in education called **Sociocultural Theory** (**SCT**). This will be explored in more depth in the next point.

5. Learning is a social act in which dialogue supports learning

In all three stories at the beginning of this chapter, another user of the language provided the source for the new language. For example, in Zhaida's case, the interaction with her friend shows how a language learner often needs to draw on the support of others to provide input when needed. This 'other' is often a more proficient or confident language user. In the language classroom, this important role is most often taken by the teacher, though it is also regularly taken by fellow learners as they interact together.

Drawing on the work of Vygotsky (1978), Lantolf (2012) sees learning as happening within interaction. That is to say, the role of others during interaction is instrumental in supporting the mental processes involved in acquisition. Regarding emergent language in the classroom, the role of the teacher is to intervene when they see a gap in knowledge and to provide support until the learners have grasped a point or can manage something on their own. Teachers are also instrumental in guiding the construction of new knowledge through **scaffolding** (Mercer, 1995). To do this, you need to offer support during interaction with learners to support the communicative success of the speaker. This may include the provision of missing vocabulary or the expansion of an incomplete sentence (Lightbown & Spada, 2006).

It can also be done through **clarification questions** or **confirmation checks** that demonstrate misunderstanding or partial understanding to the learner. Scaffolding mediates learning, and in **How to work with emergent language** (pages 53–74), we will examine the choices you have in interaction, whether you are correcting an error or helping the learner by providing language to extend their turn, or to stretch them beyond what they are currently capable of.

In **SCT**, metaphorically speaking, learning happens in the **zone of proximal development** (**ZPD**). This is the theory that learning happens when a learner is challenged beyond what they already know, but not challenged to learn something that is too far beyond them at that time. In this zone, teachers act as a mediator to help the learner at their point of need and to provide language input within the reach of their level of understanding and competence.

The example in Extract 2.2 shows an intermediate learner describing a city. In the interaction, you will see a teacher providing the learner with support through scaffolding until the learner can manage on their own. You can also see that the support the teacher offers is within the learner's capabilities. This is possible because the learner knows what they want to say, so they are primed for any input they receive. The words the teacher offers (*packed*, *busy* or *crowded*) are also within the learner's capability. In fact, it is possible that *busy* is not a new word for the learner, though the collocation could be. Here the teacher is supporting the learner by reformulating the language the learner needs to make their intended meaning clear and comprehensible.

Learner:	Can I say it is a 'back' city?
Teacher:	What's that? Can you spell it?
Learner:	P-A-C-K (Teacher writes *pack* on the board)
Teacher:	Ah a '*packed* city'? No, you can say 'the tube is packed' or 'the bar is packed'. We could say 'a busy city', or 'a crowded city'.
Learner:	It's a busy city.

Extract 2.2: Scaffolding

This co-construction of meaning is a two-way, dialogic process, where a teacher supports the learner in creating the meaning they wish to convey.

In such situations, the teacher must make on-the-spot judgements and pedagogical choices to evaluate and mediate learning, something which is known as 'dynamic assessment' (Lantolf, 2012). Dynamic assessment and the delicate skill of scaffolding learning through interaction is an important area of development for teachers, especially in responding to emergent needs. It is also an area which is not always given enough focus on initial preparation and in-service teacher development courses.

6. Working with emergent language mirrors the incidental way learners pick up aspects of the language in real life

The term 'emergent' has been used in other senses in linguistics, such as **emergent grammar** (Hopper, 1987) and the **emergent lexicon** (Bybee, 2010). Both see language development as a result of experiencing language use. In keeping with this idea are popular ideas in SLA that see language as a process rather than a product. For example, Rutherford (1987) used the term **grammaticisation** to highlight that language learning is an 'organic process' rather than a 'mechanical one' – in other words, grammar is a process of meaning making. He called for language teaching to provide opportunities for **consciousness raising**, whereby the learners are presented with examples of language use from which they, in turn, make sense of in their own way. This is one of the functions of you giving feedback on emergent language. **How to work with emergent language** (pages 53–74) outlines the techniques that you have for raising consciousness about language, while the stories at the beginning of this chapter show how examples that arise in language use can lead to awareness of new language.

In support of language learning as a process rather than the collecting of linguistic items in an orderly fashion, Larsen-Freeman (2003) put forward the idea of **grammaring**. This addresses the fact that learning a language is not about learning a fixed body of rules, but rather actively engaging with the language; she proposed that to make meaning we need **to grammar**. This is a dynamic process of meaning making that a focus on emergent language supports.

7. Working with emergent language respects the fact that language is dynamic rather than fixed

Because every language is dynamic and in constant flux, the forms presented in a coursebook can only ever be a snapshot of what is thought to be acceptable by a specific group of people at a specific time in a specific place. This 'one size' does not fit all, so by working with emergent language, teachers can take into account the characteristics of the language and how it is performed in their particular setting rather than pushing learners to use specific forms or work towards a standard or norm.

Instead, the onus can be on successful communication and interaction. Teachers can therefore use feedback to explore how learners use all their available linguistic resources to successfully make meaning. This can include a focus on useful language or mutually comprehensible forms. It can also include a focus on successful interactional strategies, such as paraphrasing or repairing breakdowns in communication, as well as the use of **translanguaging** (Sifakis et al., 2018), where learners use their L1 or other languages as a natural part of interaction. By regularly using feedback to explore what made communication successful within a specific setting, teachers encourage learners to focus more on what is possible rather than what is expected. This in turn may help learners who worry that they are not making progress or are tied down by trying to attain a set of norms or standards.

8. Focusing on emergent language can help increase learner agency

One of the goals of CLT is to encourage learners to be **autonomous**. 'Autonomy is related to independence and the learner's ability to make "free decisions"' (Larsen-Freeman et al., 2021). In order to be **autonomous**, learners need to have **agency**, the feeling that they have the freedom to act in ways they want to. By focusing on the learner's agenda in class, you can feed their **agency**. That is to say, by providing learners with the language they require to aid self-expression and complete communicative goals, you support their **agency** to act by using language. By making your learners more agentive, you are creating space for their voice in class, thereby encouraging them to take charge of their own learning. Encouraging learners to express their own meanings and exploiting naturally-occurring language also enables learners to experiment and find their voice. Illés and Akcan (2017) found that this increased participation and led to more natural, even playful, interaction between the learners and their teachers. As language or verbal play is related to affect, imagination and creativity, it should be cherished (Cook, 2000). This can be seen in some ways in the teacher's response to *You can smell the history in the air* (Extract 2.1 on page 18), where they express enjoyment of the learner's language creativity.

9. Learners often find emergent language motivating and engaging in class

Another dimension of learning important to emergent language is that of motivation, affect and engagement. Research into motivation has more recently moved on to learner **engagement** (see Mercer & Dörnyei, 2020), which is relevant to emergent language. **Engagement** can be seen as meaningful and active participation in learning, which involves the learners' cognitive, affective and behavioural abilities. When learners are working at the edge of what they know, and are ready to receive new information about language that is of present importance to them, their engagement is often visible. For example, it is common to see learners noting down emergent language that is put on the board and explored by their teacher. Furthermore, learners are often noticeably engaged when their questions are answered, or when they are being helped to communicate an idea with support from the teacher or other learner.

Learner engagement can be observed when learners ask questions about language that arises, write down emergent language or listen to what other learners have to say in moments of meaningful interaction. Working with emergent language is successful when you involve your learners in the learning process by asking questions, eliciting and prompting learners. Emergent language puts the learner at the centre of the learning process, and this is consistent with ideas on engagement (Mercer & Dörnyei, 2020). By working with emergent language, you can encourage learners to take control of their own learning. You can support this by training the learners to keep records of the language that emerges. **Exploring emergent language in lessons** (pages 75–102) provides ideas and examples of how to do this.

Conclusion

Emergent language draws together the SLA ideas of input, interaction, FonF, noticing and output, while engaging with more general learning theories such as engagement, scaffolding and the ZPD. It also draws on the notion of the classroom being a social space, where dialogue is essential to learning, and where learners are exposed to new language as affordances arise. The role of all participants in the language classroom is important in the joint construction of new knowledge, with them all learning during the processes of classroom discourse. Working with emergent language can involve the learners in the learning process by making new language relevant to their immediate needs. The key for teachers who want to work with emergent language is to create the right conditions for language to emerge – in other words, they need to create ways that generate affordances. In **Creating the right conditions** (pages 29–52), we will look at how this can be done.

Professional development

Questions for reflection

- Consider the stories at the beginning of this chapter. As a language learner, have you ever experienced emergent language in this way? What was the situation? What did you learn from the experience?
- Identify a time you have worked with a learner's output to help them say what they wanted to say. What happened? How did the learner respond?

Things to try

- Map out a couple of lessons you have done recently. Then, thinking back to the approaches and techniques you have just read about in this chapter, identify what techniques or approaches you have used to generate interaction and opportunities to work with emergent language in your classes. If possible, do this activity with a colleague and then compare your findings. What can you learn from each other?

3. Creating the right conditions

This chapter focuses on how teachers can create opportunities for emergent language, and the activities, procedures, and teaching techniques that can limit emergent language opportunities. Having discussed the importance of working with emergent language (**Why work with emergent language?**, pages 13–28), let us turn our attention to how teachers can create the right conditions for language to emerge. We can do this by looking at typical lesson stages and classroom tasks that generate emergent language opportunities.

Before we do, however, let us briefly look at how **target language** is introduced in lessons with a **specific language aim**, and how doing this can limit opportunities for emergent language.

Language-focused lesson procedures

When working with target language, it is common for teachers, materials and coursebooks to follow two well-established lesson procedures. For example, a lesson may follow a **PPP** (Present–Practice–Production) procedure. This involves the following steps:

1. The target language being presented or discovered.
2. Learners moving on to controlled practice exercises (such as gap-fills or those requiring them to reorder words to make a sentence).
3. Opportunities for freer production.

Another common procedure is what Anderson (2017) terms **CAP** (Context–Analysis–Practice). A CAP procedure involves the following:

1. The context of the lesson being established, for example through a text.
2. Learners noticing the language in the text and exploring how it is used, perhaps through a guided discovery task (see Figure 3.1 on page 30). This is the 'analysis' stage; it can be either deductive (where you tell learners the rules) or inductive (where learners work out the rules for themselves).
3. The lesson then moves on to practice, which can be either controlled or free, or both.

1. Look at the article about Dilek. Underline all the examples of the present continuous and circle examples of the present simple.

2. Look at sentences a) and b). Which sentence describes something that is generally or always true? Which sentence describes something that is happening at the moment?

a) She's taking a day off today so she's not doing anything.

b) Dilek runs a successful bakery and employs over 20 staff.

Figure 3.1: Guided discovery tasks

In the procedures described above, there is a clear focus on specific language items. There are generally accepted right and wrong answers to the discovery tasks and controlled exercises, which helps teachers prepare for the lesson and think about how they will explain answers or aspects of the target language in feedback. Lessons that follow the stages described have a clear structure and learning outcome. This can help both learners and teachers (especially ones at the start of their career) to feel secure. However, because there are generally accepted correct and incorrect outcomes to the activities and exercises, the amount of emergent language that can occur in the first two stages is limited.

As both PPP and CAP procedures have freer practice stages, there are opportunities for language to emerge. However, because the practice happens at the end of the lesson, it can often be a little more rushed than is desirable. Another drawback is that it is common for teachers to use the feedback stages after freer tasks to focus on how well the learners have used the target language, and this limits how much time they might have for anything else that emerged. In the next section, we will look at how you can create emergent language opportunities within the procedures described above, and in more communication-focused lessons.

Lesson stages

Unlike target language, emergent language does not entail planned presentation stages or pre-designed noticing, guided discovery or practice activities. So, if they cannot plan for it, how can teachers predict when emergent language might occur in a lesson? In fact, many emergent language opportunities occur during the common lesson stages described below, so teachers don't have to make radical changes to their normal practices:

- lead-ins
- responses to texts
- grammaticisation tasks
- communicative tasks
- feedback stages

Let us now look at each in turn and explore how language can occur in them.

Lead-ins

A lead-in is designed to engage learners in the topic of the lesson and to warm them up before the skills-based or language-focused stages. Lead-ins are also used to activate learners' knowledge of a topic, or to stealthily check or introduce any language necessary for ensuing tasks or activities. This is especially the case in lead-in stages that occur before learners read or listen to a text, where engagement in the topic and activation of schematic knowledge is considered necessary for them to process the text for meaning (Hedge, 2006).

One barrier to exploiting lead-ins for emergent language is the fact that many ELT blogs, methodology books and training courses suggest that lead-ins should be brief and kept to a maximum of three to five minutes. This is especially the case when a lesson has a specific language or skills aim, as the lead-in is viewed as a brief warmer to prepare learners for the more focused work that follows. In fact, a good lead-in can be as language-rich and communicative as the freer tasks that follow. It can also produce multiple learning opportunities, as you will see in the examples below.

Brainstorming activities

Brainstorming is a whole-class or group activity that encourages learners to generate ideas or words relating to the topic of the lesson. The learners are invited to contribute to the free flow of ideas, and the teacher's role is to listen to the learner contributions and perhaps record them on the whiteboard. Teachers can decide whether to accept every idea or play a more evaluative role by rejecting ones that do not fit.

Because there is a free flow of ideas, brainstorming activities present ample opportunities for teachers to work with emergent language as it arises. To demonstrate this, look at the board in Figure 3.2 on page 32. In this lesson, a group of intermediate learners studying online are going to read a text entitled 'It's like a drug'. As a lead-in, the learners brainstorm ideas for things that are like a drug. As they share their ideas, the teacher listens and displays ideas on an interactive whiteboard.

Figure 3.2: Brainstorming boardwork

You can see numerous examples of emergent language work on this board. These include:

- highlighting the form *addicted to* + gerund
- inputting lexis that can follow *addicted to*
- types of extreme sports (*water skiing, climbing*)
- words ending in the suffix *-oholic* (*alcoholic / chocoholic*)
- sharing the phrase *adrenaline junkie*

Rather than just boarding ideas and keeping this stage brief, the teacher has used the brainstorming stage as a learning opportunity to introduce new language and reformulate learner output. We will explore the rationale behind how you choose what to explore in **Exploring emergent language in lessons** (pages 75–102).

Prediction tasks

A **prediction task** is often done before learners read or listen to a text. It involves them trying to work out what the text might be about, or what they might hear or read. The prediction is designed to engage the learners in the topic of the text. It also gives them a reason to listen or read, as they do so to confirm or reject their predictions. Like a brainstorming task, there is a free flow of ideas. However, as learners are making predictions, they are pushed to produce longer turns. You can then prompt the learners to use speculative language, thereby further encouraging more complex utterances.

The following prediction task is taken from a lesson delivered by a teacher from Turkey to a group of intermediate (B2) learners studying online (thanks to Kadir Özoy). Before listening to a story told by the teacher, they first look at the mock headline in Figure 3.3, and try to predict what might have happened.

The ☆ Pavilion

BRIGHTON'S FAVOURITE NEWSPAPER

Eight Turkish youths interrogated by FBI

Figure 3.3: Prediction task

As the learners share their predictions, the teacher writes ideas on the board. This is useful as it enables the learners to discuss later whether their predictions were accurate. Writing ideas on the board also enables the teacher to work with what emerges by reformulating learner language, or by providing useful new words and phrases, as we see in Figure 3.4 on page 34. The reformulations are in bold.

He was probably with friends driving somewhere in Turkey.

We think it was a misunderstanding. He was innocent.

It was a serious incident because the FBI were involved.

He might have looked like a bad guy / a suspect.

It could be about | preconceptions of immigrants.
| prejudice against immigrants.

Maybe he committed a crime.

Figure 3.4: Prediction task boardwork

The emergent language work shows that the teacher has chosen to focus on potentially useful words and collocations, such as *misunderstanding*, *commit a crime* and *serious incident*. This is useful as the new lexis is provided at the point of need, which, as you saw in **Why work with emergent language?** (pages 13–28), can lead to better retention. The learners are also better able to understand the new language as the meaning has come from them.

Responses to texts

In the **CAP** procedure described above, the target language is introduced through a text. Before doing the noticing or discovery tasks, which focus on the target language, the learners process the text for meaning. The rationale for this procedure is that the lesson moves from a focus on meaning to a focus on form, and the language is introduced in a clear and meaningful context. This subsequently makes it easier to understand.

To check that the learners understand the text, it is common to set a series of comprehension questions. **Comprehension questions** can be divided into two categories: content questions, which prompt learners to demonstrate general understanding of what they read and listen to, and language questions, which focus learners' attention on specific forms (Freeman, 2014). Comprehension questions can include short-answer questions, true or false, multiple choice, or 'yes or no' questions. An example of typical **comprehension questions** can be seen in Exercise 1 in Figure 3.5 on page 35. The answers to the questions are given in brackets.

Hand-me-downs and queueing: Life for teens in large families

Delia's story

The mornings in my house are never calm or quiet. I have 11 brothers and sisters, so when we are all awake there is constant noise as we fight for the bathroom, eat breakfast, and get ready for kindergarten, school or work.

There are seven rooms in the house, but we all have our own beds. Even Mum and Dad don't have their own room as baby Michael is with them for now. We don't all eat at the same time in the morning, but we have a big family meal in the evening. Everyone must be there. Our parents insist on it. After that we do the chores on the rota, like washing up, putting away the dishes and making packed lunches for the next day; then we do our homework. We have a TV, but no one ever agrees on what to watch, unless there is a good film on. Some of us watch things together on our laptops, though.

1 Read about Delia's family and answer the questions.

1) How many people live in Delia's house? *(14)*
2) Does everyone have their own bedroom? *(No)*
3) When does the family eat together? *(In the evenings)*
4) What does everyone do after dinner? *(They do chores and homework)*

Figure 3.5: Reading text and comprehension questions

Comprehension questions like these are the most common question type in ELT coursebooks and materials (Freeman, 2014), so teachers-in-training on pre-service courses often learn how to use them or how to create their own. **Comprehension questions** are also found in several English language examinations, so learners need to learn how to approach them. Indeed, many teachers would not regard the use of comprehension questions as in any way controversial.

There are, however, some drawbacks to using closed comprehension questions such as those shown in Figure 3.5. Firstly, as they require learners to look for information that is directly stated in the text or worded only slightly differently, comprehension questions like these are not particularly cognitively demanding and lack a genuine challenge for many learners (Mishan & Timmis, 2015). Secondly, comprehension questions with pre-determined answers guide the learners to parts of the text chosen by the writer, rather than to those that interest them (Roberts, 2014). This reduces learner agency, as learners do not have the freedom to approach the text in their own way. Finally, because there is only one 'correct' response, they can fail to engage learners in the content or discourage them from exploring a writer's or speaker's opinions or ideas. This type of question forces all the learners to respond in the same way, regardless of their culture, what they think about the content of the text, where they come from or why they are learning the language (Norrington-Davies, 2018). To sum up, because they have set answers, comprehension questions limit opportunities for language to emerge from the interaction that follows reading or listening tasks. To generate more emergent language in a lesson, it is therefore a good idea to include other types of question alongside, or instead of, comprehension questions. We will look at these alternative question types in the following section.

Personal response questions and evaluative questions

Two types of question that encourage free responses and generate emergent language are **personal response questions** and **evaluative questions**. **Personal response questions** encourage the learner to respond with an opinion or reaction to the content of a text (Freeman, 2014). An example can be seen in Question 1 in Figure 3.6, which asks learners to decide whether they would like to live in a household like Delia's. Evaluative questions, on the other hand, require more considered responses to the text. As we see with the evaluative questions in 2 and 3 below, some judgement or assessment is required, which calls for deeper cognitive processing than personal response questions (and much deeper cognitive processing than closed comprehension questions).

1) Would you like to be part of a family like Delia's? Why/Why not?
2) What are the advantages and disadvantages of growing up in a family like this?
3) What do you think life is like for the family members below? Give reasons for your answers.
    - the parents
    - the eldest child
    - an 18-year-old
    - the youngest child
    - the only boy/girl in the family

Figure 3.6: Evaluative and personal response questions

As personal response questions and evaluative questions generate more extended communicative turns, more opportunities are created for teachers to work with what emerges. This can be seen in the first two contributions in Extract 3.1 below, made by B1 learners studying English in the UK. In both responses, the learners are clear about how they feel about the situation; both also share something about their lives with the rest of the class, which helps build rapport and generates ideas for further discussion. There are plenty of options for their teacher in terms of working with emergent language, both grammatical (*is always 20 people/I has five brothers and sisters*) and lexical (for example, where one of the learners has had to use the Spanish word *nietos* as they do not know or have forgotten the word 'grandchildren').

Learner 1:	In my house in Chile is always 20 people. Brother, sister, *nietos*, cousins, friends. No problem.
Learner 2:	I has five brothers and three sisters. Is nice because the friends for your brother are friends for you. And your old brothers always your home. Your plans your brother plans.
Learner 3:	Oh my god no! Too many people!
Learner 4:	Is big table in the house for dinner, no?

Extract 3.1: Responses to personal response questions

Two further advantages of personal response and evaluative questions can be seen in the responses from Learner 3 and Learner 4. The response of Learner 3 demonstrates how strongly they feel about the situation. The response of Learner 4 is also interesting as it shows that the learner is thinking critically about the situation and imagining aspects of living in a large family. All these responses are significant: Tomlinson (2011) suggests that any follow-up noticing or language work is more salient if the learners have been affectively and cognitively engaged in the content before they unpack it for language. One further way to generate engagement in a text is for learners to write their own questions before they read or listen.

Text summaries

Another useful text-based activity is summarisation. As well as being something people regularly do, this is an important skill in higher education, where learners need to summarise articles or academic sources. Summarisation is therefore useful training for any student preparing to go to university.

In general language classes, summarisation can be a useful way to check that the learners have identified the main or supporting ideas in a text. It can also be used to develop paraphrasing skills, and as the focus is on the meaning of the text, this is a simple way to generate emergent language opportunities. One way to make a summarisation task more fun or challenging is to set little obstacles. For example, you can ask the learners to summarise the text in a specific number of words. This can be done two or three times, with the number of words being reduced each time. You can also ban the learners from using specific words from the original text as this challenges them to come up with alternatives. You can then use the feedback to explore the learners' words and compare them with those in the text.

An example of learners summarising a text can be seen in Figure 3.7 below. In this activity, the learners have read a text about a person travelling and working in southern Africa. The learners first discuss the content of the text. Then they summarise it in 100 words. Look at the examples of how three different learners paraphrased the last sentence of the opening paragraph.

> I'd just left university and, quite weirdly, I found a job delivering vending machines to schools in Gaborone in Botswana. It wasn't a proper job, though. I knew the owners of the company and they were **putting me up** at their place, so I helped at work and **did some odd jobs** around the house.

Learner responses

1) He **lived their house** and **did small jobs** for them.
2) I **stayed with my friends** and **did chores** for them in the house.
3) He worked for them and **did jobs they need in the house, like fix a door**.

Figure 3.7: Text summarisation responses

In each summary, the learners have demonstrated that they understand the general meaning of the excerpt and some of the more complex lexis, for instance, *put someone up*. To build on this, the sentences have given the teacher several options in terms of working with emergent language either in feedback or as they monitor. For example, the teacher could briefly elicit which preposition is needed in *he lived their house* (Sentence 1) or explore the difference between *chores* and *odd jobs* (Sentence 2). Sentence 3 is a little more complex as there are several ways of reformulating *jobs they need in the house*, so this would be a useful area to explore.

Grammaticisation tasks

Grammaticisation tasks involve learners being given sentences or short texts with words but no grammar – in other words, there are no articles, tense endings, plurals, prefixes or suffixes. The learner's task is to add the grammar. An example of a grammaticisation task can be seen in Figure 3.8. It uses the same text as the summarisation task above, but this time the grammar has been omitted.

3A Look at the story below, where the grammar has been taken out. With a partner, rewrite the text with the correct grammar.

> I just leave university and, quite weird, I find job deliver vending machines to school in Gaborone in Botswana. It no proper job though. I know owner company and they put me up at their place, so I help at work and do some odd job around house.

Figure 3.8: Grammaticisation task

There is a sound rationale for using grammaticisation tasks. First, grammaticisation tasks replicate the process people naturally follow as they acquire their first language, where they begin by using words or fixed chunks of language before gradually adding the grammar (Batstone, 2006). For example, language learners start by using words with minimal or no grammar (*dog cold dog inside*) and, over time, the grammar gradually emerges (*The dog is cold. It wants to come in.*).

Grammaticisation tasks also allow for greater learner agency, as it is the learners who decide what grammar is most appropriate. This means there is useful negotiation and discussion of rules or reasons as they complete the task. In addition, the focus on form used in grammaticisation tasks makes them a useful halfway house between controlled practice exercises, where there is usually one correct answer and repetition of specific forms, and freer communicative practice.

In terms of emergent language, grammaticisation tasks enable you to work with common differences, alternatives, errors and/or interesting language produced by the learners. However, they also allow for differentiation, as varying things will emerge for different learners or level groups. This gives you the opportunity to respond to different learner needs as you monitor. You may remember from **Why work with emergent language?** (pages 13–28) that this is a key aspect of successful language learning.

Dictogloss

Another type of grammaticisation task is dictogloss. This is like the activity described above, but in a dictogloss, you read aloud a short text such as that in Figure 3.9 (note that the forward slash (/) represents a pause). The learners listen to the text and note down key words. The key words are then used as a base for the text reconstruction. Like the grammaticisation task, the reconstruction is done in pairs or groups; this allows for negotiation and discussion as learners compare what they wrote down with what forms or words best fit the context.

> The mornings in my house are never calm or quiet / I have 11 brothers and sisters / so when we are all awake / there is constant noise as we fight for the bathroom / eat breakfast / and get ready for kindergarten / school / or work /

Figure 3.9: Dictogloss

As we have discussed, in each of the grammaticisation tasks, you can work with emergent language as you monitor groups working together. By exploring the emergent language at this time, you can work with the language produced by each group of learners, thereby allowing for differentiation and reformulation at the point of need. You can also use an open-class feedback stage to explore one or more reconstructed texts and look at the emergent language together. To do this, you can use the monitoring stage to pick interesting or useful examples to share. Alternatively, you may choose to pick up on common errors or issues that would benefit the whole class.

Communicative tasks

If we want to create the perfect conditions for emergent language work, learners need to be given opportunities to take part in extensive communicative tasks that allow for genuine and meaningful interaction.

Communicative tasks are perfect for generating emergent language because they are meaning-focused and, if they are appropriately pitched, learners will be able to draw on all their available linguistic skills, resources and knowledge to complete the task. Good communicative tasks also have a communicative goal or outcome as opposed to a linguistic one, so success is judged on completing or participating in the task rather than the language used to do so (Willis & Willis, 2007). This means that learners are free to say what they want and how they say it rather than being limited by a specific set of acceptable answers or forms.

Of course, opportunities for freer, communicative practice are built into procedures such as PPP. However, as mentioned earlier, it is not uncommon for teachers to run out of time for practice or feedback on emergent language because the final practice often comes at the end of the lesson. Another drawback of using communicative tasks within a PPP framework is that where a communicative activity has been designed to provide practice of a discrete language item, learners focus more on using this item accurately than on what they genuinely want to say. This turns the communicative task into something more like a practice exercise (Ellis, 2003), thereby limiting emergent language opportunities.

Pre-task stages

Before we look at communicative tasks that generate emergent language, it is worth noting that it is not just the task itself that creates emergent language opportunities. By adopting a speaking or task cycle that includes preparation time or pre-task stages, there are further opportunities to work with what learners produce.

For example, in a pre-task stage such as that suggested by Goh & Burns (2012:153; see Figure 3.10 for a representation) or Willis (1996), learners are given opportunities for guided planning. This can involve brainstorming ideas, note taking, or rehearsal time during which teachers can monitor and prompt learners with ideas or suitable lexis or forms. This means that the teacher can deal with learner language or gaps at the point of need rather than waiting to deal with it in post-task feedback stages. This stage can also give the learner greater confidence in communicating their message during the task itself.

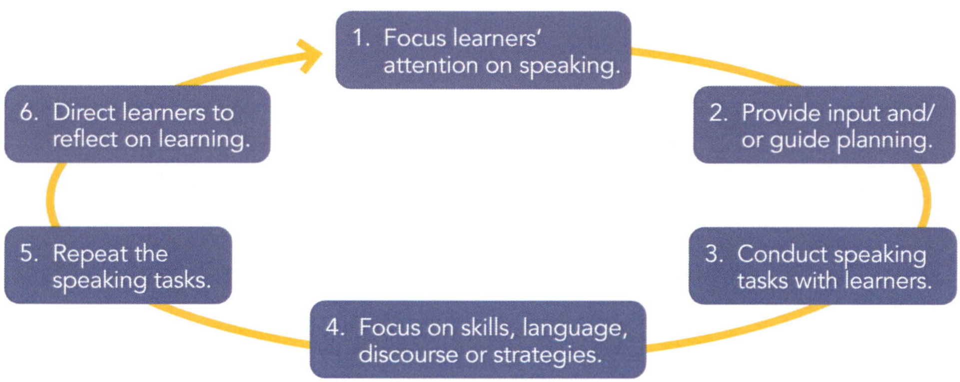

Figure 3.10: A teaching cycle

Types of task

Certain task types are ideal for giving learners extensive communicative turns and generating emergent language. As these tasks involve learners working together to communicate ideas, it is common for emergent language work to be done during the feedback stage that follows so as not to interrupt the communicative flow. However, there may be occasions when you need to intervene in order to prompt or guide your learners when communication stalls. How and when you might do this will be looked at in **Exploring emergent language in lessons** (pages 75–102).

Stories and anecdotes

As Heathfield (2014) suggests, stories and storytelling are ideal for building language learners' self-confidence as well as their language skills. Because storytelling is a common real-life activity, it is a useful skill for learners to acquire. Shared stories also help to build and strengthen relationships in the classroom as you and your learners share information about your life or culture. As stories are meaning-focused and often unique, they are also rich in emergent language opportunities.

Storytelling tasks can be set by teachers with learners given planning and rehearsal time to help them fine-tune their stories. This can be especially useful if the learners are inventing a story. However, it is also useful to set time aside in classes for the stories and anecdotes that arise as learners respond to lesson topics. As these stories are meaningful and personal, they are often rich in emergent language opportunities.

Problem-solving tasks

Problem-solving tasks are another great way of giving learners extensive speaking turns. When learners analyse a complex situation to identify what the problem is and decide on a solution, they are learning thinking and negotiation skills that will serve them in all aspects of their lives. Problem-solving tasks are also rich in emergent language opportunities as you can analyse and explore not only the language your learners use to complete the task, but also their interactional skills as they take turns to suggest, justify, accept and reject ideas.

Ranking tasks

Another task that gives learners the opportunity to develop interactional skills is the ranking task. Like a problem-solving task, a ranking task requires the learners to get together to use thinking and negotiating skills. For example, they might be asked to rank the ten most important qualities of a language teacher or to decide which job should be paid the most. As such, ranking tasks give learners opportunities to take turns and suggest, justify, accept and reject ideas.

Information gaps

An information gap is a task that relies on the exchange of information between learners. To facilitate this, each learner in a pair or small group is provided with different information in the form of a picture, an infographic, a short text, or different parts of the same text. Once they are ready, they exchange the information they have with another learner in order to get the information they are missing and to form a complete picture of a situation. This task provides opportunities for communication as the learners have to give and request information to complete the task. An example task could be two people telling the same story from a different perspective, for example, a suspect in a crime and a witness. Once the learners have heard both stories, they then decide which one is true.

Debates

Also known as an opinion gap activity (Willis, 1996), a debate or discussion gives learners the opportunity to take longer speaking turns as they offer and defend their own position and counter arguments. Debating and discussing topics is something that language users will do in academic, social and professional settings, so it is an important skill to develop. With the right topic, preparation and research time, debates can be fun activities to do in class.

Role plays

Role plays are useful as they enable language learners to practise communicating in the kind of real-life situations they will encounter when travelling to countries where the L2 is spoken or when communicating online, for example, on Zoom. They provide rehearsal time in a safe and supportive environment, where feedback can be used to build their confidence, language skills and knowledge of how typical communicative exchanges, such as ordering coffee or booking a doctor's appointment, are structured. Harmer (2009) suggests that as well as being fun and memorable, role plays offer opportunities for quieter learners to express themselves more freely and openly.

Another advantage of role plays is that they can be matched to the specific needs of learners. For example, for a group learning a language for business purposes, role plays can enable them to rehearse taking part in business meetings or negotiations; a learner travelling to another country could role play booking a hotel or shopping in a market.

Classroom writing tasks

Writing tasks also create opportunities for working with emergent language. Much like with spoken tasks, giving learners time to plan, prepare and draft a piece of communicative writing enables you to monitor and help the learners at their point of need, whether this is with language items or aspects of discourse such as organisation, style, coherence and cohesion. This can be especially fruitful where learners are planning together as you can observe their thinking and help with ideas.

Emergent language work can also be done when learners are encouraged to edit their writing before producing a final draft. As learners edit, you can move around the class helping them notice issues and reformulate their work. As in a spoken task, feedback can be given when learners complete their final version, but it is important to ensure that learners receive feedback on content and a genuine response to their writing as well as feedback on language.

Choosing and setting up tasks

Of course, it is not just a matter of giving the learners something to talk about and letting them get on with it. This will not always work as there are several additional factors that can limit how much learners are able or willing to contribute to a discussion. Teachers therefore need to have criteria that they refer to as they choose tasks for their learners. Partially drawing from Willis & Willis (2007) and Ur (1996), we recommend the following criteria as a useful checklist both for the suitability of the task and the extent to which it will generate emergent language opportunities:

- *Will the topic and task engage the learners?*
- *Is the topic and task relevant to the learners' world and real-life needs?*

- *What language items are necessary to complete the task appropriately?*
- *Can the learners do the task autonomously with minimal teacher intervention?*
- *Are learners able to freely express their ideas and opinions or draw on their own experiences to complete the task?*
- *Does the task enable all learners to participate equally?*
- *Does the task have the potential to create positive relationships between the learners?*
- *Will there be opportunities for creative language use?*
- *Does the task develop communicative or interactional strategies?*
- *Can you predict the language items that learners will need during the task? Is this language you feel comfortable exploring in feedback?*

Motivation and engagement

When choosing tasks and creating the conditions in which learners are motivated and willing to fully engage in interaction (and classes in general), Mercer (2019) describes three main factors that teachers should take into account. These are:

1. promoting learners' sense of competence
2. autonomy
3. relatedness.

A **sense of competence** refers to learners feeling that they have the skills to manage the tasks given them by their teacher. Of course, they won't all achieve the same levels of proficiency in completing the task, but they should all feel that they can do it. To further foster their sense of competence, post-task feedback can involve you asking learners to share interesting ideas and stories that they heard, thereby demonstrating that they recognise that the learners have succeeded. You can use the feedback stage to share examples of effective or interesting learner language as well as areas for improvement, thereby building learner motivation.

The second important factor is a **sense of autonomy**. Mercer (2019) says that for teachers, this means building in options for 'choice and voice' where possible. This can include 'big choices', such as letting learners choose topics they want to discuss or tasks that they would like to do. Where this is not possible, teachers should ensure that learners are free to offer their own ideas and opinions in completing tasks. If learners feel that they have a voice, they are more likely to contribute during freer tasks, which in turn generates more emergent language opportunities.

The third factor is a **sense of relatedness**. This refers to the quality and strength of relationships that learners have with both you (as their teacher) and their classmates. It is useful to spend some class time fostering positive relationships within the group. This can be done by learning about the learners as individuals and finding out about their interests and beliefs, which helps you choose appropriate and relevant tasks. It can also be useful for teachers to model tasks and behaviours themselves. For example, you can share experiences, stories and opinions before the learners do so themselves. You can also use your monitoring and feedback stages to show that you are listening to, interested in, and respectful of the ideas and opinions of your learners as well as monitoring the language they use. If possible, it is also nice to spend time before and after classes chatting with learners. As Mercer says, simply by engaging in small moments of interaction and sharing, we help to build, maintain and strengthen the personal relations within the class.

All of these factors are important for engagement and motivation to blossom in classes. They are also vital for creating the conditions for language to emerge: if learners feel they have a sense of ownership of their learning, feel confident about their skills and safe in the environment, they are more likely to participate in communicative and meaning-focused stages. If learners feel engaged, motivated and safe, they are also likely to see the value of teachers working with their emergent language, including errors. This will be the case in particular if you make it clear why they think it is useful to work with learner language through reformulations.

Feedback stages

There are differing views on when it is best to intervene and help learners with their language use. Researchers such as Loewen (2018) hold that input or feedback is most effective when it occurs at the time the learner needs it. However, various methodologists and teachers (for example, Ur, 1996; Harmer, 2009) believe it is best not to intervene when learners are doing a communicative task as this can interrupt the flow and put them off communicating. This choice is considered in greater depth in **Exploring emergent language in lessons** (pages 75–102).

Even though there is a delay, saving the feedback stage till after communicative tasks provides teachers with ample opportunity to work with emergent language. Firstly, because teachers are not involved, they have time to walk around the classroom listening to the learners and noting down interesting examples of language or errors. They can then write these examples on the board in preparation for the feedback stage. Because the errors and examples of language are on the board, it is not clear which learner said them. This means learners are not being put on the spot and their errors are not highlighted to the rest of the class.

The feedback stage also means that there is a clear switch from a focus on meaning to a focus on form, though it is important that you take time to explore outcomes and ideas in the feedback, as well as the language. Once the switch to form has occurred, any corrections or reformulations can be explicit. This creates the opportunity for you to elicit why an utterance might have been misunderstood or might be in need of reformulation. This feedback then consolidates learning that has taken place both before and during the task.

Unplanned interactions

Emergent language opportunities can also be generated by allowing for spontaneous communicative moments in class, or what might be called 'Dogme moments' (Thornbury, 2017). These are those lovely instances when the conversation is generated by the learners themselves, who become so involved in the topic or flow that they almost forget that they are still in a lesson. Allowing for unplanned conversations can often be difficult for teachers if they are following a syllabus or if they have limited time to cover items that will be tested later in the course. They can also be challenging for teachers with classes with disciplinary issues as they can be hard to manage. However, there is a sound rationale for letting Dogme moments happen.

Firstly, the discussions can add to learners' sense of competence, autonomy and relatedness, which we have seen are vital aspects of learner motivation and engagement. In addition, unplanned interactions mirror those that learners want and need to take part in when they use the language outside the classroom, where the discourse is mostly unscripted and is co-constructed by the participants (Gil, 2002). Giving time and space for spontaneous interaction means that learners have experiences that enable them to cope with the unpredictability of real-life communication outside the classroom (Illés &

Akcan, 2017). Finally, where language use is genuinely spontaneous and meaning-focused, the interactions are rich in emergent language opportunities.

Questions

Some types of question by their nature extend learner turns and provide teachers with a rich source of material to work with, while others can limit opportunities for learners to interact genuinely with the teacher. This, in turn, can limit emergent language opportunities.

Referential questions

Referential questions are questions that produce genuine contributions from learners (Thornbury, 1996), and this spontaneous, meaningful use of language by learners can in turn provide you with linguistic data to work with. This can be seen in the exchange in Extract 3.2, where the teacher asks two types of referential question to extend the learner's turn. The first question pushes the learner to justify their idea, and the second one is more personal as it checks whether the learner can relate to the idea that they propose. In each instance, the teacher has not chosen to work with any of the language the learner has produced as the message is clear. However, both questions have pushed the learners to communicate further, creating a further opportunity to work with what emerges.

Teacher:	OK, let's have another idea.
Learner:	We think exercise.
Teacher:	Really. In what way can you be addicted to exercise?
Learner:	Some people, if they don't go to the gym or running, they feel bad or nervous.
Teacher:	Ah right. Is that you, or someone you know?
Learner:	No. But I heard it.

Extract 3.2: Referential questions

While referential questions and genuine responses to learner output extend learner turns and potentially give teachers more emergent language to work with, there are other aspects of teacher responses that do not always do this. These responses are overuse of display questions, praise, echo and short wait time.

Display questions

Display questions are ones that a teacher already knows the answer to, so they are commonly used to elicit specific answers or reformulations, or to clarify understanding of language items. They are a key resource for helping teachers organise their lessons and manage learning (Lee, 2006), especially in feedback stages to comprehension tasks, discovery activities and controlled practice tasks. They are therefore an important skill for teachers to acquire. However, because display questions lack the communicative quality of referential questions and generally limit the learners to short responses with preconceived answers, their overuse can limit opportunities for learners to interact genuinely with the teacher. This in turn can limit emergent language opportunities.

Echo

Echo refers to instances when teachers repeat what learners have said. Though this may be for the benefit of the class to validate a response or share it with those that did not hear, echoing tends to end the learner's communicative turn. Echoing is also quite an unnatural response in most real-life interactions, so when teachers use it in response to stories, ideas or opinions, it can create the impression that they are not genuinely interested in what the learner has said. Overuse of echoing has also been seen to interrupt the flow of what learners are trying to communicate (Walsh, 2002).

In terms of emergent language, because an echo looks and sounds the same as a recast, where you repeat what the learner has said but with a reformulation, it is possible that learners do not notice the value or intent of the echo. Reducing the use of echoing could therefore add some value to teacher recasts.

Praise

As motivation is necessary for successful language learning, **praise** is an important way to develop and sustain it by building confidence and creating positive learning experiences. Like echo, however, **praise** in response to learner's stories, ideas or opinions often ends the speaker's turn. It can also create the impression that you are more interested in the learner's use of language than their ideas and opinions. While the genuine interaction in Extract 3.3 is quite an extreme example, it shows how praise can be inappropriate and close down communication.

Teacher:	[After pre-teaching the word *camping*] Has anyone been camping?
Learner:	Yes, I was camping for three months after the earthquake.
Teacher:	Good. Anyone else?

Extract 3.3: Example of inappropriate praise

Here, the use of praise could suggest that the teacher's initial question was a display question, designed to check that the learners understood *go camping* rather than a way of eliciting experiences. However, the learner has interpreted the question as a prompt to share an experience, so in this instance, the praise is inappropriate. It would be more motivating and natural to invite the learner to share the experience if they are willing to go further. A more natural response would also be to express shock or sympathy. Of course, if the learner shared their story, it may not be appropriate for you to then use feedback to work with emergent language (such as the difference between *camping* and *being in a camp*). However, sharing the story can add to the learner's sense of competence, autonomy and relatedness, which increases emergent language opportunities in other ways.

Short wait time

Another aspect of successful interactional competence is extended **wait time**. Wait time is the length of time a teacher pauses after they ask a question or prompt learners. Typically, this is quite short (Walsh, 2011), which limits the thinking time of learners and therefore the quantity and quality of learner responses. Short wait time and teacher interruptions also reduce the chances for learners to self-repair. Studies have shown that extending wait time even by a little can improve the quality of learner responses and lead to more learner questions with both younger learners (for example, Yataganbaba & Yıldırım, 2016) and adults (for example, Walsh, 2002).

As Walsh (2011) suggests, by asking genuine questions, responding naturally to messages, being non-evaluative, and extending our wait time and allowing for pauses, we create the conditions to elicit fuller and more complex responses from our learners. This, in turn, can produce greater engagement and motivation in classes, and generate more emergent language opportunities as a result.

The 'IRF exchange' versus cross-class interaction

Display questions, echoing and praise fit into what Sinclair and Coulthard (1975) refer to as the **IRF exchange**. This is a three-part structure of interaction that begins with a teacher **initiating a response** from the learners. The learner **responds** with an answer or idea, and the teacher **follows up** with an evaluation. An example of the IRF exchange can be seen in the exchange about camping above.

Walsh (2011) describes the IRF structure as the most common model of interaction in the language classroom. Though this structure helps teachers to organise lessons and elicit and monitor learner responses, relying on it can limit the opportunity for learners to take control of the interaction, thereby diminishing their sense of autonomy. It also limits the number of opportunities that learners have to interact across the class as they respond to their classmates' ideas and opinions.

Conclusion

As emergent language is unplanned, it can happen at any point in a lesson when there is a focus on meaning. As we have seen in this chapter, there are numerous activities, procedures and techniques that create the conditions for a focus on meaning and more opportunities to work with emergent language. In **How to work with emergent language** (pages 53–74), we will look at how teachers might intervene in these emergent language moments.

Professional development

Questions for reflection

- Which of the approaches, techniques or activities do you regularly use in your teaching? How do you work with emergent language that arises from them?
- Before you read **How to work with emergent language** (pages 53–74), consider what different techniques you might use to work with emergent language, for example, eliciting or reformulating.

Things to try

- Identify one of the approaches, techniques or activities that you have never used before and try it out. After the class, think about the following questions: *What language emerged from the interaction that followed? How did you work with the learner's output during or at the end of the stage?*

4. How to work with emergent language

This chapter focuses on the different techniques teachers use to work with emergent language, the rationale and benefits of each technique, and how teachers often use more than one technique simultaneously.

The following terms are key for this chapter, so let us check their meaning before getting into the detail:

- **intervention technique** is any response to learner language that involves reformulation or emergent language input.
- **reformulation** is any instance where you (or another learner) corrects, extends or modifies learner language. Reformulations can be explicit (in other words, you make it clear that you are reformulating) or implicit (you reformulate without signalling that you are doing so).
- **uptake** is the process by which learners notice or react to teacher reformulations. Uptake may involve learners acknowledging the intervention with a nod, using a new item or modifying their utterances.
- **repair** is any move by a learner in which they modify an error after an intervention.

Our research

In **Why work with emergent language?** (pages 13–28), we outlined reasons for working with emergent language and discussed how responding to and reformulating learner output can facilitate or speed up language acquisition. Interestingly, very little concrete guidance has been published relating to how you should go about this. There is also scant published research on how teachers currently work with emergent language in lessons, though there is a large body of research into how teachers respond to errors.

To close this gap and find out more about what teachers are currently doing, we worked with our colleague Nick Andon at King's College London to gather data and create a list of techniques and procedures for working with emergent language. We did this by observing and recording lessons taught by experienced teachers at a private language school and an ESOL (English for Speakers of Other Languages) college in London. After the classes, we transcribed the lessons and categorised the different techniques the teachers had used (Andon & Norrington-Davies, 2019). We called these **intervention techniques**.

Ten intervention techniques

This section outlines the ten different intervention techniques (listed in Figure 4.1) that we observed teachers using in response to emergent language during or after interactions with the learners. Many of the techniques we observed – for example, recasts and clarification requests – have been observed and discussed in previous studies (for example, Lyster & Ranta, 1997; Ellis, 2009; Walsh, 2011). However, we observed other techniques, such as interactional recasts and recalls, which we have not seen extensively in research literature.

1. Explicit reformulation
2. Recast
3. Clarification request/confirmation request
4. Elicitation
5. Metalinguistic feedback
6. Extension
7. Interactional recast
8. Sharing
9. Recall
10. Learner-initiated

Figure 4.1: Ten intervention techniques

Even though we noticed that teachers often used two or more techniques at the same time (see 'Mixing techniques' below), the following overview begins by looking at each one separately. Each example of an intervention has come from a genuine classroom situation, but note that some transcripts have been simplified to make the intervention clearer for the reader.

1. Explicit reformulation

Explicit reformulation refers to a moment in class in which teachers provide a clear and overt alternative form in response to learner output. This can come either immediately after the learner completes their turn during open-class interactions or during a feedback stage after learners have completed a communicative task in pairs or groups. To make a reformulation explicit, you clearly indicate that what the learner has said was unclear or inaccurate. To do this, you can use **signposting language**, as seen in Extract 4.1. The utterance being reformulated or modified is in italics with an asterisk (*) at the end. The intervention is in italics and underlined.

Learner:	He wasn't in the interview because he *lost the bus** so he can't go on time.
Teacher:	That's right, <u>but you don't say '*lost the bus*'</u>. <u>They '*missed the bus*'</u>.
Learner:	I think the boy is *afraid of his exam**.
Teacher:	I see, <u>but I wouldn't say '*afraid of' it*</u>. <u>You could say he's '*afraid about' it*, but I think it's too strong. I think he's '*worried about it*'</u>.

Extract 4.1: Explicit reformulation

The signposting phrases are designed to make it clear to the learner that what they have said requires reformulation. By making the reformulation explicit, the teacher makes it more likely that the learner will notice the intervention and potentially recognise the gap or mismatch between their existing knowledge and the L2. This noticing is known as 'uptake'. Many researchers (for example, Loewen, 2005) have suggested that uptake is a sign that the learner has taken a step towards learning through the interaction, and some studies (for example, Lyster & Ranta, 1997; Sheen, 2004) have found a positive link between uptake and learning. This creates a strong rationale for using explicit reformulations in class.

Uptake comes in many forms. The basic principle is that the learner is seen to acknowledge the reformulation in some way. They might say 'OK', thank their teacher or nod. However, an explicit reformulation might also encourage the learner to modify their output or try to use the new item, as in the examples below. Learner modification or self-correction is known as **repair**. A clear indication of uptake, repair has been seen to have a positive effect on language development (for example, Williams, 2001).

Learner:	Maybe they don't go to clubs because *they fright of Covid**.
Teacher:	Possibly, but it's not *'fright of'*, it's *'frightened of'*. They're frightened of catching Covid.
Learner:	Yes, they don't go because they are frightened of Covid.
Learner:	*I looked, but I discreetly**.
Teacher:	Oh, you mean you looked discreetly [miming action].
Learner:	Yes. I looked discreetly.

Extract 4.2: Explicit reformulation and repair

The teacher interventions in Extract 4.2 come during interaction and immediately after the learner has completed a communicative turn. To make a reformulation explicit after the learners have done a communicative task, you might note down examples of errors or unclear language as you monitor, and then write what you heard on the board in preparation for feedback. After the task, you can ask the learners to work out what is problematic about the examples on the board before you provide reformulations. This intervention type will be discussed further when we look at elicitation on pages 60–61.

2. Recast

A **recast** is an implicit reformulation. In a recast, teachers reformulate all or part of a learner's utterance, most commonly on completion of their turn. Unlike in an explicit reformulation, there is no overt indication that there has been an error or that the teacher is reformulating the learner's contribution. In addition, recasts are not introduced by phrases such as *You mean* … or *You should say* …. A recast could be provided in response to a range of issues, from an unclear or incorrect sound, through to a word, phrase or full utterance. What connects them is that they are brief and implicit, and the learner is generally free to carry on with their turn, as we see in the first two examples in Extract 4.3 (on page 57). The learner may repair or modify their output, but this may not always happen.

Learner:	Is his house but he *rent** to me.
Teacher:	He *rents it* to you.
Learner:	Yes, and I don't pay much.
Learner:	I think it's *a regression**.
Teacher:	*A regret*.
Learner:	Yes. It's a regret.
Learner:	They eat a lot of beef and lamb [pronounced as **læmb***] ….
Teacher:	**læm**
Learner:	… and chicken is *very famous**.
Teacher:	*Chicken is very popular*. What else do they eat?

Extract 4.3: Recasts

In the first and third examples in Extract 4.3, the learner lacks an explicit sign that they need to modify their output because the teacher does not overtly indicate that there has been an error. In fact, it is possible that the learner has not even noticed that their utterance has been reformulated. This is one of the potential issues with recasts: some studies (for example, Sheen, 2006) suggest that as they are not necessarily noticed by the learner, they are not as likely to lead to uptake. However, you may choose to use recasts for a variety of reasons.

The first reason is time. If you have limited time with their classes, you may feel that recasts are the most efficient way to give feedback on as many emergent language episodes (most commonly errors) as possible during the time available. There is also no time lost on negotiating the form, as you can quickly and efficiently provide the correct alternative (Long, 2006). You may also be wary of using a more explicit technique that stops the learner from continuing their turn. Recasts may also be used in contexts in which teachers do not want to make the reformulation too obvious so that the learner does not lose face or motivation. This is a reason for recasting that has been put forward by many teachers who work with teenagers.

There is also evidence that learners do notice recasts. This is especially true in contexts in which learners have been primed to notice more implicit modes of correction, or when the recast is accompanied with a clue, such as rising intonation (Sheen, 2006) or a change in facial expression. Sheen also found that where a recast only focuses on one item, for example, a single word or sound, there is more evidence of uptake and repair among learners. Asari (2012) suggests that a recast accompanied by clues such as intonation or a change in facial expression should be known as a 'cued recast', and that it is more likely to promote uptake. Indeed, a cued recast might actually be seen as an example of explicit reformulation as the teacher has used a clear device to signal there has been an error or need for some kind of reformulation.

Despite the fact that learners do notice some types of recast, if more explicit forms of reformulation are more likely to lead to learner uptake and facilitate language acquisition, you should consider how you might use these more frequently. This would involve a change for many teachers, as studies tend to show that recasts are the most common way of working with learner errors.

3. Teacher clarification requests/confirmation checks

Clarification requests indicate to a learner that what they have said has been misunderstood by their teacher or another learner. A clarification request includes phrases such as *What do you mean?* or *I'm sorry, I don't understand*. These phrases may be accompanied by the teacher indicating that they do not understand with their voice or facial expression. A clarification request helps the learner to notice that what they said has not been understood, thereby pushing them to reformulate or repair their utterance themselves and to get the communication back on track.

Clarification requests are an important technique for you to use for two main reasons. Firstly, this type of explicit feedback on language helps the learner to notice the gap between their performance and the L2. This creates an overt learning opportunity as the learner is encouraged to reformulate and solve the problem they are facing. Second, clarification requests mirror real-life behaviour, thereby preparing the learner for communication breakdowns they will naturally face when using the L2 outside class. Examples of clarification requests and learner responses can be seen in the example in Extract 4.4 (on page 59), taken from an elementary (A2) class during open-class discussions.

Learner 1:	I like coffee but into … **mi:li:ks***
Teacher:	*What do you mean?*
Learner 1:	I put in … [mimes poring]
Teacher:	Ah … milk. You have coffee with milk.
Learner 1:	Yes.
Learner 2:	milky coffee
Learner 1:	Yes. I like milky coffee. [To teacher] You like?
Learner 3:	… is on the first floor … *I think a dark* **beðrʊm*** is located above the kitchen.
Teacher:	*Are you saying bedroom or bathroom?*
Learner:	**beðrʊm*** [mimes sleeping].

Extract 4.4: Clarification requests

In the first example above, because the teacher asks for clarification, the learner realises that they have not been understood, so they mime the action of pouring milk. This is their way of solving the communication breakdown. The teacher picks up on this and provides a more comprehensible form (*coffee with milk*). Interestingly, another learner joins in to give the phrase *milky coffee*, which Learner 1 notices and uses – a clear sign of uptake. With the conversation back on track, the learner then feels confident enough to ask the teacher if they like milky coffee too.

A **confirmation request** is similar to a clarification request and serves the same function. However, confirmation requests are different in that they indicate that an utterance has been partially understood or the listener is slightly unsure about what was said. In a confirmation request, you might use a signposting phrase such as *Are you saying that …?* or *So you mean …?*, as can be seen in Extract 4.5.

Learner:	He works in a *law case**.
Teacher:	Oh, *you mean he's a lawyer?*
Learner:	Yes. He is lawyer.

Extract 4.5: Confirmation request

4. Elicitation

Elicitation refers to techniques that teachers use to encourage the learner to reformulate their output themselves, as opposed to giving the learners an alternative form directly. To elicit a reformulation, you might ask clarification questions or give prompts before strategically pausing to allow your learners to modify their utterance, as in Extract 4.6. As with an explicit reformulation, elicitation enables the learner to notice the difference between their performance and the L2 and encourages them to close that gap by repairing what they said. Though eliciting may take a little extra time and, in some cases, interrupt the communication, there is ample evidence suggesting that encouraging learners to self-correct or modify their output is effective in promoting acquisition (for example, Lyster, 2004; Sheen, 2006).

Teacher:	Where did you read that?
Learner:	*On the computer*?*
Teacher:	OK. <u>*But maybe not on the computer. You can say I read it …?*</u>
Learner:	Online.
Teacher:	Yes. You read it online, or you saw it online.

Extract 4.6: Learner self-correction

To make elicitation more overt, it is common for teachers to use the board to display an error or unclear word. This can be done during a communicative turn, as you can see in the first example in Extract 4.7. It is also common to use elicitation after learners have completed a communicative task or discussed a text, as in the second two examples. To do this, a teacher monitors their learners as they are interacting and notes down examples of errors or miscomprehension. They then write the items on the board so they can be discussed during feedback. This is often known as delayed feedback.

Learner:	If you take the phone, you might *stop them from … look the answer**.
Teacher:	Absolutely, *but look here* [writing on the board]. <u>*What do I put here? Stop them from look -------- up the answers.*</u>
Teacher:	[Pointing at the board] OK, you said one way to study better is to *raise a group chat**. <u>*We need another word, not raise. What do you think?*</u> ➔

Learners:	[Shouting answers together] Make? Start?
Teacher:	Start a group chat sounds good [writes on the board].
Teacher:	OK, I heard this [pointing at the board], *He had a difficult criação**. <u>*What word could we use here?*</u>
Learner 1:	Childhood?
Learner 2:	Background?
Teacher:	Good ideas. I think upbringing. He had a difficult upbringing.

Extract 4.7: Elicitation with written prompts

Note that in the third example in Extract 4.7, the teacher uses their knowledge of the L1 (Portuguese) to try to elicit the corresponding English word from the learners. This shows how useful the learners' L1 can be both in the performance of the task, where it was used to keep the conversation going, and as an elicitation technique.

As well as inviting the learners to reformulate what was said, you can use other techniques to signal that there has been an error and elicit a response. As in a recast, one technique is to echo the error but with questioning intonation, as we see in Extract 4.8. This invites the learner to reformulate what they said as it shows them that the listener has noticed a problem. You can also use a facial expression or gesture to reinforce the intervention. These paralinguistic prompts help to make the intervention more explicit, which in turn makes it more likely that the learner will notice what the teacher is doing and can attempt to modify their output.

Learner:	They *go** there after the gym.
Teacher:	[Using a questioning tone] <u>*They go?*</u>
Learner:	They went

Extract 4.8: Elicitation with questioning intonation

5. Metalinguistic feedback

This is another explicit technique. Here, you draw attention to the error, and then use grammatical or linguistic terminology to provide information about it, for example, *You can't use a noun here. What type of word do you need?* or *You need to use a different tense*. These prompts signal to the learner the nature of the issue to help them come up with a more appropriate or comprehensible form. As with the examples of elicitation above, **metalinguistic feedback** can be immediate or delayed.

In the first example in Extract 4.9, which occurred in a delayed feedback stage, the teacher uses two metalinguistic prompts. The first one, *This is the present continuous*, highlights the nature of the error and the tense that the learners needed to use. They then use elicitation to prompt the learners to provide the correct verb form. In the second example, the teacher uses a linguistic term to highlight what is wrong with the utterance before providing the correct form themselves.

Teacher:	[Pointing at the board] I heard someone say '*Where is he live now?**' Not 'live'. <u>This is present continuous, so what verb form do you need here?</u>
Learners:	*Living*. [Teacher reformulates on the board]
Teacher:	What job do you think he does?
Learner:	*Maybe he's model. Or singer*.*
Teacher:	Maybe. <u>Remember you need the article. He is a model. Maybe he's a singer</u>.

Extract 4.9: Metalinguistic feedback

One of the main reasons for using metalinguistic feedback to elicit reformulations from learners is that metalanguage is a key feature of many language courses and coursebooks. Language learners who use coursebooks have quite a sound knowledge of metalanguage, such as the names of tenses, so it can act as a useful and simple prompt to elicit reformulations. Metalinguistic feedback can also make it easier for you to show why a specific form is more appropriate. There is also support from studies (for example, Ellis, Loewen & Erlam, 2006) for the positive effects of metalinguistic feedback on learners' grammar.

6. Extensions

Extensions are interventions where you respond to a learner's use of a word or form by providing or eliciting alternative ways of saying the same thing. This can be done in response to an error, as you will see in the example in Extract 4.10, where the teacher provides the learners with two alternatives to the word they originally used.

Learner:	If you take it to class the teacher will *seize the phone*.*
Teacher:	I see. So, they take the phone, or you could say they confiscate your phone. 'Seize' is maybe a bit strong.

Extract 4.10: Extensions with error correction

However, extensions are different from other types of intervention as they do not necessarily follow an error or communicative breakdown. As you can see in the first example in Extract 4.11, the teacher initially responds with interest to what the learner has said. They then switch to a focus on language by providing an alternative way of saying the same thing. The interaction and response create the opportunity for the teacher to introduce and explore what they think is a useful pattern. This is clear in the first example where the teacher elicits other things that teachers might stop learners doing. This is designed to encourage the learner to notice the new pattern and have a go at using it themselves. In the second example, the teacher accepts the word the learner has used, and then introduces another way of saying the same thing.

Learner:	The teacher takes the phone because we might look for the answer.
Teacher:	I see. So, they take the phone to [writing on the board] *stop you looking for the answers, or to stop you cheating. What other things might they stop you doing?*
Learner:	On the weekend I like to wake up later.
Teacher:	Ah me too. You can say that, or you can say you *have a lie-in*. What time do you lie in until?

Extract 4.11: Extensions that provide alternatives

7. Interactional recast

This is a type of recast, so it is implicit. In **interactional recasts**, you provide an alternative form while maintaining communication and encouraging the learner to extend their speaking turn. In other words, rather than simply echoing what the learner has said you provide the reformulation at the same time as they respond to the message.

Learner:	We have to give our phone to the teacher at the start of class
Teacher:	Oh, <u>*so you had to hand them in?*</u> What happened after that?
Learner:	We take back after class.
Learner:	My grandfather had a … *hall of cine** and *he have to use his hand, like this, to hidesome people or action**.
Teacher:	Wow, <u>*so he censored the film with his hand?*</u>
Learner:	And I still remember … I still watch the film in his hand. Not the audience, who are older, but a four-year-old boy, I can watch.

Extract 4.12: Interactional recasts

The advantage of an interactional recast is that the learner is free to carry on with their story or turn, as we see in the second example in Extract 4.12. The teacher is also able to show that they are interested in what the learner is saying and are following the story. This type of back-channelling, where the listener interjects to show that they are following, is typical of genuine interaction, so the teacher is modelling behaviour which the learner can pick up on and integrate into their own communicative practices.

However, during our observations, we did not notice a single instance of learner uptake following an interactional recast. The same thing has been observed in other studies, for example, Asari (2012), though she used the term 'interrogative recast'. Note that this apparent absence of uptake does not necessarily mean that the learner has not noticed the reformulation; however, it may suggest that interactional recasts are less effective as a corrective technique than other, more explicit types of intervention.

8. Sharing

Sharing refers to instances where a teacher has noticed examples of interesting or useful language that their learners have used in pairwork or a small group task. Because the rest of the class will not have heard the words or phrases, the teacher uses the feedback stage to share them. As we saw above, this stage is often known as **delayed feedback**. Though delayed feedback often includes a focus on errors, sharing also involves you looking at examples of interesting language that you believe the rest of the class would benefit from learning.

The exchanges in Extract 4.13 show examples of sharing from online classes in which the teacher has put the learners in breakout rooms to talk about jobs they have done. As the teacher moves from room to room, they notice their learners using interesting new words or discussing the difference between them. Having helped the learners with these words, the teacher decides that these would be useful lexical items for everyone. They therefore ask the original group to share the words with the rest of the class in feedback.

Teacher:	*OK, Cesar's group was talking about the difference between babysitters, childminders and au-pairs. Can you tell us the difference?*
Teacher:	I like this word. Francis, *what did you say about your houseplants?* You said you always kill them. *What was the phrase you used?*
Learner:	I don't have green fingers.
Teacher:	Nice [writing on the board]. What does it mean?
Learner:	I'm not good with plants and gardens. I can't grow nothing.

Extract 4.13: Sharing

One reason for sharing is that it adds variety to feedback stages as the learners are not just looking at and reformulating errors. It can also be very motivating for a learner to be invited to share a phrase they have used with the rest of the class, and it promotes opportunities for learners to learn from each other. Sharing, therefore, can be very motivating and a good way of building rapport in a group.

9. Recalls

Recall is another type of elicitation technique. It refers to an instance in which learners have misused or cannot recall a lexical item or grammatical form that a teacher believes they have been exposed to in previous lessons. As a prompt, the teacher uses phrases such as *Do you remember the word for ...?* or *What was the word we used for that?* to elicit from the learner or class, as you can see in the example in Extract 4.14.

Learner 1:	So I didn't wake up because *my alarm doesn't start**.
Teacher:	I see. That's OK. *But we saw this before. My alarm didn't go ...?* [Pauses to elicit] ➔

Learner 1:	I don't know.
Learners:	*go off.*
Teacher:	Yes. *Your alarm didn't go off.* You set it, but it didn't go off.

Extract 4.14: Recall

It can be difficult to decide when to use eliciting as a technique, as obviously it is not possible to elicit a language item that the learners do not know. However, with recalls, a teacher can be more confident about eliciting as they believe that their learners have encountered the item before. This means they are prompting learners to remember, making the elicitation more likely to succeed. Recalls are also a useful way of recycling language from previous lessons. Through repeated exposure, it is more likely that the learners will remember the items in the future.

10. Learner-initiated interventions

The final type of intervention is different from those described above as it is a learner rather than the teacher who triggers the emergent language episode. This can be done by directly asking you for help with a word or phrase, for example, with questions such as *How do you say …?* or *What is the word for…?* The learner may also indicate that they are unsure of how to complete their utterance by pausing and looking at you or another learner for guidance.

Learner:	[Looking at a text] He said it was a blustery morning, and everyone is …. <u>*Is blustery the same as busy?*</u>
Teacher:	*Blustery?* No, *blustery* is *windy*. So, the weather was *blustery*.
Learner:	<u>*It's the weather?*</u>
Teacher:	Yeah. Cold and windy.
Learner:	Oh, OK.
Learner:	Yeah. So I remember he was with glasses and he walk with … stick … like a stick. [mimes a walking stick] <u>*How do I say this?*</u>
Teacher:	*He had a walking stick*. Or *he used a cane*.

Extract 4.15: learner-initiated interventions

Arguably, a learner-initiated intervention may be the most powerful of all the intervention techniques: rather than looking for where learners might need assistance, you can directly respond to a call for help at the learner's point of need, which we have seen is important for language acquisition (Ellis, 2016). As the learner wants to use the word or phrase, especially in the context of a story they want to tell, it is possible that the reformulation or input that you give will also be more memorable. Studies have also shown that the highest rate of successful uptake was observed when the learner initiated the intervention (for example, Gholami & Gholami, 2018). This creates a powerful argument for encouraging learners to initiate interventions during lessons.

As you have just seen, you can make use of several different intervention techniques in order to work with emergent language. You can choose to work with emergent language either in response to something you notice in learner output or to the questions learners might have. The intervention techniques we have discussed can be broadly split into two categories: explicit and implicit interventions. In the next section, we will examine this distinction in more detail.

Explicit interventions

Explicit intervention techniques (Figure 4.2 below) are used to make it clear to the learner that their teacher is modifying, reformulating or responding to the learner's use of a specific language item or form. By using these techniques, the teacher is drawing the learner's attention to a language item and encouraging **noticing**, **uptake**, and possibly **repair**.

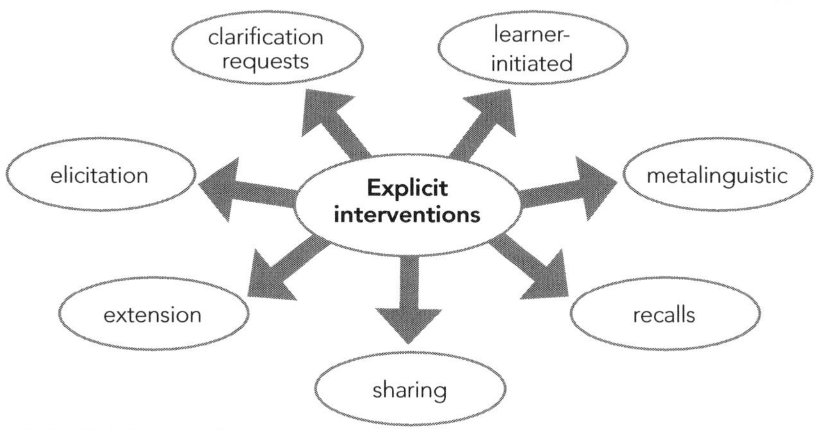

Figure 4.2: Explicit intervention

The explicit interventions in Figure 4.2 are designed to give learners new information about language in response to their output. In most cases, it is the teacher who provides the input. However, it is also possible for the teacher to elicit the reformulation or repair from the learners. As this move involves an overt indication from the teacher that they are looking for a reformulation, elicitation is included here.

While some teachers worry that explicit reformulations might disrupt the communication in some way, the advantage of using them is that the learner is more likely to notice the intervention. As we saw in **Why work with emergent language?** (pages 13–28), it is believed that noticing, or noticing the gap, is a prerequisite for language learning as it acts as a catalyst for subsequent change in knowledge or performance (Schmidt, 2001). Studies have also consistently found that interventions that encourage learners to notice the gap between their performance and the L2 can contribute to L2 development (for example, Loewen, 2005; Egi, 2010). This is particularly the case for elicitation; indeed, it has been argued that learner responses that follow prompts or elicitations involve a deeper level of processing than other forms of reformulation (see, for example, Lyster & Mori, 2006). In addition, studies such as Yoshida (2008) have shown that learners in some instructional settings actually prefer to think about their errors and attempt to correct them. There is, therefore, a theoretical and evidence-based rationale for using more explicit interventions in response to emergent language.

Implicit interventions

Though there is much support for more explicit reformulations, there is also a rationale for using more **implicit intervention techniques**. For example, teachers might opt for a more implicit technique so as not to interrupt the communication too much. They may also feel that **recasting** is an efficient way of providing more input in a lesson as less time is taken up eliciting modifications or **repair** from learners. Many teachers also prefer recasts as they do not put learners on the spot. Finally, we should be careful not to take the criticism about lack of **uptake** at face value; it may well be that even if learners fail to show uptake, **noticing** is taking place.

It is worth repeating our earlier caution about the use of the term **echo** here. As we saw in **Creating the right conditions** (pages 29–52), **echoing** is when a teacher repeats a learner's well-formed response to a task or question, perhaps to validate the answer or to ensure that the rest of the class has heard. This is a common practice for classroom teachers (Walsh, 2011). However, there may be drawbacks to using this technique. If you regularly use what appears to be the same technique to both validate the learner's answer (echo) and reformulate it (recast), it is less likely that the learners will notice the gap when you are reformulating (Egi, 2010). Along with the fact that echoing often ends the learner's turn and can even suggest a lack of interest in the message, its use as a response to learner output should be called into question.

Mixing techniques

In the overview of intervention techniques above, we looked at each intervention technique individually. However, our observations showed that rather than regularly using one technique in isolation, most teachers use more than one type of intervention (Norrington-Davies, 2020). This mirrors findings in other studies (Sheen, 2006), and will be the focus of the rest of this chapter.

Extract 4.16 is taken from an open-class brainstorming task on whether mobile phones should be allowed in class. As the interaction is between a teacher and their learners, there are opportunities for the teacher to work with language as it emerges.

Learner:	*Maybe students are not ... eh ... curious.*
Teacher:	*What do you mean?* [clarification request]
Learner:	They must control themselves.
Teacher:	*I think it could be curious, but I think 'they're not interested in the lesson'* [explicit reformulation], *or 'they're not paying attention'* [extension].

Extract 4.16: Mixing techniques in a brainstorming stage

First, we see the teacher use a clarification request as they are unsure about what the learner means. This prompts the learner to explain, which in turn prompts the teacher to pause the meaning-focused interaction to provide input through explicit reformulation. The teacher then offers further input through extensions. This mixing of techniques helps the learner notice the gap between their performance and the L2 before giving them the opportunity to close it. The extensions also provide the whole class with alternative forms, thereby extending the lexical range of all the learners.

The next example (Extract 4.17, thanks to Richard Gallen) of technique mixing is taken from an ESOL class in East London, predominantly made up of Bangladeshi adult learners. In this stage of the lesson, the learner is telling the class about a childhood memory of the time when her cousin fell off a roof while trying to reach a guava.

As she tells her story, the learner is unable to recall the word *roof,* and asks for assistance. This prompts another learner to provide the word, which the teacher explains, following a further learner-initiated request for help. The teacher then quickly checks their understanding before the speaker is free to carry on with the story.

Learner 1:	She were on the, um … [mimes 'roof'] *what's that?* [Learner-initiated]
Learner 2:	*Roof* [explicit reformulation]
Learner 1:	Roof, yeah.
Learner 3:	*What mean roof?* [Learner-initiated]
Teacher:	Ah, *roof*. *The roof is the top of the building* [drawing a picture and writing 'on the roof'] *so if you've got the building here, the roof is this part* [explicit reformulation]. *Is that correct, Shahida?* [Confirmation request].
Learner 1:	Yes.
Teacher:	OK.
Learner 1:	Then she saw her niece on the roof and try to get guava and she asked her 'What are you doing there …?

Extract 4.17: Mixing techniques following a learner-initiated intervention

In Extract 4.17, we see an example of uptake and modified output as the learner uses the input to continue the story. This is an interesting exchange as, rather than interrupting the flow of the conversation, the learner-initiated intervention and the switch in focus from meaning to form contributes to the communicative flow rather than impeding it. This shows that not all explicit interventions break the flow, as some teachers feel. In fact, they are a natural part of classroom discourse.

Switching from meaning to form

The switch from meaning to form is a common occurrence in class; Extract 4.18 shows how this can happen in a lesson. It is taken from a conversation class in which a group of adult learners are discussing past school rules. Here, the speaker is describing how the learners used to hide their phones around the school to avoid having them confiscated by teachers.

Learner:	If we want we bring it like we bring drugs or something. We hidden. We try … We have many ways to … *make it?** [Learner-initiated through questioning intonation]
Teacher:	*to hide it* [Recast]
Learner:	*hid it**.
Teacher:	*hide it* [Recast]
Learner:	to hide it

Extract 4.18: Switching from meaning to form after a learner-initiated intervention

In Extract 4.18, the learner pauses their story and asks for help because they do not know which verb to use. This switches the focus from meaning to form, which enables the teacher to recast as there is no need to explain that they are providing a more suitable form. The context makes the action, and therefore the meaning, clear. The teacher recasts again when the learner mispronounces the verb. Following this brief switch in focus, the learner continues their story, going on to tell the class that their school was full of phones hidden in air vents.

In our research, we did not see as many examples of recasts as were seen in other papers. What we did notice was that recasts usually occurred when the interaction had switched from a communicative or meaning-focused mode to a more form-focused one. This can be seen in Extract 4.19, which continues the interaction between the teacher and learner that we saw in Extract 4.4 (on page 59). Here, the teacher uses a clarification request to show that they do not understand which room the learner is talking about. Once the misunderstanding has been cleared up, the teacher uses a recast to modify the learner's pronunciation. Again, because the focus has switched from communication to form, the recast has become more salient. This helps the learner notice the reformulation and modify their output.

Learner:	… is on the first floor … I think a dark **beðrʊm***. Is located above the kitchen.
Teacher:	_Are you saying bedroom or bathroom?_ [Clarification request]
Learner:	**beðrʊm*** [mimes sleeping]
Teacher:	**bedrʊm** [recast]
Learner:	**bedrʊm**

Extract 4.19: Switching from meaning to form after a clarification request

In our research, we noticed numerous examples of emergent language episodes causing a switch from interaction mode (where the learners were genuinely communicating with each other or their teacher) to a focus on form. Once the teacher and the learners had dealt with the language point that caused this switch, we saw the class happily move back into interaction mode. This showed us that rather than impeding the flow of communication, the switch to a focus on the language through reformulation actually facilitated it, as the learners often felt better able to finish their stories or complete their turns. These findings present a further rationale for using more explicit modes of reformulation in response to emergent language.

As we have seen, short, explicit interventions are not only unproblematic, they are even appreciated by learners. However, there are occasions when a teacher might want to delay the switch from interaction to form and deal with the emergent language later. For example, a teacher may prefer not to interrupt a learner who is giving a presentation, or they may want to explore an area of language further. In Extract 4.20, the teacher uses a feedback stage to explore some of the language the learners have used in a recently completed communicative task. While the learners have been performing the task, the teacher has been monitoring and noting down examples of interesting language or errors without interrupting the learners. The teacher has then written the examples on the whiteboard to draw the learners' attention to them later during the feedback stage. As we saw in our summary of intervention types earlier in the chapter, this is known as **sharing**. As the example below is grammatical, the teacher uses metalinguistic feedback to elicit the form from the learners.

Teacher:	[Pointing to the whiteboard] *I like this one: If we didn't use our phones, we didn't die*. [sharing] You're talking about the present but there is future too, so *I think we can change this verb* [metalinguistic feedback/eliciting].
Learner:	*won't.*
Teacher:	Um, *if we didn't use our phones we won't die?* I think that's OK. *I'd go with wouldn't*. [Explicit reformulation]

Extract 4.20: Mixing intervention techniques

A further point of interest in Extract 4.20 is the fact that the teacher is quite indirect when working with the learners' language and offering reformulations. The teacher does not state outright that what the learner has said is wrong. Nor do they tell the learner what the correct answer or form should be. Instead, they use the more tentative phrase *I'd go with wouldn't*, as they offer their reformulation. Our research showed a lot of examples of teachers using phrases like the one above, or *For me, this sounds OK*. This hedging suggests a desire on the part of some teachers not to strictly impose standards or norms as they work with emergent language. Instead, their focus is on improving comprehensibility or helping the learners get their message across.

Conclusion

In this chapter, we have looked at the discoursal moves that a teacher and learner can make in order to address and exploit affordances for emergent language. Over time, you will develop and expand your repertoire of intervention techniques, and it is through examination of classroom interaction that you will become more aware of what you do in class and why you do it. For example, you could see when it might be better to use explicit or implicit intervention techniques or when it might be effective to mix techniques. In Part 2, we will look in detail at how to how to do this. First, though, having looked at how experienced teachers work with emergent language, let us address two questions:

1. What items of language should you focus on?
2. How might you modify or reformulate what the learners have said?

These two questions will be answered in **Exploring emergent language in lessons** (pages 75–102).

Professional development

Questions for reflection

- Look at the ten intervention techniques. Which ones do you use most regularly?
- Which techniques do you think would be most suitable for your teaching context? Why?
- It is said that experienced teachers tend to be more comfortable than less experienced teachers when correcting learner errors (e.g. Rahimi & Zhang, 2015). Why do you think this is?

Things to try

- Look back at the **Ten intervention techniques** on pages 54–67 and select three to try out in class this week. After you try them out, reflect on how the students responded, for instance: *Did they incorporate the emergent language into their speech? Did they correct themselves? Did they ignore the reformulation?* etc.

5. Exploring emergent language in lessons

This chapter focuses on how teachers choose what emergent language to focus on, how teachers can clarify the meaning, use, form and pronunciation of the emergent language they choose, and how teachers can review and recycle emergent language.

The key terms that feature in this chapter are as follows:

- **monitoring** is a technique that teachers use while learners are working together in pairs or small groups. The teacher observes and assesses the learners as they work together, and gathers examples of emergent language.
- **horizontal extension/syntagmatic extension:** a technique that teachers use to draw attention to the word order, grammatical features and patterns in an utterance. This is done by looking at a sentence from left to right and analysing what is possible in terms of word order and form.
- **vertical extension/paradigmatic extension:** a technique that teachers use to expand lexical range. The teacher slots new or alternative words into the appropriate spaces in a sentence. This can also create opportunities for learners to notice patterns.

As we saw in **How to work with emergent language** (pages 53–74), teachers have several options for how they intervene in response to emergent language episodes. In this chapter, we will explore what language they might focus on and what information they give learners about the new forms they choose to analyse. To do this, we will look at a lesson we have taught and the emergent language it generated. As you look at the lesson, you will also be invited to complete a series of reflection tasks designed to get you to think about how you might work with the language that emerged. Let us begin by looking at what items of emergent language a teacher might focus on.

Choosing what language to focus on

In this section, we will explore what is perhaps the most difficult question regarding emergent language, and one we are regularly asked: out of everything we hear during a task or while interacting with learners, what emergent language should you focus on? There are several reasons why you might choose to focus on certain items of emergent language over others. This can depend on the context in which you work, or it might be based on a set of principles or beliefs about how languages are learnt. These options are summarised below.

Language that causes miscommunication

There is a sound rationale for prioritising learner language that has caused or might cause misunderstandings or miscomprehension. This is especially the case where the focus of a course or lesson is to develop communicative and interactional skills. Prioritising language that might cause miscommunication helps learners potentially avoid or reduce the chances of this happening outside the classroom, especially if they are also provided with strategies for overcoming communication issues, such as using clarification requests or confirmation checks. Prioritising miscommunication over errors of form, for example, also teaches learners that they do not necessarily need to be completely accurate in order to convey their message. This is important as the desire to speak 'accurately' is something that holds many learners back from taking risks and developing their skills through interaction.

It is interesting to note that in our research with Nick Andon into how experienced teachers work with emergent language (Andon & Norrington-Davies, 2019), all the teachers we observed regularly responded to language that caused or could potentially cause miscomprehension, and this accounted for the high number of clarification requests and explicit reformulations in our data. Follow-up interviews suggested that dealing with miscommunication was a high priority for these experienced teachers. This was partly down to their contexts, as all the teachers worked with small classes of adult learners who prioritised communication. Many teachers suggested that an utterance that clearly conveys a message could be viewed as a success, even if they included what some might consider non-standard forms or errors. They felt instead that it was better to prioritise language that had an impact on comprehension rather than focusing on minor or surface errors of form that do not.

Language or interactional skills that are relevant to the teaching context

The teaching and learning context provides a strong rationale for the type of emergent language a teacher might choose to work on. So, for learners who want to develop their communication skills, focusing on causes of miscomprehension is often a priority. These teachers might also choose to focus on language or interactional skills that will further aid communication skills or help learners better perform specific communicative tasks. On the other hand, teachers preparing learners for an exam might choose to focus more on the specific forms that are tested in the exam. This can mean that there is a greater emphasis on accuracy in these classes, as the marking criteria may include norms and standards of language use that their learners will have to adhere to in order to pass. This is especially true for writing tasks. Emergent language and exam classes will be discussed in greater detail in **Emergent language in different teaching contexts** (pages 197–216).

Repeated issues with the same or similar forms

If you notice a repeated issue or overuse of a specific form, this suggests that the learners have a gap in their knowledge or performance that you, as their teacher, can help to close. The fact that the issue has occurred as they are communicating also means that the language item can be taught at the point of need. As we saw in **Why work with emergent language?** (pages 13–28), this can have a positive impact on language acquisition. On a practical level, focusing on common or frequent issues means that you can provide input that is beneficial to most learners. In this sense, communicative tasks can be seen as diagnostic tools, as they enable teachers to assess their learners, diagnose needs and decide on useful input for future lessons. Picking common areas also means that the focus of the feedback is concrete, and the learning in the lesson can be neatly packaged as a kind of retrospective outcome.

Language that is interesting or useful

Many teachers use their intuition, experience and knowledge of the learners to pick up on language that they think their learners will find useful or interesting. This is a valid rationale, especially when we consider that any language input that closes a gap in the learner's knowledge or skills is useful. New lexis encountered in a clear context is also easier to absorb (McCarthy, 1990) and, as it is the learners who have generated the context, there is the potential to make the new items more memorable.

While teachers should take a prominent role in choosing what they feel is interesting and useful language to focus on, it is important to keep in mind that learners should also have a voice in this aspect of lessons. For this reason, they should be encouraged to ask questions about language that they notice in texts (both in or outside class) or about words or phrases they would like to use during a task. Teachers should factor in time during a lesson to respond to such learner-initiated interventions.

One perceived drawback of teachers using their intuition to pick up on useful or interesting language is that it can make it harder to identify a specific learning outcome at the end of the lesson (something that some learners, and many teaching institutions like and expect teachers to do). As such, teachers should encourage learners to record new items in a lexical notebook under topic-related headings. They should also find time on courses to recycle the emergent language items that come up. This means that the learners have a concrete record of the new language they have learnt on the course. Advice on how to do this will be given in more detail in the final part of this chapter.

High-frequency language

When choosing what to focus on, teachers should also take into consideration how frequent the items are, as it is widely agreed that the most frequent words in any language will naturally be the most useful ones (McCarthy, 1990). The more frequent a word, the more likely the learner will need to use it or come across it again in interactions and in texts.

Of course, many teachers rely on their intuition when deciding how frequent a language item might be. But how might teachers learn about frequency to help them make informed decisions? The good news is that information about frequencies of lexical items and grammatical structures can be found in different corpora of the language concerned, such as the British National Corpus (BNC). English-corpora.org provides a list of free corpora. Useful information about the frequency of English lexical items can also be found in several dictionaries, such as the *Longman Dictionary of Contemporary English* (2014, Pearson) and the *Oxford Advanced Learner's Dictionary* (2020, Oxford University Press).

Previously taught content

A common area that teachers choose as a focus of language feedback is grammatical, lexical or discoursal features that the learners have already encountered on the course. This is done because things are better learnt in the long term if learners encounter them repeatedly. This repetition needs to happen over a period with space in between each instance; as such, when an item comes up again in a communicative task, it can be useful to explore it in feedback, either through an explicit reformulation (if it is used ineffectively) or through sharing, as an example of successful communication. As we discussed in **How to work with emergent language** (pages 53–74), this intervention is known as a **recall**.

Another reason for introducing an item in feedback is that the learners may not have used it, possibly because they have forgotten it or because they have found another way to convey their message. In such instances, teachers can use elicitation techniques to encourage the learners to recall the word or phrase, as can be seen in the exchange in Extract 5.1. Recalling useful language in this way can be useful not only as a way of recycling the language, but also to give learners a greater range of options for future communication.

Learner:	Davide, you said your flatmate only thinks about himself. He doesn't care about you. Can anyone remember the word for this?
Teacher	Yes, he's inconsiderate.

Extract 5.1: Elicitation and recall

Language influenced by the learner's L1

Early theories in **SLA** included the notion that L1 interference, also known as negative transfer, was the prime or even sole cause of error. For some time, this meant that many researchers maintained that errors produced by negative transfer were the ones that most needed to be dealt with. Though research has since shown that many L2 speaker errors cannot be traced back to the L1 (VanPatten & Williams, 2015), it can still be useful to point out to learners instances where the influence of their first language might have produced an unclear utterance, or occasions where a word they have chosen in the L1 may not work quite so well in the L2.

For example, **false friends** can often be a source of misunderstanding during intercultural interactions, whether by changing the meaning of what the speaker is trying to say or by altering the connotation. An example of miscommunication caused by a false friend can be seen in the exchange in Extract 5.2, which occurred as learners worked together in the lead-in stage of the lesson described in the next section of this chapter. Learner 1 is South Korean and Learner 2 is German.

Learner 1:	I think this man is a renter
Learner 2:	Is not possible. He's too young.
Learner 1:	Why is he too young?

Extract 5.2: Miscommunication caused by a false friend

In Extract 5.2, Learner 2 has been confused by the word *renter,* which is close to the German word *rentner*, which means *pensioner*. They have therefore misinterpreted Learner 1's meaning. This creates a kind of chain reaction, as Learner 1 subsequently believes that Learner 2 thinks the man in the picture is too young to rent a flat. As false friends can lead to miscomprehension, drawing attention to those used in classes and developing techniques and strategies to raise awareness of them can contribute to L2 development and intercultural competence (Yaylaci & Argynbayev, 2014). The same can be said of learners who draw on idioms in their own language to create a version in the L2. Because many idioms are culturally bound, they often do not work when translated into the L2. False friends and other aspects of the learners' L1 can also be interesting to look at in their own right, as they can raise learners' awareness of the similarities and differences between languages they are familiar with and the language they are studying.

Task-specific language

A final area that you might choose to focus on is task-specific language. For example, if your learners have been asked to debate a topic or negotiate an outcome, it can be useful to provide feedback on the way they made suggestions, justified ideas, expressed agreement or disagreement, or held or relinquished their turns. The feedback might then include reformulations of ineffective or inappropriate phrasing, for example, if the learners have sounded a bit rude when disagreeing. It might also include extensions, where you provide alternative ways of saying the same thing. This might be done if the learners are showing a lack of range or are overusing a specific phrase.

It has been suggested that providing feedback on task-specific language is the same as what teachers would do after the productive stage in a PPP lesson. However, there is a difference: in the PPP procedure, the learners are potentially more conscious about the need to use a specific language item as it has just been explored. This might even cause them to deliberately use an item as they read it off a board or lesson notes. During the feedback stage after the production stage of a PPP lesson, the teacher often refers back to the input when exploring the learner's errors. However, when the focus is genuinely on emergent language, this is not the case.

Examples of emergent language work in a lesson

In this section, we look in more detail at the language items that you might choose to work on in a lesson and the rationale for your choices. To do so, let us examine a lesson we taught with a face-to-face class of adult intermediate learners (B1) studying in London. As you go through this lesson, you will be invited to complete a series of tasks to enable you to think about how you might work with the language that emerged. The topic was flat sharing, which is a common situation for these particular learners. Look at the material in Figure 5.1. What language do you think might emerge at different stages?

Flat-sharing

Activity 1

Look at the pictures. What might be the relationship between the people?

Speaking 1

- Where are you living at the moment? Are you sharing a flat, or are you staying in a student hostel or homestay?
- Have you ever rented a house or flat with other people? What was it like?
- What different interests do/did you have?
- If you have never rented a flat with other people, what do you think it would be like?

Speaking 2

- What are the advantages and disadvantages of sharing a flat with other people? Talk to your partner and fill in the table with your ideas.

Advantages	Disadvantages

Speaking 3: Part 1

- **Student A:** Read the situation on your role card and describe your problems to Student B.

Student A
- My flatmate has parties two or three times a week.
- He never does the dishes or tidies up.
- He takes my food out of the fridge and eats it.

- **Student B:** Listen to Student A's problems and give them advice.

Speaking 3: Part 2

- **Student B:** Read the situation on your role card and describe your problems to Student A.

Student B
- My flatmate cooks very strong-smelling food.
- She smokes in the living room and puts her ash in plates and cups.
- She uses my things without asking.

- **Student A:** Listen to Student B's problems and give them advice.

Figure 5.1: Sample lesson material

Language emerging from Activity 1

Activity 1 is a lead-in task, designed to engage the learners in the topic and generate ideas. In **Creating the right conditions** (pages 29–52) we saw how the lead-in/brainstorming task can create the conditions for emergent language as the learners are free to interpret the pictures as they wish and are invited to share their own ideas and opinions. A brainstorming task like this could be done as an open-class activity; alternatively, learners can be given a short amount of time in pairs to decide who the people in the pictures might be. The teacher can then use the feedback stage to encourage the learners to share their ideas. Note that the examples of feedback in this section were done in open class, so the reformulations were given immediately. However, the teacher also has the option of taking notes and working with the emergent language afterwards.

Before you read about how the teacher worked with the emergent language generated in Activity 1, look at **Reflection task 1** and answer the questions.

Reflection task 1: Language generated from Activity 1

1. Look at the learner contributions below, taken from the open-feedback stage. Which emergent language items might the teacher choose to respond to?

Learner 1:	*I think they are roommate.**
Learner 2:	*They might be boyfriend and girlfriend.*
Learner 3:	*Maybe one owns the house ... and the other rent it.**
Learner 4:	*Yes we think flatmates, or maybe they are a couple.**
Learner 5:	*We agree they are flat<u>MATES</u>.**

2. How might the teacher intervene in each instance?
3. What information could the teacher give about the emergent language? How might the teacher explore the meaning, use, form and pronunciation of the language during this stage?

As in any brainstorming session, some of the words came fully formed from the learners, for example, *flatmate* and *roommate*. This means that the teacher can explore how the learners came to this conclusion before they board the items. There would be no need for any significant interventions or reformulation, except, perhaps, to discuss the fact that the two words are from different varieties of English.

Learner 3's contribution is worth looking at in more detail. Learner 3 has been able to communicate their message, but either they do not have the specific words they want to use or they have forgotten the words. Therefore, the teacher has a strong reason to intervene and reformulate in order to close a gap in the learner's knowledge. The teacher might also believe that the reformulation will provide useful words for these particular learners, who are living and studying in London.

How might the teacher intervene in this instance? As the reformulation will happen live, teachers can choose from a variety of techniques. These are outlined below, along with a possible rationale for each choice. Each intervention type is in bold.

- **Explicit reformulation:** *Good idea. We call these landlord and tenant. The landlord owns the house and they rent it to the tenant.* In this case, the teacher may suspect that the learner does not know the words, so provides them directly.
- **Confirmation request:** *You mean this one is the landlord, and this is the tenant?* In this instance, the teacher briefly makes sure they understand what the learner means. The teacher might do this if they suspect that the learner knows the words but has not been able to recall them.
- **Eliciting.** *OK, what is the word for the person who owns a house and rents it to someone else? What do we call the person who rents the house?* To use elicitation, the teacher must suspect that the learner knows the words or has come across them but was not able to recall them in the moment of interaction. This technique gives the learner time to think. It also probes to see if anyone else in the group knows the word. This is an important move to encourage learners to share and foster cross-class communication. If no one can supply the words, the teacher closes the gap and tells them the words. It is important to do this quickly rather than turning elicitation into an impossible guessing game; if the learners don't know the lexis, it is better to supply the language promptly and move on.

In each case, the teacher has been quite explicit in their reformulation. This has the advantage of drawing the learners' attention directly to the item, so they are more likely to notice it. Of course, it is important to feel that the learners are comfortable having the gaps in their knowledge addressed in this way, but if it is done in a supportive way, the advantages for learning are significant.

Regarding other items that come up in the learners' contribution, teachers might use the same procedures as above to provide the word *couple* for Learner 2. The teacher might also choose to deal briefly with the misplaced stress in *flatmate* (Learner 5). The teacher has the option of simply **recasting** here – in other words, repeating the word with the stress on the first syllable but making no other comment. Alternatively, they can elicit or show how the word is stressed. This could be followed up with some brief drilling, so the learners have the chance to say the reformulated version.

Note that there are some small, morphological errors with the missing plural form of *flatmate* (Learner 1) and the third person *s* in *rent* (Learner 3) – though they are relatively easy to deal with, there is a rationale for ignoring these items as they do not unduly affect the meaning. Of course, a teacher may choose to focus on these items, but it is important not to spend too long on minor points such as these at the expense of giving the learners genuinely new or unknown language.

The next thing to explore is how teachers can work with this new language – in other words, what aspects of meaning, use, form or phonology do they decide to focus on? Figure 5.2 shows what the board looked like at the end of the lead-in. The teacher has not displayed every idea that came up, though they could if they wish. Instead, they have displayed only the items that they reformulated. Note that as there is no specific language aim for this lesson or words that the learners will need to understand for a later stage, the teacher does not need to introduce any other words at this point of the lesson. However, the teacher can still elicit or provide certain items if they think they are useful.

Figure 5.2: Lead-in board

Language emerging from Speaking task 1

Speaking task 1 is an extensive communicative stage in which learners discuss their current living arrangements and share stories about their past experiences. As the learners do the task in small groups, their teacher monitors and notes down emergent language. The teacher can also use this time to note down how they might reformulate what they have heard. We will offer some tips on how to do this in **Development tasks, ideas and commentaries** (pages 129–196).

Before you read about how the teacher worked with the emergent language generated in Speaking task 1 (see Figure 5.1 on pages 81–82), look at **Reflection task 2** and answer the questions.

Reflection task 2: Language from Speaking task 1

1. Look at these notes that the teacher made while they were monitoring. Which language items could the teacher choose to work on in feedback? What might be the rationale for their choices?
    1) *When I was study I have to live with other people.*
    2) *We know each other after live.*
    3) *I share a flat with other friends.*
    4) *I lived with other people.*
    5) *All is common places in the house.*
    6) *We had many common features/We had a similar culture and we like a lot the same things.*
    7) *When I was at the university, we argue a lot with housemates.*
    8) *We argue together.*
2. What information could the teacher give learners about the emergent language they chose to draw to learners' attention? How might the teacher explore the meaning, use, form and pronunciation of the language during feedback?

The notes in Reflection task 2 shows that a greater range of language items have emerged in this stage. The items are also more complex and less predictable. Teachers would therefore need to think more carefully about what they choose to work on and how they would reformulate each one.

As well as exploring various lexical and grammatical items in feedback, teachers can also draw attention to features of phonology. With so much choice, this means that it is often hard for teachers to make a decision. One criterion a teacher can use is to address any repeated errors or slips. For example, in this lesson, learners repeatedly make errors with past tenses. As the teacher has heard this issue repeated more than once or by more than one learner, they might judge that it would be useful to remind the learners of the correct form of the past continuous in the first example or the past simple (or *used to*) in the second two:

*When I was study …**

*I share a flat with friends**

*We argue a lot**

It is unlikely that the message would be completely misunderstood in these examples. However, the lesson material is for intermediate learners (B1), so the teacher can assume that they are familiar with the past continuous and used to. This would make it more likely that the teacher could elicit the reformulations, which can be motivating for learners. Furthermore, since these forms have been taught before, the learners should be able to produce them more accurately. As we saw earlier, recycling previously taught items at a later time increases the likelihood of the learners remembering them.

So, how might you work with the language once you have noticed it? With the first example, you could return to the learner's utterance and repeat it, using an upward inflection in your voice to draw attention to the error and elicit a reformulation. Having written the reformulated sentence on the board, you can elicit the form before asking clarification questions to check the learners understand how the tense is being used, as below:

What tense is this? How do we form it?

Why are we using past continuous? Are you telling us background information?

You could also draw attention to features of phonology by asking the following focusing questions:

Listen to me saying this sentence. […] Did you hear how I said 'was'? **wɒz**. *Is it weak or strong?*

Following this, you could use drilling techniques to encourage the learners to repeat the utterance. This might be done to provide a different mode of input and to aid memory. See the end of this chapter (pages 96–101) for some ways to use repetition to aid the learning process.

In the utterance *I share a flat with friends*, there are several ways in which you could deal with *share* being in the wrong tense. You could simply elicit the past simple form from the learners, thus dealing with the issue quickly. Another way would be to explore *used to* as an alternative. If you believe that your learners have encountered this form before and are avoiding it, eliciting it here would remind the learners about it. If not, it would be a good time to introduce it. This would extend range and push the learners to use a more complex past form:

*I **shared** a flat with friends.*

*I **used to share** a flat with friends.*

Having checked that the learners understand the emergent language, you can use the board (as shown in Figure 5.3 below) to provide further clarification by displaying the forms, exploring patterns and eliciting further examples.

Figure 5.3: Board after Speaking task 1

When dealing with emergent language, you can use two techniques to help learners better understand the meaning and use of an item and how it is formed. These techniques do not have to come in a particular order; this will depend on the language you are working on.

1. You could explore the syntax (for instance, subject + verb + object). This is called exploring the **syntagmatic relationships** or using **syntagmatic extension**. This is done by looking at the sentence you are working with from left to right and examining the grammatical patterns that are possible horizontally from the first to the last word, as shown in Figure 5.4:

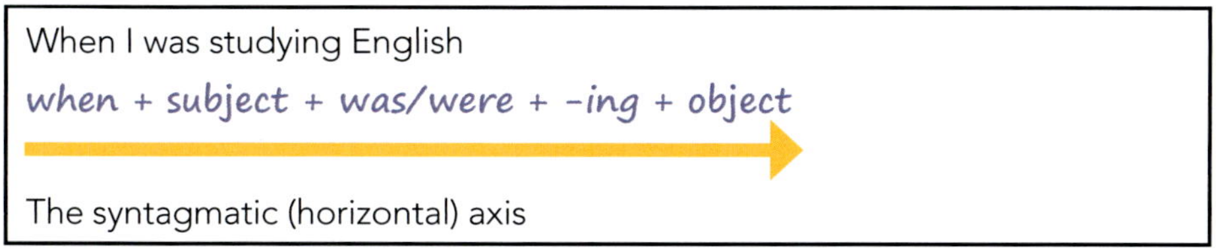

Figure 5.4: Syntagmatic extension

2. The second choice is to use **paradigmatic relationships** or **vertical extension**. Looking vertically is a technique you can use to substitute, extend and explore other possibilities in terms of the meaning of an utterance. In the example in Figure 5.5, the teacher has elicited other examples of the past continuous to describe the background to an event. The different examples help extend the learner's lexical range. The repeated instances of the verb + *-ing* also helps the learners to notice this pattern, thereby reinforcing the form of the second verb used along the horizontal axis.

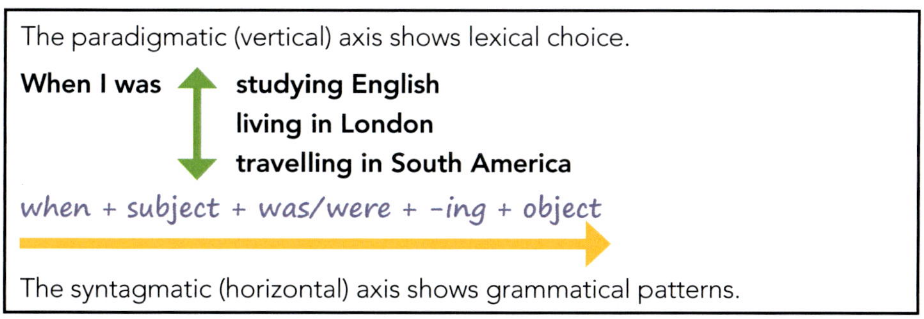

Figure 5.5: Syntagmatic and paradigmatic extension

Looking at language forms through the horizontal and vertical axis is an effective way of dealing with meaning and use while mapping on the form. This technique can also help teachers assess what the learners know and what might be useful and new, as the original sentence is added to with input from the learners. Putting vertical and horizontal extensions on the board also provides a systematic record for learners to use when recording language in their notebooks.

Vertical and horizontal extensions are also useful when dealing with lexis (see Figure 5.6 below). To explore this, let us look at another issue that came up in this stage of the lesson. Below, you can see an example of learner language that you might choose to work with, possibly because what the learner said was unclear and may be misunderstood:

*We had some common features. We had a similar culture, and we like a lot the same things**

In response to this output, you could choose to introduce the lexical chunk *have something in common*, which would be best given to the learners as a whole chunk. You might choose this lexical chunk because you feel it would be useful for learners at this level. You might also judge that the chunk is relatively high frequency.

To introduce this item, you could write down verbatim what the learner said as you monitored. Then, in feedback, you could draw attention to the utterance and explore what the learner was trying to say. You could then try to elicit or simply give the learners the phrase *we had a lot in common*.

Having supplied the phrase, you can move on to clarify the meaning and elicit extensions by asking questions such as *What is the opposite of 'have lots in common'?* By eliciting, you can see if anyone in the class can supply the negative form. If nobody is able to do so, you can then provide the new language yourself. You can also present other examples to consolidate meaning and use, for example, *have little in common*. Providing other examples enables teachers to look at what is paradigmatically possible. By doing so, you give the learners alternative ways of using the new language to express what they want to.

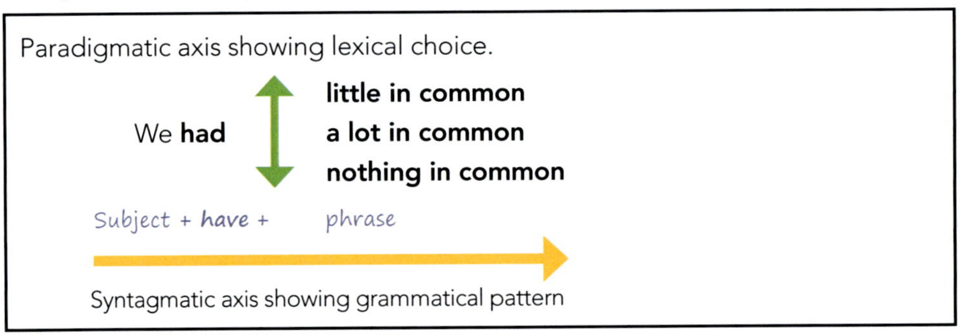

Figure 5.6: Syntagmatic and paradigmatic extensions

To further clarify meaning, you can give examples from your own life or elicit stories from the learners about people you had something in common with. By encouraging greater attention to the language, this increases cognitive depth, which can make language more memorable. This also serves to shift the focus from the form back onto meaning. If there is time, other interesting discussions can arise in class as a result.

Language emerging from Speaking task 2

Speaking task 2 was another communicative stage in which the learners discussed the advantages and disadvantages of living with other people (see Figure 5.1 on pages 81–82). As in Speaking task 1, the teacher monitored and noted down emergent language episodes as the learners worked together. They then used the open-class feedback stage to respond to ideas and opinions and work with some language they had noted down.

Before you read about how the teacher worked with the emergent language generated in Speaking task 2, look at **Reflection task 3** and answer the questions.

Reflection task 3: Language from Speaking task 2

1. Look at the notes below that the teacher made while they monitored. Why might the teacher have chosen these items to work on in feedback? What might be the rationale for their choices?

    1) *Some people never put away their rubbish.**
    2) *Some people are noise people.**
    3) *They can be not clean people.**
    4) *Your housemate might fraud you (pronounced* ***ˈfraʊwʊd****). You understand? They go your room and buy something for them from your name. They* ***fraʊwʊd*** *you.**
    5) *You have to the same bathroom and everything.**
    6) *You all pay the bills.**

2. For one of the examples, the teacher chose to intervene to help one of the groups as they worked together. Which item might have prompted them to offer immediate support and what might be the rationale for this choice?
3. What information could they give about the emergent language they chose? How might they explore the meaning, use, form and pronunciation of the language during the feedback stage?

As in the feedback to Speaking task 1, the teacher has a varied and unpredictable set of items to deal with, and there is a rationale to reformulate any or all of the items listed above, as each emergent language episode could provide some interesting and useful language for a group of B1 learners. However, there is a strong reason to deal with items 1 and 4, as each of these utterances has either caused miscomprehension (item 4) or has the potential to do so (item 1).

In item 4, the mispronunciation of the word *fraud* has meant that the learners in the group have not understood the speaker's message. As the teacher observes this happening, they have a rationale to intervene directly to help get the conversation back on track. This could be done with a clarification request (in other words, the teacher asks the speaker what they mean before supplying an alternative), for example, *someone might steal your identity*. Alternatively, if the teacher wants to move this on so the learners can get back to the task, they could directly supply a suitable word or phrase with an explicit reformulation. However, there is a rationale to also drill the word *fraud* so that the speaker is more likely to be understood the next time they use it.

In item 1, it is easy to interpret what the learner means when they say, *put away the rubbish*. However, as there is some potential for misunderstanding, the teacher has a rationale to deal with this item. The teacher might also intuit that these are quite high-frequency words for the level and certainly for the context (house sharing).

As you will see from the board record in Figure 5.7, the teacher has chosen to use the feedback to share the phrase *someone might steal your identity.* The teacher might do this because they consider it a useful phrase to share. However, it would also encourage the group who originally encountered the phrase with the opportunity to recall it and teach it to the rest of the class. This means that the phrase has been re-encountered, and this can add to the chances of it being recalled later. To deal with the meaning of fraud and to offer extensions, the teacher might choose to look at the collocation *commit fraud*.

You can also see that the teacher has chosen to use the feedback stage to clarify the difference between *throw something away* and *put something away*. To do this, they have used the same technique of vertical extension that we saw being used in the feedback to Speaking task 1 (see pages 86–91). This technique has two benefits. The first enables the teacher to elicit things that you would put away and things you would throw away, thereby helping the learners to demonstrate their understanding of the difference in meaning. Going beyond the word in this way also shows the learners that each of these multi-word verbs takes an object.

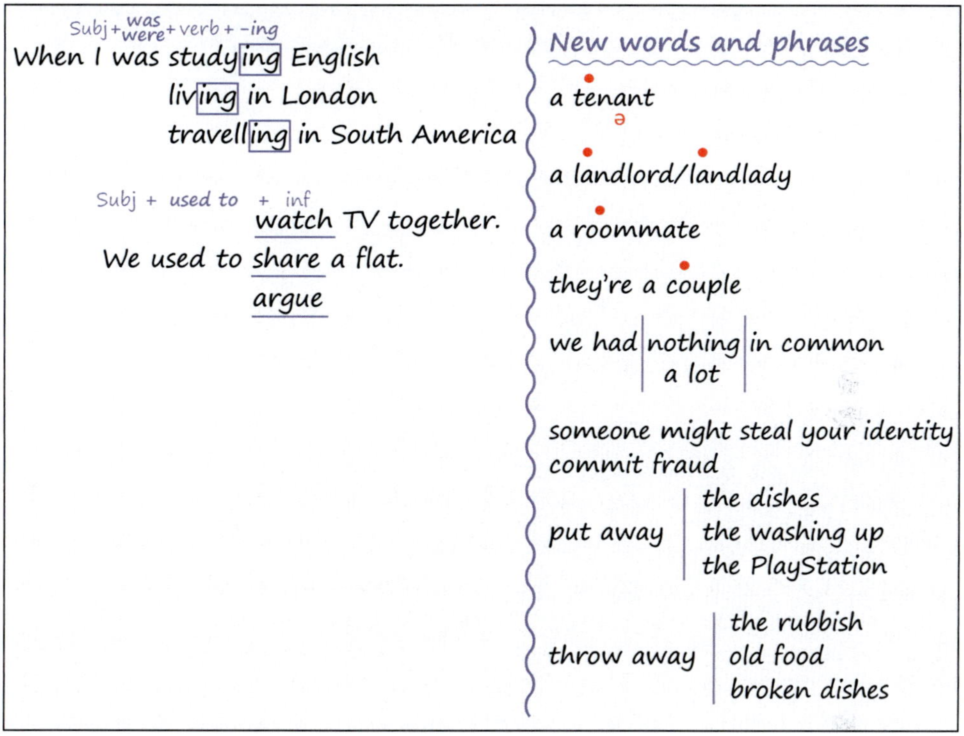

Figure 5.7: Speaking task 2 board record

Language emerging from Speaking task 3

In the final stage of the lesson, the teacher created a role play in which the learners gave advice to someone having an issue with a housemate. As they monitored the task, the teacher once again noted down emergent language they might explore afterwards. They then used the open-class feedback stage to respond to ideas and opinions and work with emergent language.

Before you read about how the teacher worked with the emergent language generated in Speaking task 3 (see Figure 5.1 on pages 81–82), look at **Reflection task 4** and answer the questions.

Reflection task 4: Language from Speaking task 3

As the learners worked together, the teacher noted down examples of emergent language. Just before the learners finished speaking, the teacher wrote the following six examples on the board to look at in feedback.

1) You should to tell the landlord about the parties.
2) You should have a meeting with all the people in the house.
3) Don't do the dishes also. It will get messy for everyone.
4) Put your name on the food.
5) Get a fridge for your room ... or lock the fridge.
6) Put fire alarm in the room so he can't smoke.

1. Look at the examples of emergent language above. Why might the teacher have chosen to look at these items?
2. What other ways of giving advice might the teacher introduce in the feedback stage? How might they explore the ways in which these items are used?

There are two reasons why teachers may have chosen to look at these items. The first is that they are directly useful for the task at hand. This means that the learners will be able to see that they have been successful in giving advice, and the teacher can open a discussion about how useful each piece of advice might be and whether it would work or not.

The learners have been broadly successful in using *should*, bar the odd misuse or slip with *to*. They have also repeatedly used the imperative, which is a very common way of giving advice, especially among people who are close to each other. However, the teacher may choose to introduce or elicit other ways of giving advice. This could be done to add to the options the learners have, and thereby increase their lexical range. Introducing new language through extensions also means that the learners will be primed to understand the new items as they already know what they mean. This is certainly the case with this lesson, where the teacher can be confident about discussing the appropriacy and pragmatic use of any different phrases they introduce because the learners already know the meaning and function from the context. The learners will therefore be able to map the meaning and function of the new language to their existing knowledge.

To introduce other ways of giving advice, you could simply elicit by asking the learners if they can think of any other ways giving advice. If your learners are having trouble with this, you could add little prompts on the board (see Figure 5.8 below). For example, you could write the start of a phrase on the board or add gaps, as shown below. You can also use metalinguistic feedback to elicit that *could* or *ought to* can be used as well as *should* in the final example. To do this, you can ask a question like *What other verb could I use here?*

I suggest you ______________.
Why ________ __________ phone the landlord?
Have you __________ putting your name on your food?
You ________ have a house meeting.

Figure 5.8: Prompts on the whiteboard

As we saw in Speaking task 1 (see Figure 5.1 on pages 81–82), teachers can then explore the meaning and use of the items and look at the forms and patterns in each one. In terms of clarifying meaning and use, this might involve asking questions to ascertain that a phrase like *Have you tried calling the landlord?* Is more tentative than *Call the landlor*d, which is very direct. When exploring this, you can show learners the difference by discussing who you might use an imperative with and who you would not. Drilling can also be used to model the intonation and reinforce how some of the phrases sound more direct than others.

To look at the form, you can use vertical extensions to model and raise awareness of patterns. This can be seen in the final board (Figure 5.8 on page 96), where the teacher has used several vertical extensions to show the common features within the new phrases, for example, *Have you tried* + *-ing* and *Why don't you* + bare infinitive. This is important because the lexical chunk dictates the grammar patterns that follow, in this case, verb + *-ing* (see Hoey, 2012).

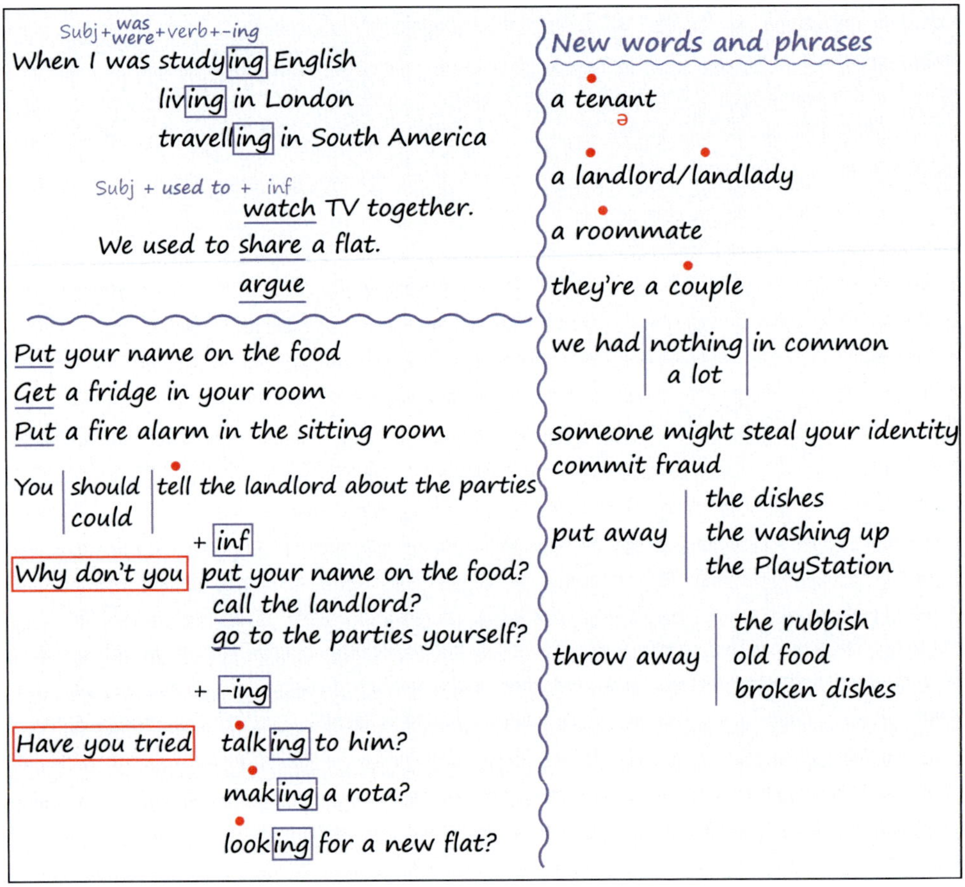

Figure 5.8: The whiteboard at the end of the sample lesson

Ideas for memory work and recycling emergent language

You have seen how teachers might choose what emergent language to explore in a lesson. Regardless of why you have chosen an item, it is also important to consider what you might then do with that language to make it more memorable. Let us move on to explore some ideas for recalling, recycling and reviewing emergent language.

Recognition and controlled repetition

It is widely believed that repetition in the form of drills can help learners commit new language patterns to working memory (for example, Bilbrough, 2013). There are different techniques that can be used for oral repetition of emergent language. These include:

- **silent drilling** where the learners repeat language to themselves two or three times silently.
- **choral drilling** where the class repeats a chunk of language after you.
- **individual drilling** where the learners repeat language individually or in pairs.
- **shadowing** where the learners mouth the words alongside the teacher as the teacher says a chunk of language.

Lexical notebooks

Training learners to record new language is important to enable the learner to be more autonomous. Figure 5.9 shows an example of a learner's lexical notebook.

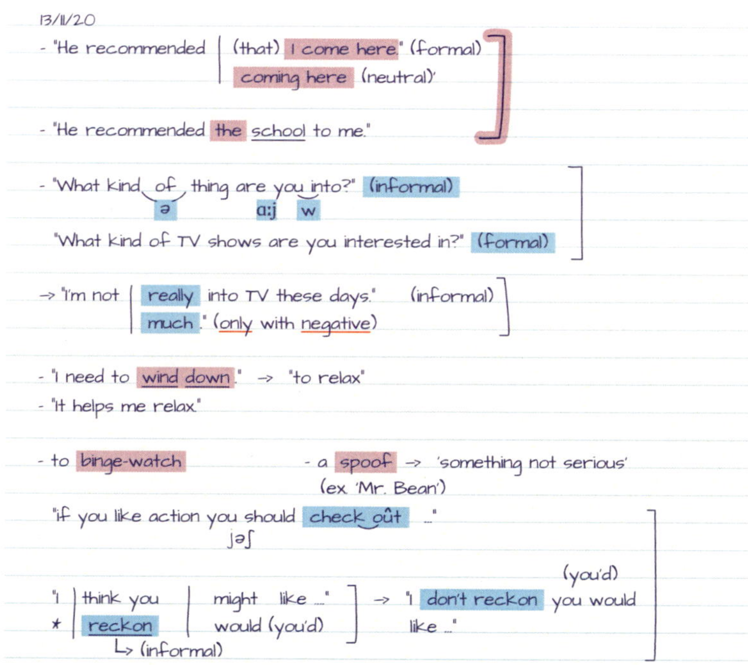

Figure 5.9: Learner's lexical notebook

To make the language in a lexical notebook more usable in the future or easier to review, the following criteria are useful to follow:

- Display language in a chunk to provide clear examples of meaning, use and language in context. Then encourage your learners to record the language in the same way.
- Organise your board so that learners can copy from it easily.
- Use horizontal extensions to highlight features of grammar, lexis and pronunciation for learners to note down in their book.

Recall

Here are ten simple ways of encouraging recall in a lesson (adapted from Chinn & Lamb, 2014). All of these activities are commonly used by teachers who use the **Lexical Approach**, a methodology that sees the teaching and analysis of lexical phrases and chunks as key to acquiring a language. In each example, the lexical chunks are based around giving advice. In a lesson, you can use one of these techniques or a combination of them. All work well on the classroom whiteboard, but if working online, you can simply use a blank document either on the screen or shared using a file-sharing app.

1. **Using prompts:** On the board, write the key words from an utterance or give the learners a gapped sentence. The learners then complete it. This is a type of grammaticisation task, as suggested in **Creating the right conditions** (pages 29–52).

   It/good/idea ____________________.

   Have you_____(try)______(ask) your tutor?

2. **Exploring options with vertical extension:** As described earlier in this chapter, you can encourage learners to recall possible alternatives in a chunk by using vertical extension, for example, *should*, *need to*. You can then have a feedback session to see if the learners can recall the difference in meaning.

   You could call the landlord.

   ____

   ____

3. **Open cloze:** A simple way to draw learners' attention to language and get them to recall what has been taught is to produce a gap fill. For example, you can take out key parts of the fixed expression and

encourage learners to remember what goes in the gap. It is also useful to gap tricky parts of speech to encourage learners to remember items such as function words, prepositions or auxiliary verbs.

If I ________ you, I ________.

If you are looking ________ advice ...

I think ______ good thing to do is ...

4. **Reordering a sentence:** A jumbled sentence or chunk can help learners recall it or remember syntagmatic patterns.

   You already thought have about probably this.

   (You've probably already thought about this.)

5. **Error correction:** Revisiting common errors that you have heard or that you know learners regularly make with a chunk or pattern can encourage learners to focus on accuracy. This can be done as a game or a quiz at the start of a class or at the end of the week.

   Why you don't try read more?

   doing try don't Why you that?

   (Why don't you try doing that?)

6. **Choose the correct answer:** Giving learners a choice can help refocus them on language you have looked at before. In the example below, the learner is first prompted to consider the context in which the language arose and why one form is preferable to the other.

   Maybe it would / should be good to call the landlord.

7. **Personalisation:** Personalising language can be a way to encourage cognitive depth and to make it more meaningful (and therefore more memorable) to the learner. Sentence completion activities are useful for doing this.

   When you find a new flatmate, you should ________ .

8. **Matching:** If the language lends itself to being split into two logical chunks, you could encourage learners to match them. This can help them recognise and remember syntagmatic relationships.

   It's a good — *you try finding a new house?*

   Why don't — *idea to find a new house.*

9. **Deletion:** Rub out half of a pre-boarded collocation or part of a chunk, and then ask the learners to recall it. This is good for helping learners memorise the language.
10. **Progressive deletion:** Erase parts of a chunk and ask the learners to identify what is missing. Repeat this process until the whole chunk has disappeared and the learners recall all of it, as in the example below:

    / ___ / *have nothing* / ____ / *common.*

    / ___ / *have* / ___ / ___ / *common* /.

    / ___ //___ // ____ //___ //___ /.

Lexical cards

Another technique involves teachers recording language on cards during the lesson and bringing them back into a subsequent class for revision (see Figure 5.10 below). These can then be used in the following ways:

- Use one of the techniques for drawing attention to language mentioned above, such as a jumbled lexical chunk, a matching task or a gap fill.
- Give the learners cards to test each other.
- Encourage learners to create their own cards.

Note that it is useful to record prompts on the back of the cards so the learners can use them without you.

Figure 5.10: Lexical cards

Test your partner

At the end of a lesson, learners record the language in their notebooks. On the following day or in subsequent lessons, the learners can test their partner on the emergent language. Alternatively, pair up learners who attended when the language emerged with ones who were absent. The learners who attended can teach it to those who didn't.

Write mini-dialogues

Learners put the language that has emerged into mini-dialogues, which they present to the rest of the class. This provides an opportunity for you to see if there is more work needed in the use of the language item.

Create a poster

Learners work in groups to produce posters of the language that they thought was interesting that week. Following this, they present their posters or circulate around the class visiting each other's posters and compare which items of language they chose. This can show you which language was useful and memorable to the learners. This can also allow the learners to assess what needs to be revisited.

Backs to the board

This is a class competition where learners guess the phrase that is written behind them by another learner on the board. This activity helps with recall, and the element of competition can generate energy in the class.

Conclusion

In this chapter, we have looked at ways in which you might note down learner language used during communicative stages and discussed the options teachers have when choosing what emergent language to focus on or prioritise. We also looked at the techniques you can use to clarify the meaning and use of the new items, and how you might deal with any relevant features of form and phonology. We also looked at how you might aid memorisation, recycle and review emergent language in later lessons.

Working with emergent language requires a combination of skills and techniques, and each one can take time to master. Experience and practice matter, but to help speed up the process of developing emergent language skills, there are several useful strategies and tasks that you can use. In the next part of the book, we will provide tips, tasks and strategies to help you understand, monitor, develop and hone your skills for working with emergent language. We will also offer advice for teacher educators on how they can develop emergent language skills of the teachers they work with.

Professional development

Questions for reflection

- Which rationale for choosing emergent language items do you think is most important in your context? Why is this the case?
- Which of the techniques for clarifying and displaying language do you use in your teaching? How have your learners responded? Consider why they responded in this way.

Things to try

- After you have taught a lesson, take a picture of your boardwork. Notice what emergent language you have on the board and ask yourself the following questions: *What language did you record? Why did you choose to work on this language? How did you use the board to record and draw attention to the language?*
- Try out a technique for working with emergent language that you have never used before. Afterwards, think about how successful it was. How did the learners respond?

Part 2:
Practical applications

6. Teacher development and emergent language

This chapter focuses on the challenges encountered by teachers when working with emergent language, the role of reflective practice in teacher development and the principles underpinning it, and the different ways in which teachers can investigate how they work with emergent language.

Given all that we are covering in this chapter, let us define the key terms you will encounter:

- **reflective practice** is the process of exploring and reflecting on your teaching in order to make it more effective or better meet your learners' needs.
- **skills acquisition** is the process of moving from conscious control of a skill to automaticity.
- **critical incident** is an unplanned event in a lesson that teachers see as interesting or challenging. By noticing and formally reflecting on critical incidents, it may be possible for you to uncover new insights about your teaching or the learning process and come up with solutions to problems.

In this chapter, we consider the role of reflection in teacher learning and highlight the different ways in which teachers might go about investigating the ways in which they work with emergent language. **Development tasks, ideas and commentaries** (pages 129–196) then provides a series of tasks to help raise teachers' awareness of their treatment of emergent language and develop their skills in this complex area. Each task is accompanied by answers or insights and reflections from teachers who have tried out the task. These commentaries will enable the reader to compare what they learnt from doing the task with the findings of another teacher. Though you may wish to go straight to choosing a task from **Development tasks, ideas and commentaries** (pages 129–196), we recommend beginning with this chapter, which focuses on CPD, and the general ways in which teachers can investigate classroom interaction and emergent language in their teaching.

Teaching as a complex and open skill

At any given moment in class, there are multiple decisions teachers make as they constantly assess the situation to make the most effective choices for learners. As Malderez and Weddell (2007) observe, teaching is a 'complex, open skill'. First, it is 'complex' in the sense that it requires multitasking throughout a lesson. This is particularly true when it comes to working with emergent language, as from the moment a teacher notices an error or potentially useful language item, numerous decisions have to be made, for instance:

- *What is the learner trying to say?*
- *If there is an error, do I ignore it, or is it worth correcting?*
- *Should I intervene now, or would it be better to wait?*
- *What phrase would work better here?*
- *How explicit should I be?*
- *Is this language useful to everyone?*
- *What phrase would be appropriate for this level?*
- *How should I present the new item on the board?*
- *How will the learner feel about my intervention?*

Second, teaching is an 'open' skill because there is no one way of carrying out a classroom action and there are often several choices available to teachers. For example, there are numerous ways to draw attention to emergent language, as you saw in **How to work with emergent language** (pages 53–74). Therefore, if we are to develop as teachers, we need to experiment with different ways of carrying out classroom practice in order to extend and deepen our teaching repertoire to best meet the needs of our learners.

Whenever you learn new techniques or skills as a teacher, you need to practise them. If you take a skills acquisition approach (Anderson, 1982) to teacher learning, the process of learning is first to become consciously aware of a new technique or idea you wish to use and then to try it out. The process of practising the new teaching skill helps you refine it and eventually internalise it so that it becomes more automatic. The knowledge you gain from this can be referred to as 'procedural knowledge'. As this type of knowledge can be accessed quickly, it affords you more thinking space, putting less demand on your attentional resources (see Randall &

Thornton, 2001). As a result, you are better able to attend to what your learners are saying and what message they are trying to get across, as well as considering what to reformulate and how to intervene.

However, when you try out new ways of doing things, it can be a rather messy and clunky business – you are consciously trying to control what you are doing and you lack the fluidity that practice gives you. This can be disheartening, sometimes leading you to reject the new element of practice and to revert to what is familiar, comfortable and safe. It is important to remember, though, that the clumsiness involved in implementing a new teaching idea is completely normal. It is part of the process of refining a new technique so that it can become part of your classroom skill set. The more techniques you can add to your skill set, the greater the array of choices you have at your disposal when responding to learners' emerging needs. To advance from a novice to expert teacher, it is advisable to develop the ability to improvise when the unexpected happens in class, and this can be done by adding to your repertoire of skills. In this way, you are empowered and better able to meet your learners' emerging needs.

Teachers' concerns about working with emergent language

One of the main concerns expressed by teachers we have worked with is that dealing with emergent language is difficult, leading many to avoid creating the space in class to do so. A number of specific issues have been highlighted, including the following:

- *It's hard to hear what learners are saying when they are talking together in class.*
- *I find it hard to think on the spot.*
- *I'm indecisive about which language items I should focus on.*
- *Sometimes I don't know whether the intervention should be on the spot or delayed.*
- *Sometimes I'm not sure what an appropriate or useful reformulation would be.*
- *I am unsure if I should share a piece of emergent language with the whole class or give feedback to the learner individually.*

- *I struggle to find the time to work on emergent language as there is so much else to cover on the syllabus.*
- *I don't know if my learners like me focusing on emergent language, or if they think it's a waste of time.*
- *No one has shown me how to do it and I don't feel I really know what it is.*

These are all valid concerns, as dealing with unplanned language alongside other important activities and teacher actions puts a strain on our attentional resources and working memory. Dealing with emergent language often gets put aside when teachers are focusing on other teaching activities, such as monitoring to see if everyone is on task during a speaking activity, offering support when learners are confused about a task, deciding whether to change the order of stages or activities, or concentrating on what is coming next in the lesson.

However, responding to learners is something all teachers do, and to some degree, most teachers are dealing with emergent language whether they are aware of it or not. For example, teachers answer learners' questions about language, supply new vocabulary when there is a gap, and correct learners when they make errors. This is all part of interaction in class and, if we take a sociocultural view of learning, we can view learning as happening within interaction (see **Why work with emergent language?**, pages 13–28). Because learning occurs in interaction, the role of the teacher in creating opportunities for interacting and supporting learners' development is key. Research into classroom interaction (for example, Walsh, 2011, 2013) has revealed the intricate skills of teachers in scaffolding and supporting learners when helping them express their ideas verbally. This is why teachers need to develop an awareness of what constitutes successful interaction. In fact, Walsh (2013) calls for developing an awareness of classroom discourse to be at the centre of all language teacher education courses.

It is by exploring classroom interaction that teachers develop what van Lier (2000) calls 'microscopic understandings' of what we do in class. In turn, these microscopic understandings afford teachers more intuitive and sensitive responses to learners in interaction. In the next section, we will provide you with practical ideas for this type of microscopic investigation regarding their treatment of emergent language. It is important to note that this kind of investigation can benefit both newer and more experienced teachers. Both can gain insight into their classroom interaction and discover new aspects of practice, and both can unearth features of their practice they might not be aware that they possess.

For example, consider the teacher who videos themselves and notices that they use a lot more explicit feedback on emergent language than they initially thought. This could lead them to consider the principle behind their actions and what their beliefs are. The principle they discover could be that they believe it is important to signal to learners that a certain item of language should be noted. This kind of realisation can lead to more conscious decision making, and ultimately lead teachers to be more aware of what they are doing in class. As a result of this experience, they were able to articulate this belief to teachers they worked with, which in turn added to their practice as a teacher educator.

Ways of investigating emergent language in class

There are many theoretical approaches and models of how teacher development takes place. In the following section, we will identify the key ideas that have underpinned our approach to investigating emergent language.

The ideas that follow in this section draw inspiration from the work of academics and practitioners who have encouraged teachers to become researchers of their own practice. These include Steve Walsh's work on **Classroom Interactional Competence (CIC)** (2011); Steve Mann and Steve Walsh on **Evidence-Based Reflective Practice** (2017); Leo van Lier on the role of **emergence** in language learning (2004); Dick Allwright and Judith Hanks on **Exploratory Practice** (2009), which encourages teachers to investigate small areas of classroom practice that puzzle them; Michael Wallace (1998) and Ann Burns (2009) on approaches to **action research**, where teachers formulate a research question regarding classroom practice that they want to systematically investigate; and Richard Smith and Paula Rebolledo on **exploratory action research** (2018), which combines the ideas of action research and exploratory practice, and encourages teachers to share discoveries they have made with peers.

Reflective practice

The importance of reflection in teacher development has a history dating back to the 1930s, when John Dewey introduced the idea of reflection for learning as a deliberate and active process. However, it is only in more recent history that various models have been put forward to describe types of reflection, and to explain how reflection works and when it might happen (see Anderson, 2020). One example is that of Schön (1983), who surmised that reflection can be in the moment in class (**reflection-in-action**) as well as after class (**reflection-on-action**; see Farrell, 2022). In reflection-in-action, a teacher might watch a video of themselves teaching. While watching the recording, they might become aware of a particular intervention type they did not know they were using, for instance, **clarification requests**. The **post-lesson reflection** may then lead teachers to think about the effect of this technique and whether they could be using it more frequently. Reflecting in- and on-action can also help teachers address issues with their teaching. For example, to reflect on-action, a teacher might watch themselves after a class and decide that they need to increase their wait time after asking questions or **eliciting** during interactional moments. Through this process of reflection, teachers can plan how to implement something new into their practice. This planning stage has been called **reflection-for-action** (Killion & Todnem, 1991).

It should be noted that in some cases, the term **reflective practice** has been over-used; indeed, some approaches to it, such as written post-lesson reflection, have been criticised or viewed as unhelpful as they are often enforced by the institution or training course, and this can lead to teachers paying lip service to the process of reflection while not fully embracing the concept (Walsh & Mann, 2017). This kind of pressure can subsequently lead to a lack of willingness on the part of the teacher to engage in deeper personal learning. For example, a teacher may be required to fill out a post-lesson reflection after being observed by an academic manager as part of a cycle of school-wide observations. However, because teachers often view this kind of observation as a form of assessment, they might write down what they think the observer wants to see rather than what they really think (Hobbs, 2007). This lack of real engagement in reflection has caused many researchers and educators to suggest that reflection should become more teacher led.

Writers such as Mann and Walsh (2017) have also called for reflection to become more evidence based. Evidence-based reflection involves teachers identifying examples of classroom practice and examining them in detail. For example, a teacher could record a feedback stage in a recording of their lesson and, as they listen to it, note down the types of question they used to prompt and involve learners. They could then decide which prompts and questions were useful, and which could be improved on. This differs from institutionalised reflection in that the focus is on encouraging teachers to explore their practice to stimulate development for themselves. Gathering data from their own classrooms helps teachers become more interested in investigating what they do in class as the reflection is more meaningful to them. We will look at how you can do this later in this chapter.

Teachers often need support and encouragement to develop reflective skills, and there are many activities and tools that can be used to support teachers to engage meaningfully with reflection. Focused tasks and activities can lead to more evidence-based reflection as they help us to examine a specific aspect of our practice and look objectively at what we do in class. This can lead to what Wallace (1998) calls 'illuminative' discoveries, in which we gain deeper insight into an issue we were already aware of, and 'heuristic' discoveries, when we learn something new about our practice.

Some views on teacher development focus on a learning cycle such as that shown in Figure 6.1, and we would encourage you to consider this cycle when planning to include analysis into your teaching, or when advising and supporting teachers in their development. It is important to note that as with all theoretical models, it should not be followed unquestioningly as the process of development is rarely linear or purely cyclical. The process of learning through experience can be recursive, and sometimes the starting point is unpredictable (see Mann & Walsh, 2017). Nevertheless, models such as Kolb's experiential learning cycle (1984), later developed by Gibbs (1988) – see Figure 6.1, which is an adapted version – can provide us with some prompts when analysing classroom practice.

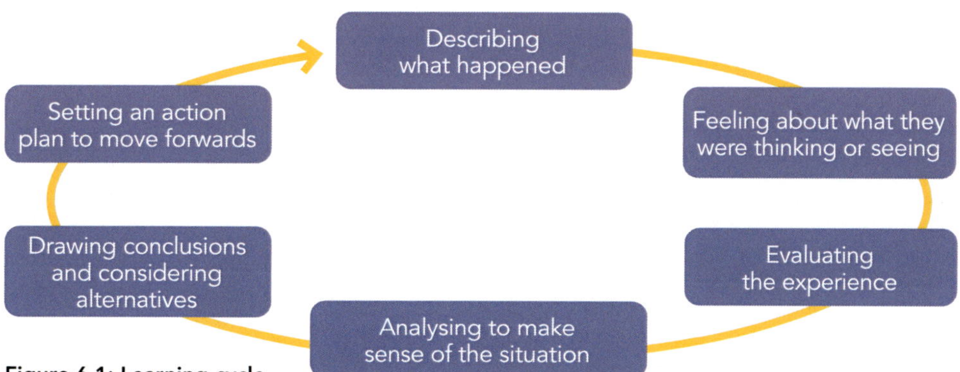

Figure 6.1: Learning cycle

By considering the steps above, you begin a process of discovery with a classroom experience or 'critical incident'. For example, say you correct a learner, and they ignore your correction. This incident plays on your mind after class and you feel unsettled about it. From this point, you can start to evaluate what was involved in this critical incident. For example, you might start to think about why there was no uptake, which might prompt you to examine your role in the incident. Perhaps you only gave a subtle recast, and the learner was paying too much attention to getting their meaning across to attend to form. Through this process of reflecting, evaluating and analysing the situation, it is possible to draw conclusions. In this case, it could be that you needed to be more overt about your intervention. Alternatively, you could have delayed the intervention until the learner had finished what they were trying to say, thereby freeing up the learner's attentional resources and thus making the correction more explicit. From here, you can plan to experiment with more explicit intervention in the future.

In order to support your reflection, you can use the following questions as prompts:

- *What happened during the critical incident?*
- *What was going through my mind at the time?*
- *How did I feel?*
- *Why did I think/feel that?*
- *What was good/bad about the situation?*
- *What sense can I make of this situation?*
- *What can I do differently next time?*
- *What skills do I need to address this?*

Emergent language story 1: Luiz

Luiz is an experienced teacher from Brazil who had become interested in developing the way he dealt with emergent language. When teaching a high-level class, he noticed that the learners were not paying much attention to the emergent language that he explored. This led him to question the way he intervened. Luiz stated:

[I noticed] students need a more direct approach. If you're too subtle, your students don't pick it up. ➔

So how did Luiz come to this conclusion? Through classroom experience, he identified something that was puzzling, so re-evaluated and analysed why his learners seemed not to notice the emergent language he was highlighting. From there, he was able to conclude that he had favoured an implicit approach to highlighting emergent language and maybe a more direct approach was necessary. He trialled this in class and noted an increase in learner responses. This cycle and outcome were repeated in subsequent classes, which enabled Luiz to come to the conclusion that a more direct approach was more effective for this group of learners. Through this microscopic investigation, there was a clear shift in Luiz's classroom practice. Although it was a seemingly small shift, Luiz saw it as significant to the way he gives feedback and to his students' learning. He noticed that the learners were noting down the language he highlighted, and that there were better signs of acknowledgment and uptake. It is sometimes the small adjustments in our practice that create significant shifts to the way we approach classroom practice.

Once Luiz had identified a problem, he was able to draw on his experience to monitor and address this area in his classes. The following part of this section outlines ways in which you can gather data about your teaching. Like Luiz, teachers are strongly encouraged to explore their own context and to choose relevant areas to investigate within it. The idea behind the tasks in this section of the book is to put teachers in the driving seat of their own development and encourage them to become researchers of their own emergent language practices.

Investigating your teaching and collecting evidence

There are many ways to gather data from your classroom practice to help you home your reactive skills to learner output. These include the following:

- videoing yourself and watching it afterwards
- recording learners interacting
- peer observation
- encouraging dialogue with others
- recording your board by taking a photo of it
- using lesson transcripts

Videoing yourself

One of the most effective ways of gathering data about your teaching is to use video to capture real classroom action. Videoing in language teacher development has been made relatively easy with the advent of smartphones, and now, with so much teaching happening online, it is even easier to record ourselves teaching. The potential of using video in language teacher education has been demonstrated by the work of Steve Mann and his colleagues (Mann et al., 2019), who suggest that the technology that is available to many teachers today makes the process of recording lessons much easier than in the past. We have also found videoing ourselves extremely informative in examining our own practice, and the same can be said of teachers we work with.

Videoing yourself is probably the best way to get a genuine impression of your classroom practice. It is also a good idea to video your own everyday classes rather than setting up special ones. This is because videoing your normal lessons will be more likely to capture evidence of real teaching. It is also advisable to video a number of lessons or sections of lessons with a class you are familiar with. This way, it is more likely that genuine moments of interaction will yield examples of you working with emergent language. If, like many teachers, you don't have enough time to analyse large stretches of classroom interaction, you can simply use short video or audio recordings to provide useful snapshots of your teaching practice. These snapshots are best obtained in moments when learners are interacting together or with you in whole-class interactional moments, such as in a feedback session after a communicative task. To annotate your videos, try using an app such as Panopto or EVO; these platforms allow you to note down elements you notice about interaction and mark where you found them. Consider the following advice when videoing yourself and your classes:

- *Get permission from the learners (and your school, if appropriate).*
- *Avoid overplanning or 'scripting' your lesson, so as to make space for genuine interaction.*
- *Consider how you will record the sections of your lesson. Smartphones tend to be the most effective, as many people have them and it is easy to quickly review what you have recorded.*
- *If you are using a portable video camera (such as a GoPro), make sure you have microphones near the learners.*

Remember that for many people, yourself perhaps included, being videoed is daunting, and it can feel embarrassing to watch yourself teaching. Initially, you may be fixated on mannerisms you are not aware you have (or in the case of one of the authors, 'I'm never wearing that shirt again!'). However, after getting over the initial discomfort of seeing yourself on camera, you will move beyond the superficial elements and begin to notice deeper patterns of behaviour. As a result, you can begin to question yourself about the choices you have made in a lesson, and this is the exciting part of development. As with everything, you have to plunge in if you want to reap the reward; some of the development ideas and activities in **Development tasks, ideas and commentaries** (pages 129–196) can support you in doing so.

Emergent language story 2: Holly

On her diploma course, Holly chose to work on demanding more of her learners in feedback sections of her lessons. She would do this by pushing and probing during these interactional moments to see the limits of her learners' language abilities. Her tutors encouraged her to video herself, but she was reluctant to do so. Finally, she did record herself in an experimental lesson which focused on her interaction with the learners, and she set herself the task of identifying what she called 'learning movements' in her lessons. From observing her body language, Holly noticed that she avoided eye contact with learners in feedback, and that she seemed distracted when interacting with them. This led to her missing opportunities to help learners with their emerging language needs. She also noticed that she sometimes cut learners off, and that she tended to focus on one particular learner to give answers, whereas a more balanced interaction would lead to more extensive learner participation.

However, it was not only the negative aspects of her behaviour that became apparent. She also noticed that when she was more relaxed and 'interacting more genuinely', the learners were more involved in the feedback and took longer speaking turns. Holly noticed more emergent language opportunities in these moments than in others. The idea of being 'genuine' in interaction is interesting; without the teacher's interest in what the learners have to say, language is less likely to naturally emerge. Holly came to value this point through observing herself. This is an example of how video provides a simple yet powerful means to investigate the nature of our teaching.

Recording your learners

You can also record your students interacting together. Recording students can have a number of positive effects. First, it can help you notice where there are opportunities in your class to exploit emergent language. Second, it can help you to attune yourself to your learners and to raise your awareness of language strengths or any issues that they have. This can aid your future lesson planning. Third, recording students can help you identify learning preferences or behaviours that you might miss as you are focusing on other aspects of teaching during your lessons.

One effective way of gathering information is interviewing learners and analysing long turns. This is something teachers can use on their own or on preparation and development courses. You could try using a two- or three-minute clip of a learner being asked questions to show to teachers as an awareness-raising task. When interviewing a learner (or group of learners), begin with easy questions, and then move on to questions that require more complex answers, for example, moving from asking about simple personal details to asking them to comment on hypothetical situations. The aim is to get the learner to talk for an extended period of time, as this is more likely to provide you with opportunities for emergent language. At lower levels, there are naturally a lot of opportunities to work with emergent language. If you capture a snapshot of the learners speaking, and then listen to the recording, you will notice opportunities where you could reformulate learners' language. At higher levels, where there are fewer slips and errors, you can identify opportunities for pushing learners linguistically by exploring alternatives.

Another way of gaining an insight into learners' needs is to video- or audio-record learners interacting with each other as they work on a task. By recording learners doing tasks, you then have time and space to review it after the class. This will help them notice learners' interactional competence and management of discourse, as well as linguistic features such as grammar, lexis and phonology. It will also help you become more attuned to your learners and identify their needs.

Recording learners doing tasks is also an effective tool for teacher developers or managers. For teacher developers working on training courses, the recordings can be used to help course participants identify language that could be reformulated, either on the spot or in a delayed feedback stage. It also creates discussion opportunities as the teachers-in-training talk about what language they would choose to reformulate, when they would do it and how. In this way, teachers can learn from one another by sharing ideas and comparing choices. For more information on this, see **Using lesson transcripts** on pages 124–127.

A recording can also be an effective alternative to an observation. For this kind of observation, the manager or senior teacher who normally observes lessons instructs the teacher observee to audio-record their learners doing a task. The 'observer' then listens to the recording, perhaps transcribing an excerpt or making notes. They then give the teacher a short reflection or discussion task, which the teacher does while listening to the recording. In terms of working with emergent language, this can be as simple as asking the teacher what they reformulated during a class feedback session, and what they might do differently now they have had time to think about it. Alternatively, the observer could ask the teacher observee to plan a follow-up lesson based on an area they have identified that the learners need to develop. This idea is an interesting alternative to observation as the focus is on the learners and how the teacher might respond to their performance, as seen in Fenella's story below. This technique takes away the pressure for the teacher observee to perform, or to try to plan the perfect lesson – a common issue in observations. Discussing a future lesson plan also creates an opportunity for the teacher to discuss their planning process and the rationale underpinning their decisions.

Emergent language story 3: Fenella

At the time of this emergent language story, Fenella was a newly qualified teacher with some prior teaching experience. She noticed when she was reflecting in-action (in the moment in the lesson) that she was able to pick up on issues the learners were having with grammatical forms, such as tenses and subject–verb agreement. However, on listening to a recording of her learners talking to each other, she noticed what she felt was a more important and useful area to focus on.

She commented: 'I noticed that the students were having problems using past forms in the lesson and I was able to deal with it [during the lesson]. However, I wasn't aware of the problems Pati was having responding to Marco. When Pat spoke, Marco made it clear he was listening, but Pati didn't do this when Marco spoke, so occasionally Marco had to stop speaking to ask if Pati understood. So, this is something I could do in a future lesson. I could use model conversations in a future lesson to help with this.' ➔

By listening to the recording, Fenella was not only able to identify an area for language development, in this case an interactional strategy – she also had the space to consider how she might address this issue in a practical way in future lessons.

Videoing or audio-recording learners affords us the opportunity to see beyond a teacher's action – in other words, intervention – and allows us to see the context in which the action occurred. This contextual information can provide factually rich evidence to explore questions you may have about how to react to learners more effectively. By looking at classroom interaction, you can objectively view what is happening in class and, as a result, you are armed with more choices for future episodes.

Recordings from a previous lesson can also be used with learners in a subsequent class, after you have reviewed them. You can then play segments for the learners to explore what they have said. This can open up an opportunity for learners to notice gaps in their performance and gives you the opportunity to reformulate learner language. This idea can work particularly well in a small class, and in one-to-one situations. Recording a class, or part of a class, and reviewing it later also gives teachers time to consider useful reformulations, and this can be a strategy to help with the concern teachers have about reacting in the moment. This practice also helps teachers become more confident with their reformulations and helps them develop their ability to react in the moment in future classes. A recording can be made of a whole lesson or of short segments of lessons, the latter being less time-consuming for busy teachers.

Peer observation

A feature of many teacher education programmes and development initiatives is peer observation. This can involve one of the following:

1. observing other teachers on a preparation or development course,
2. observing a more experienced teacher in your institution or on a training course,
3. observing colleagues as part of an in-service teacher development scheme within a department or school.

Video is also often used as an awareness-raising tool on teacher education courses, where teachers-in-training watch recordings of experienced teachers in action. There are a number of commercially produced videos that are used to train teachers. However, while they do usefully demonstrate lesson procedures and techniques, these kinds of videos tend to be rather neat and tidy, missing out the messy, complicated off-plan moments that lead to emergent language in lessons. This is often because the teacher has a strict aim to meet and teaching point to demonstrate, so the lesson has been carefully planned and perhaps even rehearsed. The other drawback is that the teaching context in the video might be very different from the context of the observer. This can lead to the observer rejecting techniques because they do not see how they might be applied in their classrooms. For this reason, it is usually best to do peer observations in-house where possible.

When setting up peer observations, it is worth considering how nerve-racking it can be to be observed. Even for experienced teachers, it can be daunting to have someone else in your class. One way to address this is to team teachers up and encourage them to prepare for lessons together. They could consider which parts of their lesson might generate emergent language and then video these sections. They could then share the recordings with each other when they are happy with them. Although the buzz of the physical environment of the classroom might be absent, the reduction of pressure on the teacher who is being observed is greatly reduced, meaning that teacher might be more relaxed and comfortable working with learner language. This can remove what has been called the **special lesson syndrome**, where teachers display their techniques rather than being natural and reacting in the way they normally would in an unobserved class.

Another option is for teachers to team-teach a lesson that they have prepared together. Teachers teach the same class together, taking it in turns to lead feedback stages. For some teachers, this can be a less threatening way of being observed. It also provides an opportunity for them to observe their colleague, as well as to be observed themselves. This paired video recording or live lesson can be an effective way for teachers to review parts of the lesson, as there is always one teacher observing who can note which stages contained moments of, or opportunities for, emergent language.

Sharing ideas: dialogue with others

Human learning is viewed by many as a social activity (Mercer, 1995), and in recent years there has been a move in educational research and practice towards what has been termed 'dialogic teaching, learning and reflection' (see Alexander, 2008; Walsh & Mann, 2017). **Dialogic teaching** can be intrapersonal – in other words, using a reflection instrument such as a checklist of classroom behaviour you want to examine – and thinking about what you can learn from it. It can be interpersonal as well, where new understandings can be arrived at through discussion with others. Although the term **dialogic** was originally used in relation to educating children, Walsh and Mann make a strong case for its application to teacher education.

One dynamic senior teachers and managers can explore involves pairing a less experienced teacher with a mentor. This can benefit both experienced and less experienced teachers. Firstly, less experienced teachers can benefit through dialogue with the more experienced teacher. Secondly, experienced teachers can come to new understandings or affirm older ones through the discoveries of less experienced teachers. Sharing ideas can foster a sense of community and create a culture of bottom-up development in an organisation. It can also demystify what happens in other teachers' classrooms and create an atmosphere of cooperation and collaboration. Through discussions about emergent language with colleagues, a greater understanding of the 'what' and 'how' of emergent language can be gained; teachers can become aware of other possibilities and approaches to classroom interaction and the kind of language that can be worked on.

Emergent language story 4: Alex

Alex is a teacher with two years' experience working at a private language school in the UK, where she mostly teaches one-to-one classes. During her first months in the school, she joined a teachers' discussion group that regularly met to talk about aspects of teaching that the group wanted to discuss. The topic for the meetings was often chosen during sessions, or teachers could request an area that they wanted to explore.

Due to the nature of her classes, Alex found she was working with emergent language a lot, and was always looking for ways to improve and be more responsive to the immediate needs of her learners. However, she was concerned that she wasn't sure what to do with language that had emerged and had already been recorded on the board. Alex therefore requested that the next group discussion would be on emergent language. This would enable her to learn from her peers about how they dealt with it. ➔

'I wanted to ask for other teachers' experiences of Dogme and learn about how to take the language that emerged and was boarded further. I learnt about some activities other teachers use to achieve this.'

After the meeting, Alex tried out ideas her colleagues had suggested. One technique she started using regularly was gapping parts of the emergent language that she had put on the board as a way of revising it and helping learners remember it at the end of lessons. She said: 'I did a gap-fill exercise with some (emergent) language today to test their retention, which I think was well received, and felt more complete in terms of doing something with the language and making sure I could check their knowledge.'

Alex was fortunate to have a teacher discussion group to draw ideas from. This kind of professional development within schools is valuable as it allows for sharing not only good practice but also beliefs. Joining or following discussions on local or international ELT blogs and forums is another way of gaining insights into other teachers' practices. If joining a group is not possible, try finding a colleague who can be a critical friend – someone with whom to share ideas and talk about your development with emergent language. This will be looked at in the next section.

Working with a colleague: cooperative development

When working with a colleague, it is important to approach dialogue with sensitivity and without judgement. In this way, an equal and fruitful collaboration can be fostered. The work of Julian Edge has a lot to guide us through what he terms 'cooperative development' (see Edge, 1992; 2002). We have adapted the following stages from Edge for successful collegial discussion. Each colleague has a turn to speak and the other colleague listens, prompting and encouraging the other to explain further. The stages of this type of discussion include exploration, discovery and action.

- **Exploration (reflecting and focusing)**

  In the initial stage of the conversation, a teacher reflects on an issue to do with emergent language in their lesson and explains it to the listener. For example, an observation task has revealed that the teacher uses lots of 'echo'. The discussion that follows can help to establish why the teacher might be echoing. For example, is it to validate learner responses? Is the teacher echoing what the learner said to make it clear for the other learners? As the conversation progresses, the listener can ask questions such as: What is the effect of the echo? How did the learners respond? In this way, the teacher is prompted to focus on specific evidence from their lesson and to explore what happened.

In their 2017 IATEFL talk, *Dialogues and Diagrams in Teacher Education*, Chinn and Lamb suggested using questions to prompt discussion. The following adapted questions can be used by the listener to facilitate evidence-based discussion regarding emergent language:

1. *What issues arose in your class regarding emergent language?*
2. *What do you think the cause of this was?*
3. *What evidence do you have to support that?*
4. *How do you know that is the case?*
5. *Can you think of an example of that from the lesson?*
6. *How did the learners react?*
7. *Are there any other examples of that?*
8. *Why do you think this point is important / unimportant in class?*
9. *How would this relate to (previous sessions / what we discussed yesterday)?*
10. *What is a way of resolving this issue?*
11. *What is a solution to this problem / puzzle?*
12. *What is an alternative to …?*
13. *What are the strengths and weaknesses of …?*
14. *What do you want to know more about?*
15. *How can we explore this further?*

- **Discovery (thematising)**

  In this stage of the discussion, teachers can work together to summarise what has been discovered. New understandings may become apparent, and through discussion, themes can be established, for example, *Although I was trying to encourage the learners by echoing what they said, the echoes were an interruption, and they ended the learner's turn.*

- **Action (goal-setting)**

  Finally, teachers can come up with some practical ideas to target the issue, for example, if echoing is a problem, you can consciously try not to echo and instead prompt the learner to say more. You could also simply practise back-channelling unobtrusively, with active listening noises like 'Uh huh'.

Some guidelines for successful teacher collaboration might include the following:

1. Brainstorm what is puzzling you about your emergent language work.
2. Choose a task for self-reflection (see **Development tasks, ideas and commentaries**, pages 129–196, for ideas).
3. Video yourself or observe a colleague.
4. Do your chosen reflection task as you watch the lesson.
5. After you have gathered some data, share your experience with a peer using the guidance above on cooperative development.

Recording your board

A simple way to examine the emergent language that you deal with in class is to take pictures of your boardwork at key moments in a lesson, for example, after a feedback stage, or at the end of the class. If you are working online, you can save the chat or keep a copy of any language items you highlighted on a presentation tool or online whiteboard. Saving a copy of your board provides you with hard evidence of what happened in a lesson, and allows you to reflect on what you have written there.

In fact, recording your board helps you develop your teaching in several ways. At a basic level, you can look at the language you have recorded and think about whether you have organised it effectively. If not, you can take some time to reflect on how you would reorganise it. Your board is the record learners take away from the lesson, so it can be seen as a model for how your learners should record emergent language. The better the board is, the better the record the learners take away.

Examining your board also gives you time to think about what you have chosen to focus on. As you do this, ask yourself questions such as, Was this new language useful for the learners?, Was it suitable for the level?, Could I have extended the patterns I looked at? and Are these typical or common collocations or phrases? Over time, you can use board records to examine the kind of language you typically respond to. For example, does it tend to be lexical, grammatical or discoursal?

On longer courses, keeping a record of what emerges in your classes can also help you think about what can be recycled or tested in future classes. Using the questions suggested above, think about which language items might be most useful for the learners. Then consider how you might recycle them in a future class or how to test them at the end of the course.

Using lesson transcripts

Transcription (when recorded bits of lessons are written out for examination) has long been used in teacher training and education, with Ellis (1986) suggesting that they can be used for awareness raising in development sessions. This technique has proved to be an effective way of drawing attention to features of classroom interaction on teacher education and training courses. From a teacher education perspective, having a number of transcripts that have been analysed for learning opportunities provides the trainer with various ways of sensitising developing teachers to classroom interaction.

Another way transcripts can be used is to video yourself teaching and then, as you watch back, to create transcripts of interaction moments in class. Scott Thornbury (1996) used transcripts to encourage participants on an in-service training programme to examine the extent to which teachers' lessons were communicative; this resulted in better awareness of interaction features in their lessons. This is an important aspect to consider with regards to emergent language because if the discourse is tightly controlled by the teacher, and there is overuse of display questions, underuse of genuine questions and a lack of space for learner-initiated-turns, it is unlikely that any language will emerge. Thornbury showed that through transcribing parts of their lessons, teachers became more aware of how to make their classes more communicative. And by transcribing short sections of discourse, you can become more aware of the intervention choices you make in class. In the same way, teachers can be helped to notice when more emergent language moments could have been acted on. For example, you might notice when you could have intervened or when a learner required more support in communicating their idea.

Transcribing lessons can be time-consuming for teachers, but once a transcript has been made, it can be used again by those in charge of teacher development. For example, a Director of Studies could make a short transcript after observing a teacher. This can then be examined in the post-lesson conference. It is important to note that a transcript can be very short, as long as it fully demonstrates features of interaction. There are various ways in which to transcribe spoken language. Based on the advice of Walsh (2011), the following recommendations can be made:

Produce a basic transcript

If you want to record basic interaction, you may wish to simply write down the gist of the exchanges. This would be suitable if you were looking for more generic features regarding emergent language, such as identifying the language that emerged, the intervention used and the learner response.

Basic transcripts can be produced by observers as they watch lessons. The transcript in Figure 6.2 was created during assessed teaching practice on a CELTA course. During this stage of the lesson, the learners were performing a task in which they discussed future plans and ambitions. As the assessed teacher was monitoring another group, the observer noticed two learners struggling to decide which form to use to talk about a future plan. The observer decided that this exchange would be interesting to share with all the teachers on the course. They therefore made a basic transcription after the lesson, which they then used in an input session. The teachers on the course were asked to discuss what they thought the learner was trying to say and what they might have done had they noticed this exchange as they monitored. In summary, the transcript created the conditions for the teachers to discuss the value of monitoring as learners do communicative tasks and to think about when it might be useful to intervene.

Sorour:	(By the time I'm 30) I'll be quitting smoking … no
Kenta:	no?
Sorour:	no
Kenta:	no what?
Sorour:	not 'I'll be quitting smoking'
Kenta:	no
Sorour:	will be …
Kenta:	… will be quit …
Sorour:	… will be quitted
[long pause]	
Kenta:	you will be quit [nodding]
[long pause]	
Sorour:	you understand? →

Kenta:	Yeah. You will be quit
Sorour:	I will be quit
[long pause]	
Sorour:	[to self] is not that

Figure 6.2: A basic transcript

As discussed above, creating transcripts can be time-consuming, but this transcript was created in 2013, and the trainer is still using it on training courses today.

Using a transcription code

When transcribing lessons, it is useful to use a transcription code to help you note specific features of the interaction, as in shown in the examples listed in Figure 6.3 (adapted from Walsh, 2011).

T	Teacher
L	*Learner (not identified)*
L1, L2, etc.	*Identified learner*
LL	*Several learners at once*
/ok/ok/ok/	*Overlapping and simultaneous utterances by more than one learner*
[Do you understand?]	
[I see]	Overlap between teacher and learner
=	Turn continues, or one turn follows another without a pause
...	A pause of one second or less
[4]	*Silence; length given in seconds*
?	*Rising intonation – question or other*
!	*Emphatic speech; falling intonation*
[[4]]	*A stretch of unintelligible speech given in seconds*
P, L, M	*Capitals are only used for proper nouns, such as Pedro, Lili and Marta*

Figure 6.3: Transcription code examples

When transcribing interaction, it is useful to go beyond simply noting down who is speaking and what they say. For example, you might want to note down pauses, interruptions or overlaps, as shown in the lesson extract in Figure 6.4, as this can give greater insight into teacher and learner actions in class. You can also add to it by annotating and highlighting interesting features of intonation or body language, for example, if there is learner uptake, (for instance, when they are nodding or writing down emergent language that has arisen). Once you have transcribed a chunk of discourse between teacher and learners or learner with learners, you can begin analysing it for intervention types.

T:	So, we are trying to understand what is happening in the pictures … and now we are trying to understand what is happening in picture number … OK?
L1:	[Oh ok!]
T:	Who can tell her what we know so far?
L2:	Errrr [[6]] she is … er … party … er [[5]] Maddison … taking [[3]] and Daniella … [the learner is unintelligible]
T:	OK ... so … they are at a barbecue party and Maddison is talking about Daniella … and she is saying that Daniella is [a problem].
L3:	= [Is a problem because] … Er … she … er watch … She, she look … er … watch … er … she … don't take [[1]].
T:	= OK she's not happy … OK that's enough for now … Let's listen to the recording.

Figure 6.4: Transcription code in use

Note taking

Rather than creating a whole transcript, you can just make relevant field notes regarding emergent language moments in class. You might even note down isolated utterances from teachers and learners. Figure 6.5 shows notes that were made by another teacher while watching a fellow diploma candidate teaching – the observed teacher had just asked a learner what they did in the morning.

Learner 1:	I watered the flowers.
Teacher:	*Ah you have a garden?*
Learner 1:	*No garden just … [mimes an oblong box].*
Learner 2:	*Balcony?*
Teacher:	*Do you have a balcony?*
Learner 1:	No balcony. Just the … [mimes oblong box].
Teacher:	A window box [boards this]!
*The learner wrote it down in his book and the other learners nodded.	

Figure 6.5: Field notes

Conclusion

In this section, we have looked at different techniques that teachers can use to investigate, reflect on and develop specific aspects of their practice. We have also outlined the principles underpinning this form of teacher development. **Development tasks, ideas and commentaries** (pages 129–196) will provide specific activities and tasks that teachers and teacher educators can use to develop emergent language skills. Before you move on to that chapter and choose activities and tasks for yourself, consider the following continuing professional development questions.

Professional development

Questions for reflection

- What would you like to learn more about emergent language in your classroom? Which techniques described might help you investigate this?
- Have you ever recorded yourself teaching? If you have, what did you notice about your teaching? Did it lead to any changes in your practice? What advice would you give teachers who haven't recorded themselves before?
- How might you support other teachers in your context to explore emergent language? What do you need to consider? What advice would you give them about organising their board? How would pairing teachers up to work with emergent language work in your context?

Things to try

- Which of the ideas explored in this chapter are feasible in your context? Pick 1–2 ideas and try them out in class. Afterwards, reflect on what went well and what could be improved upon for future use.

7. Development tasks, ideas and commentaries

This chapter contains lots of practical ideas that you can use to gather data on your teaching and to develop your reactive skills. The exploration activities are designed for teachers to use, but they can equally be used by teacher educators and mentors on development initiatives and teacher training programmes. The activities have all been used by teachers at various stages of their careers, and the commentaries after each task provide an insight into some of the discoveries these teachers made when using them. The suggested procedure is that you pick an activity, try out the idea, reflect on it, and then read the accompanying commentary.

The ideas are flexible in nature, aiming to help teachers sensitise themselves to learner language, to explore teaching choices and possibilities regarding emergent language, and to develop and practise strategies for working with emergent language. Each task also comes with a suggested variation that offers either an alternative way of doing the task or suggestions for how teacher trainers can use the task on teacher development courses or INSET sessions.

Task	Type of reflection	Aim
1	Engaging in dialogue 1: self-reflection and discussion	To raise awareness of your emergent language beliefs and practices
2	Engaging in dialogue 2: recalling a recent event	To recall a critical incident with emergent language and explore how you dealt with it
3a 3b	Engaging in dialogue 3: critical friends and critical questions	To use a critical friend to investigate your emergent language practices
4	Engaging in dialogue 4: learner questionnaire	To find out your learners' views on emergent language and how you intervene ➔

5	Using lesson transcripts 1: Choosing what language to work with	To identify what emergent language to work on and how you might reformulate different utterances
6a 6b	Using lesson transcripts 2: identifying intervention types	To raise awareness of different types of intervention
7	Using lesson transcripts 3: identifying interventions in longer transcripts	To analyse how a teacher manages a stretch of classroom discourse and works with emergent language
8	Using lesson transcripts 4: deciding when to intervene	To identify where you might intervene in student–student communication
9	Observation task: what did the learner say? What would I say?	To sensitise yourself to learner language and consider how you would reformulate it
10	Recording yourself teaching: identifying your intervention practices	To provide you with evidence of how you work with emergent language
11	Video/peer observation: designing your own task	To help you work on identified areas of weakness
12	Task planning 1: pre-empting emergent language	To help you pre-empt the possible emergent language in a task
13	Task planning 2: pre-empting learner language in your classes	To help you pre-empt the emergent language in a task and monitor learners performing the task
14	Tuning into learners: monitoring and giving feedback on content	To develop your ability to listen to learners and note down what they say
15	Improving your boardwork 1: learning how to effectively display new language	To examine how to effectively display emergent language on the board
16	Improving your boardwork 2: organising your board	To develop boardwork skills by taking pictures and redesigning the board
17	Using the board: blanking the board	To help you reflect on how you might review emergent language at the end of a lesson
18	Learner training	To help learners record and organise emergent language

Engaging in dialogue 1

Task 1: Self-reflection and discussion

Rationale

This task is designed to help you examine your beliefs, and to prompt you to think about when and how you respond to learners' language needs. Even before we become teachers, we have deeply ingrained ideas of the role of a teacher and what teaching and learning involves, which is to a great extent based on our extensive experience of being learners ourselves. This is what sociologist Dan Lortie termed **the apprenticeship of observation** (Woodward et al., 2018). According to Lortie, when we become teachers, we often emulate and reject the teaching and learning roles that we have experienced ourselves. For example, if you were often corrected as a learner, you might do this regularly in your classes. Alternatively, if teacher correction had a negative impact on you, you might decide not to correct your learners much.

Our experience of being teachers also leads us to form subconscious beliefs. These beliefs are not always easy to articulate as they have formed over extended periods, and we may not regularly examine them or talk about them. However, self-reflection can give us an insight into the teaching techniques we choose and why we use them. In the case of emergent language, it can help us think about how useful it might be for our learners and what the best intervention techniques are for them. This can help us make better-informed choices when responding to learner output.

Task 1: Self-reflection and discussion

A. Procedure

1. Look at the Task 1 discussion questions and make notes.
2. Share your answers and ideas with a colleague.
3. When you have completed this task, read the Task 1 commentary and compare your ideas with those of other teachers.

B. Discussion questions

1. How often do you correct learners?
2. What affects your decision about when to correct learners?
3. As well as working with errors, how often do you deal with emergent language, for example, by providing alternative ways of saying something or exploring interesting patterns that come up? →

4. What affects your decision about when to work with emergent language?
5. How do you offer support to learners when they have trouble communicating? Can you think of an example?
6. What affects your decision to help learners?

Photocopiable task

Teacher training variation

Give the teacher trainees time to reflect on the discussion questions before putting them into groups to compare and discuss ideas. If there is time, you could do this task twice, once at the beginning of the course and then again at the end. The teachers-in-training can then see how their beliefs have developed over the course of the training programme.

For teachers working in the same institution, a group task like this will enable them to reflect on, and perhaps agree on, best practice for the teaching context. For teachers from diverse contexts, the discussion will enable them to compare practices and explain potential differences.

Task 1 commentary

Zoe and Jack are experienced teachers who did Task 1 at the start of their Cambridge Delta course. Both have been teaching for several years and work in different teaching contexts, including English for Academic Purposes (EAP), English for business and exam classes. As you will see in their story below, they focused on the doubts they both have about intervening, and the worry that it 'disrupts' the flow of the lesson. However, they also believe that how and when they intervene depends on the type of learners they are working with.

Task 1 emergent language story: Zoe and Jack

Zoe and Jack agreed that they felt more comfortable intervening in exam classes than in general English classes. This was because they felt that they have more licence to focus on accuracy in learner output as it can help their learners do better in their exams. In fact, they often justified corrections and interventions in these classes by telling the learners that 'this phrase will get you extra marks in the exam' or 'this error will lose you marks'. They also said that they felt more uncomfortable correcting learners in a general English class. In fact, both worried that correcting the learners could be patronising, and this feeling stopped them from responding more to learner language.

In Zoe and Jack's discussion, you can see a direct correlation between beliefs and classroom action, in this case the avoidance of error correction because it feels uncomfortable. However, by having the discussion and uncovering beliefs, you have a starting point for new discussions on why you might work with errors or emergent language, and how learners in different contexts might feel about it. By exploring and sharing your feelings, you can uncover the reasons behind your classroom actions, and in doing so, open up other possibilities in your practice.

When we have used this task on training courses, we have noticed a number of different beliefs and practices emerging, and it is interesting to see how they differ from teacher to teacher. Look at the list below. Are any of your responses the same? Which ones do you agree or disagree with and why?

- *We should only correct errors when they are connected to target language or lesson aims.*
- *It's OK to focus on any language items that come out of a communicative activity.*
- *The type of error is important, for example, if it is a repeated error.*
- *It's helpful to intervene when learners don't know a word.*
- *It's OK to use L1 and translation.*
- *It's important to deal with errors immediately as this has the most impact.*
- *You shouldn't interrupt the learners' flow, so work on emergent language should happen when they have finished speaking.*
- *Teenagers don't take correction well, so it should be delayed and anonymous.*
- *Some learners might not appreciate being put on the spot.*
- *Some learners need a push.*

Engaging in dialogue 2

Task 2: Recalling a recent event

Rationale

Teachers build up episodic knowledge through classroom practice (Randall & Thornton, 2001). This in turn allows them to be more able to anticipate what will happen in class and to improvise in the future. A typical method of reflection is to explore 'critical incidents', which Farrell (2008) defines as any unplanned event that happens during classes. By exploring critical incidents, language teachers can form new understandings of things they have previously taken for granted in their teaching (Farrell, 2008).

Emergent language episodes constitute a critical incident as, by nature, they are unplanned. The following task encourages teachers to recall such incidents in their classes. By doing so, it encourages them to think about the context in which the incident occurred, reflect on how the language was dealt with, and discuss and evaluate the learners' responses.

Emergent language can often be missed by teachers, as they are dealing with multiple other events at the same time. Then, when the moment has passed, they might not be able to remember it. Teachers might also feel these moments are unimportant; however, disregarding them can mean that they may be missing out on providing learners with valuable linguistic support. This task, therefore, encourages them to focus on what might at first seem mundane or unremarkable and to uncover something of value.

Task 2 follows a description or reflection procedure, where a teacher first recalls what happened in the lesson. After exploring what happened, the teacher is prompted to explain their choices and consider the reactions of the learners. By looking at critical incidents, teachers can become aware of moments in class where emergent language can take prominence. This kind of activity works best when shared with colleagues.

Task 2: Recalling a recent event

A. Procedure

1. Look at the recall questions and make notes.
2. If possible, share your answers and ideas with a colleague.
3. Summarise your thoughts or your discussion and highlight anything you find interesting.
4. When you have completed the task, read the Task 2 commentary and compare your ideas with those of other teachers.

B. Recall questions

1. Can you think of a time when you taught an item of language that was new to the learners that you hadn't planned to teach?
2. What happened? Describe the event. ➔

3. How did you deal with the language? (For example, did you give the learners the meaning, elicit an alternative word or phrase, or write the new item on the board?)
4. How did the learners respond? (For example, did they go on to use the word or write it down?)

Photocopiable task

Teacher training variation

Give teachers time to reflect on the recall questions before putting them into groups to compare and discuss their ideas, as described in the rationale above. For teachers working in the same institution, a group task like this will enable them to reflect on, and perhaps agree on, best practice for the context.

Task 2 commentary

Reflecting on a critical incident is a way of stimulating recall of an event in class. This can be useful to help teachers reflect on what language came up, how they felt in the moment, and how the learners reacted. An example of this can be seen below, when an EAP teacher, who regularly stuck to the textbook, recalls the learners' attitudes when she experimented with 'going off-book'.

The first thing she noticed was how engaged her learners were when she spent time on emergent language, saying 'When I was looking at the language, they seemed so invested and usually I don't see them like … they were writing notes.'

A critical incident can also help focus teachers on what was problematic for them in class. Using the questions in the task prompted another teacher on a Diploma course to remember an issue she had when she couldn't hear the learners talking, and was therefore unable to deal with language that emerged. This prompted her to decide that it was OK to sit nearer to learners as she monitored, which she had been reluctant to do as she worried that she would be getting in the way.

By exploring a story from a lesson, we also get to examine the specific techniques we use (often subconsciously) to work with emergent language. In the following extract, the teacher is working with an intermediate-level general English class with a variety of L1s. The learners have just finished a game, and the teacher has noticed an opportunity to clarify the difference between two similar words. In her story below, she recalls the event and how she clarified the language.

Task 2 emergent language story: Irina

I asked them after the game was finished if they enjoyed it and one of them said 'yes it was fun' and the other one said, 'it was funny', and I thought OK, let's see what the difference is. So first I put them in pairs to discuss what they thought the difference was ... they only came up with the part of speech: *fun* is a noun and *funny* is an adjective, but they couldn't quite pinpoint what the difference [in meaning] was, and they thought it was two different ways of saying the same thing. And then I gave them two alternatives: one of the words means haha like a joke and the other means having a good time and then I asked them: 'Who else can be funny? Can a person be funny? Can a joke be funny? Can a joke be fun?' This helped them understand.

You can see that recalling the incident has helped Irina reflect on several classroom events. She can recall how she drew attention to the language items and uncovered the limits of the learners' understanding. This prompts her to reflect on how she helped the learners by using questions to explore the meaning, thereby potentially strengthening any belief about the use of questions as a technique for clarifying meaning.

But recalling a critical incident also provides a starting point to evaluating techniques and considering alternatives, especially when it is done with a colleague. For example, recalling this incident might have prompted Irina to consider that rather than putting the learners into pairs to discuss the difference, it would perhaps have been more expedient to tell the class the difference directly. This would save time, of course, but the learners would have missed out on the opportunity to work something out for themselves. However, it is by exploring alternatives that teachers are able to evaluate what might work best for their learners and broaden the choices available to them when picking up on emergent language.

Engaging in dialogue 3

Task 3a: Critical friends and critical questions

Rationale

To explore an emergent language episode, it is important to probe for evidence surrounding the event. To help you do this, it is useful to ask another teacher to act as your 'critical friend'. Note that 'critical' does not mean that they criticise you; rather, it refers to their importance (see Woodward et al., 2018). The role of the critical friend is important in that they help you to explore the event in depth and to better understand it. To enable you to do this, the critical friend asks a set of questions that encourage you to reflect on the event. These are outlined in the task below.

The questions in this task start by focusing the teacher on an emergent language incident, issue or puzzle from a lesson. The critical friend prompts the teacher to give examples to elaborate on the moment. This is a type of stimulated recall (see Mann & Walsh, 2017) as it serves to prompt the teacher's memory about the event and to provide evidence of what happened. From here, the prompts encourage the teacher to move beyond observable facts in the lesson to questioning or exploring actions, and considering alternatives or solutions to the emergent language issue. Note that the first questions focus on lower-order thinking skills – in other words, remembering the event. They then move to engaging higher-order thinking skills, such as analysing the situation and solving problems. Finally, the conversation is summarised, and points are noted for further enquiry.

The following tasks are designed to help you to engage in cooperative development and to use critical thinking questions to explore emergent language incidents and techniques in your teaching. Task 3a is an awareness-raising task, as it provides an example of a group of teachers engaged in the task. Task 3b, which has been adapted from questions developed by Melissa Lamb (Chinn & Lamb, 2017), is designed to help you run your own cooperative development session after a lesson.

Task 3a: Critical friends and critical questions

A. Procedure

The cooperative discussion in columns 1 and 3 of the table below (in B) occurred after assessed teaching practice on a teacher development course. Look at the discussion and answer these questions:

1. What is the emergent language incident that the teacher recalls?
2. Look at the question at the top of column 2. What is the purpose of each of the critical friends' questions? Write your ideas in column 2. The first one has been done for you.
3. Look at the teacher's responses in column 3. What impact does each question asked by the critical friend have on the teacher? Complete column 4 with your ideas. ➔

4. How has engaging in cooperative development helped this teacher in terms of beliefs or practice?

When you have completed the task, compare your answers with those in the Task 3a commentary.

B. Analysis of a cooperative discussion

Critical friend question	What is the purpose of the question?	Teacher response	What impact does it have on the teacher?
1. Tell me something you noticed in the class.	*To prompt the teacher to identify an emergent language incident.*	a) The learner said: *I went to 'French'.*	*Teacher recalls the event.*
2. Why did you pick up on this item of emergent language?		b) I heard it more than once from two different learners.	
3. Why do you think they said that?		c) I'm not sure about what they would say in their L1. Maybe the words are similar.	
4. How did the learner react?		d) There was some nodding when I corrected it (and) clarified the meaning.	
5. What could you have explored more?		e) I could've explored more examples, e.g., *French wine.*	
6. Did you teach it as an isolated word?.		f) Yes, I think I wrote up an isolated word.	

➔

7. What would be an alternative?		g) I could put the word up in a sentence. Maybe I could've looked at more examples of other countries to extend their knowledge.	
8. What did you learn about your teaching from this incident?		h) I think I generally focus on words in isolation, and I need to think about context and co-text.	
9. What can you do next time?		i) Make sure I put the word in a meaningful context.	

Photocopiable task

Task 3a commentary

The exchange in section B of Task 3a occurred during post-teaching feedback on a training course. By plotting the dialogue in a table, you can see how each question prompts recall and reflection from the listener. It is possible to also see the impact the discussion has on their thinking about practice (see Figure 7.1 on pages 140–141).

In Question 1, we had the critical friend prompting the teacher to recall an emergent language incident (*I went to French*). After speculating on the potential cause of the error, the critical friends use Question 3 to encourage the teacher to consider how their actions impacted on the learners. This enables the teacher to point to evidence of learner intake.

In Questions 4–6, the critical questions have a real impact on the teacher as they consider how they could have explored the ways in which the adjective *French* is used. Note that rather than being advised or told to explore new language in context and using **extensions** to look at language at sentence level, the teacher comes to this conclusion themselves. As a result, the feedback session is more powerful as a developmental tool. The critical friends seem to recognise this, as in Question 8, they bring the discussion back to techniques by prompting the teacher to think about what they might do in the future, and the exchange ends with the teacher making an action plan for future classes.

By reflecting on critical questions, it becomes apparent that teachers can have agency in the feedback. Firstly, they have chosen which part of the lesson they want to focus on. They have then used the prompts to come to their own conclusions about how they could have dealt with the emergent language, and finally, they have suggested how this incident might impact on their future practice. Overall, the exchange has had a clear impact on their cognition and potentially on teacher's future practice.

Critical friend question	Purpose of the question	Teacher response	Impact on teacher
1. Tell me something you noticed in the class.	*To prompt the teacher to identify an emergent language incident.*	a) The learner said: *I went to 'French'.*	*Recalls the event.*
2. Why did you pick up on this item of emergent language?	*To uncover the rationale for choosing to intervene.*	b) I heard it more than once from two learners.	*Provides a rationale for choosing to work with the error.*
3. Why do you think they said that?	*To help the teacher explore why the learner may have made the error.*	c) I'm not sure about what they would say in their L1. Maybe the words are similar.	*Speculates on the cause of the error.*
4. How did the learner react?	*To prompt the teacher to consider the impact of the intervention.*	d) There was some nodding when I corrected it (and) clarified the meaning.	*Recognises the impact and evidence of uptake.*
5. What could you have explored more?	*To prompt the teacher to examine their techniques.*	e) I could've explored more examples, e.g. *French wine.*	*Considers alternative techniques to extend learner understanding.*

6. Did you teach it as an isolated word?	*To clarify the previous response.*	f) Yes, I think I wrote up an isolated word.	*Recalls how they dealt with the error and correction.*
7. What would be an alternative?	*To prompt the teacher to explore an alternative technique.*	g) I could put the word up in a sentence. Maybe I could've looked at more examples of other countries to extend their knowledge.	*Considers alternative techniques to extend learner understanding.*
8. What did you learn about your teaching from this incident?	*To prompt the teacher to identify their learning.*	h) I think I generally focus on words in isolation, and I need to think about context and co-text.	*Expresses how this exchange might impact in their general practice.*
9. What can you do next time?	*To prompt the teacher to make an action plan.*	i) Make sure I put the word in a meaningful context.	*Suggests how they will change their practices.*

Figure 7.1: Analysing a cooperative discussion commentary

Task 3b: Critical friends and critical questions

A. Procedure

1. After teaching a class or watching a recording of yourself teaching, get together with a colleague, who will act as your critical friend.
2. Using the questions below, the critical friend prompts you to explore the emergent language episode in class. When you have completed the task, read the Task 3b commentary and compare your findings with those of other teachers.

B. Critical thinking questions

1. What interesting example of emergent language occurred in your class?
2. What intervention type did you use to deal with it?
3. Why do you think it was important to deal with this emergent language incident in the lesson?
4. How did the learners respond to your intervention?
5. What were the advantages of using this intervention type? ➔

6. Were there any disadvantages?
7. What might have happened if you'd used a different intervention type? Why do you think this?
8. Were there any other examples of this incident in the lesson?
9. Have you noticed any similar incidents in previous lessons?
10. What would you like to know more about regarding this incident?
11. What can we do to explore this area further?
12. How might exploring this area further help develop the way you deal with emergent language?

Photocopiable task

Teacher training variation

After a teacher has completed an assessed lesson, those who observed it can use the questions to prompt the teacher to explore an emergent language incident. By handing over to the teachers-in-training and giving them the roles above, you facilitate a genuine group discussion as all the participants have the tools with which to take part. You also ensure that the post-lesson discussion focuses more on the needs of the teachers-in-training and their feelings about the incident than the trainer's. It's a good idea to ask the observers to refrain from giving advice, as the object is to encourage the observed teacher to recall and evaluate the critical incident rather than for the other participants to draw attention to their strengths and weaknesses.

Task 3b commentary

Teachers have commented that this kind of reflection can be difficult at first, but that it gets easier the more you do it. Another commented that it helped them realise that the questions enabled them to be more objective in the way they saw their lessons, and to find answers to some of the issues that came up in class.

Task 3b emergent language story: Jia and Miao

Jia and Miao did this task on an in-service training course and found the questions useful for grounding the conversation and examining moments from lessons in detail. They also said it stopped them from just talking about aspects of class management, like setting up tasks. From their discussion, one thing Maio noticed about her teaching was that she often reformulated or provided emergent language verbally after learner-initiated interventions. However, she rarely recorded the emergent language on the board. ➔

Together, they wondered if this would mean that the learners would not remember the incident. This prompted them to create an action plan to deal with this issue in the future.

Engaging in dialogue 4

Task 4: Learner questionnaire

Rationale

It is a good idea to find out what your learners think about the way you work with emergent language and give corrective feedback. This can be the case in particular with teenagers or younger adults who may be more self-conscious about seeing their output reformulated in open class. Another reason to find out your learners' preferences is that studies (for example, Li, 2017) have shown that teachers and learners' beliefs about corrective feedback are often unaligned, with learners being much keener on it than their teachers. There is, in fact, little research into learner preferences for correction, though this may perhaps be down to the fact that most studies would be very local and therefore not transferable to most learning contexts. It may be better for teachers to do their own research with their classes and institutions.

The questionnaire below, which has questions adapted from Lee (2013) is designed to help you find out if your learners think errors should be corrected, when they think they should be corrected, and who they think should do the correcting. There are also questions that are designed to uncover how learners feel about some of the emergent language interventions that we saw in **How to work with emergent language** (pages 53–74), for example, **extensions** and **learner-initiated interventions**. Note that this questionnaire would be suitable for B1 learners and above, but if you wanted to use it at lower levels you could translate it into the learners' L1.

Task 4: Learner questionnaire

A. Procedure

1. Look at the learner questionnaire below. Think about how your learners might answer the questions.
2. Hand out the questionnaire to your learners. This could be done in class or as a homework task. ➔

3. Look at the results and think about the following questions:
   - Was there anything that surprised you?
   - Do your beliefs about emergent language and correction match those of your learners?
   - How might the results change your practice with these learners?
   - When you have finished, look at the Task 4 commentary for another teacher's findings.

B. Learner questionnaire

This questionnaire looks at the way your teacher helps you with your language. Put a tick in the column that best describes how you feel about each statement. When you have finished, give your answers to your teacher.

Name: ______________________ Class: ______________________

Statements	Strongly agree	Agree	Don't know	Disagree	Strongly disagree
1. I think I learn more when the teacher corrects my speaking.					
2. I don't like it when the teacher corrects me in front of the class.					
3. I want my teacher to correct the errors I make the most often rather than all my errors.					
4. When my teacher doesn't understand me, I think they should tell me on the spot rather than afterwards.					→

5. When the teacher hears a mistake, I want them to tell me the correct form rather than giving me the chance to find it myself.					
6. When the teacher hears a mistake, I like it when they give me a chance to find the correct way before they tell me.					
7. I like it when the teacher gives us different ways to say what we said.					
8. I like it when the teacher gives us feedback on our language at the end of a discussion rather than immediately.					
9. When I don't understand something or don't know what to say, I think it is useful to ask the teacher for help.					
Thank you!					

Photocopiable task

Task variation

This task can be done as a discussion in class. The learners interview each other and fill in the questionnaire with their partner's answer. The teacher then uses a feedback stage to explore their answers and opinions. With B1+ learners, you could also use a feedback session to discuss your approaches and reflect on why you might use different intervention types.

Task 4 commentary

The interesting aspect of this task is that regardless of whether there is a mismatch between what you and your learners believe, the findings are valuable: either you are prompted to reflect on your learners' actions and change (in the case of a mismatch) or your learners' confidence is boosted because there is a match and the learners are happy with what they are doing. It can also build confidence in the techniques you are using, even though some results might still encourage you to make small tweaks to what you are doing in class. This can be seen in Başak's story below.

Task 4 emergent language story: Başak

Başak teaches at an institute in Eskişehir in Turkey. She was not particularly surprised by her findings, which showed that her learners had generally positive views about receiving corrective feedback and focusing on emergent language. She felt that a lot of this alignment was down to conversations she had with the learners at the start of the course where they discussed previous learning experiences and what they enjoy or don't enjoy doing in class. Başak commented, *'It helps to talk about how you learn and what helps you more. This helps me as I can find out more about them, but they can find out more about themselves. We can then work something out so that their experiences are less difficult'*.

In terms of the impact on her practices, Başak was interested in a comment in one of the questionnaires, where a learner wrote, *'I like it better when you try to make our good sentences better'*. Başak was pleased to hear this, so she will continue to make time to work with well-formed language and reformulate it or offer extensions.

Başak was also interested in the learners who felt differently to her and the rest of the class or had answered 'don't know' to some of the questions. For example, one learner said that she did not like to be corrected in front of the class. Başak noted that this learner was quite reserved and often needed encouragement to take part in conversations. Though Başak did not feel that she did put this learner on the spot, she said that she would be careful not to do so in future. She also felt it would be useful to talk to learners who answered 'don't know' so she could explore their feelings further.

To summarise, Başak was happy to see that her beliefs and practices mostly matched those of her learners, and this reinforced her confidence in the intervention techniques she was using. The results also prompted her to think more about one of the learners in her class and how she might work with her in future. Most of all, the process of doing this task reinforced her belief in the value of talking to your learners about teaching and learning.

Using lesson transcripts 1

Task 5: Choosing what language to work with

Rationale

One of the chief concerns that teachers have regarding emergent language is that it is difficult to choose what language to pick up on and how you might reformulate it. This task gives you time and space to think about the language you might choose to reformulate and how you might do so. It also gives you the opportunity to reflect on the rationale that underpins your choices.

Task 5: Choosing what language to work with

A. Procedure

1. Read the transcript from the lesson below. What does Marco say about his father's expectations? What did he want to do?
2. Read the text again. What emergent language would you address in feedback? Note down how you would reformulate the items you have chosen. If it helps, you can do this directly on a whiteboard.
3. Now consider what techniques you would use. Would you elicit a reformulation or tell the learners directly? Would you add any extensions?
4. With another teacher, discuss the items you have chosen and how you reformulated them. What criteria did you use to choose items to reformulate and how you reformulated? When you have finished, read the Task 5 commentary and compare your ideas.

B. Extract from a lesson transcript

This extract is taken from a pre-intermediate (B1) class. In this extract, Marco, an Italian learner, is telling another learner about his parents' expectations for him when he was young.

Marco:	Eh … my father want to when I grew up she ... he want to ... I will be a lawyer but I don't studied law so I … he … now he is afraid about [laughs] ... that. Umm. He … my father pay for a private school where I studied when I was young but after the school I have to play drum so I don't study law and … [long pause] I am a musician but no a lawyer.

Photocopiable task

Teacher training variation

Teachers first work in pairs or groups to choose the items they want to reformulate and to decide how they will do so. They then present their ideas to the rest of the group. This could be done through a simple presentation or exchange of ideas. Alternatively, groups could create board plans that they share. For teachers working in the same institution, this task would also be a useful way to help a team agree on what they believe to be best practice for the context.

Task 5 commentary

The first part of this task asked you to identify areas of language you would choose to address in feedback. It is interesting to note how different teachers choose different areas to reformulate. This shows that there are not really any right or wrong answers to the task. Your choices will depend on several factors, as you saw in **Exploring emergent language in lessons** (pages 75–102), which can e teased out with the following questions:

- *What might be the most useful area for the learners to look at?*
- *What error is most common?*
- *Which areas caused / might cause a misunderstanding?*
- *Which areas are easiest to address?*

Based on some of these factors, the following areas could be addressed. First, we might pick up on the initial part of this learner's turn, focusing on the accuracy of Marco's use of tense and aspect. He uses an erroneous grammar pattern, for example:

Eh … my father want to when I grew up

she … he want to …

When [1]I was growing up my father [2]wanted me to become …

[1]past continuous

[2]past simple

It would be useful for learners at this level to focus on these language points as it is highly likely that they have encountered or studied them before. Tense, time and aspect could be further explored by looking at other grammatical structures in the extract.

In addition, this short text also provides an opportunity to examine lexical choice. For example, you could probe to find out if the learner really means *afraid about*, or if they actually mean *worried about* or *concerned about*. We have observed that issues such as these are often ignored by teachers as they understand the general meaning, but this can also mean that they miss an opportunity to develop the learner's understanding of the meaning and use of specific lexical items.

Eh … my father want to when I grew up she ... he want to ... I will be a lawyer but I don't studied law so I … he … now he is afraid about (laughs) ... that.

Another example of how a teacher can address a more complex issue is demonstrated below, when Marco says, *I have to play drum*. It is unclear here if he is describing a strong desire or an obligation (although we suspect it is a desire). In this instance, it would be a good idea to use a **clarification request** to ask Marco what he means, thereby giving him the chance to explain and possibly reformulate. By identifying examples like this, you can help your learners become more aware of how errors affect meaning and can cause miscomprehension.

The second part of the task asked you to think about how you would work with the emergent language, and again, there is no right or wrong answer. The following ideas would all work well (note, the intervention techniques are in bold):

1. For the issues with tense and aspect, you can write the errors on the whiteboard for learners to look at in feedback (**sharing**). You could then ask the learners to work together to decide how they would reformulate the utterance. This would be an example of **explicit reformulation** and **eliciting**. You could also use **metalinguistic feedback** by telling the learners that they need to change the tense and aspect.
2. For the use of *afraid about* versus *worried about*, it would be useful to use **extensions** to explore how *worried about* might be used, as shown in Figure 7.1. For learners at this level, *afraid about* may be a trickier prospect to explore in depth as it is often followed by verb + *ing*, as in *I'm afraid about confronting them*. As corpus data also shows that *worried about* is extremely common, whereas *afraid about* is not, it would perhaps be better to focus only on *worried about* rather than spend time comparing the two items.

He's worried about	*my future*
	1. my plans
	2. me

(Refer back to Figure 7.1 on on pages 140–141 for extensions with *worried about*.)

3. As mentioned earlier, for the use of *have to* in *I have to play drums*, a **clarification request** would allow you to find out what the learner really means. To follow up, you could also use **extension** by modelling examples of how Marco could express either his obligations or desires (see Figure 7.1, on pages 140–141). You could then use **elicitation** by asking which sentence is a strong desire and which is an obligation.

   I felt I just had to play the drums (strong desire).

   All I wanted to do was play drums (strong desire).

   I can't come out as I have to go to my drumming class (obligation).

   (Refer back to Figure 7.1 for extensions for *I had to play the drums*.)

Using lesson transcripts 2

Task 6a: Identifying intervention types

Rationale

As well as developing practical skills and exploring different teaching approaches and procedures, teacher education programmes should also help build understanding of key concepts and develop teacher knowledge (Richards & Farrell, 2005). When it comes to emergent language, before you start examining your teaching and finding out how effectively you are working with it, it is important to be able to identify the different intervention types a teacher might use during a lesson. It is also useful to consider why a teacher might choose each intervention type at different stages. The following two awareness-raising tasks will help you do this. Both tasks can be done individually or with a colleague, though it can be useful to have the final discussion in a larger group, if possible.

Task 6a: Identifying intervention types

A. Procedure

1. Look at the list of ten intervention types below. Can you remember what each one involves? You can use the descriptions in **How to work with emergent language** (pages 53–74) to help you.
2. Look at the definitions in C and match them to the intervention types in B.
3. When you have finished, look at the answers on page 155. ➔

B. Ten intervention types

1. Explicit reformulation (live or delayed)
2. Recast
3. Teacher clarification/ clarification request
4. Metalinguistic feedback
5. Elicitation
6. Extension
7. Interactional recast
8. Recall
9. Sharing
10. Learner-initiated

C. Definitions of intervention types

a) The teacher indicates to learners that their utterance has been misunderstood or only partially understood. The learner is then invited to explain what they mean.
b) The teacher uses grammatical or linguistic labels or terms to provide information about the nature of the error or utterance.
c) After a learner has completed a turn, the teacher focuses on alternative or more common ways of saying the same thing.
d) The teacher implicitly provides a more appropriate form whilst maintaining communication or extending the communicative turn.
e) While monitoring, the teacher picks up examples of interesting or useful language from a learner and shares it with the rest of the group.
f) The teacher provides a clear and overt alternative form. As the teacher provides the new form, he or she clearly indicates that what the learner had said was inaccurate or could be expressed differently.
g) A learner asks for help with a word or phrase, or indicates that they are unsure of how to complete their utterance.
h) The teacher provides an implicit reformulation of all or part of a learner's utterance, minus any indication of error. This is usually done immediately after the learner produces the utterance.
i) The teacher prompts learners to recall or use words or phrases that they believe the learners have encountered in previous classes.
j) Rather than explaining or reformulating themselves, the teacher uses different techniques to draw out the meaning or correct form from the learners.

Photocopiable task

Teacher training variation

If you are working with newer teachers or suspect your teachers are new to the concept of emergent language, you could take a flipped approach by instructing them to read **How to work with emergent language** (pages 53–74) before you meet. You could simplify the task by reducing the number of interventions and descriptions you look at. Another way of doing this would be to split the teachers into different groups with different interventions and definitions. Once each group has read about their intervention, they could get together to exchange the new information.

Task 6b: Identifying interventions from transcripts

A. Procedure

1. Look at the underlined utterances in the transcripts in C. Which intervention type listed in B does the teacher use? Write your answers in Column 3. You can use an intervention type as many times as you need throughout the task. Note that there may be more than one intervention type in an exchange, and you can use an intervention type more than once.
2. Check your answers against those on page 155. Why might the teacher choose to respond in this way in each instance? How might each intervention help the learner?

B. Intervention types

1. Explicit reformulation
2. Recast
3. Teacher clarification/confirmation request
4. Metalinguistic feedback
5. Elicitation
6. Extension
7. Interactional recast
8. Recall
9. Sharing
10. Learner-initiated

➔

C. Matching interventions to transcripts

Exchange			Type(s) of intervention
a)	**Learner 5:**	[Explaining why mobile phones should be banned in class] Maybe students are not curious.	*Clarification request*
	Teacher:	What do you mean?	*Reformulations*
	Learner 5:	They must control themselves.	
	Teacher:	I think maybe … Curious, it could be curious, but I think *they're not interested in the lesson, or they're not focused.*	*Extension*
b)	**Learner 7:**	She were on the … what's that [mimes 'roof'].	
	Learner 9:	Roof.	
	Learner 10:	What mean 'roof'?	
	Teacher:	OK, the roof is the top of the building [drawing a picture] ... the roof is this part … Is that correct, Shahida?	
	Learner 9:	Yes.	
	Teacher:	OK.	
	Learner 7:	Then she saw her niece on the roof and try to get guava and she asked her …	
c)	**Learner 2:**	[Discussing sneaking phones into school] If we want, we bring it like someone might bring something illegal or bad. We hidden. We try … we have many ways to … make it?	
	Teacher:	*to hide it*	
	Learner 2:	*hid it*	
	Teacher:	*hide it*	
	Learner 2:	*to hide it.*	

➔

d)	**Learner 2:**	[They are …] not allowed in the school. All the school.	
	Teacher:	The whole school?	
	Learner 2:	Yeah. Not allowed … to bring … our phones.	
	Teacher:	Really? So where do the phones go?	
e)	**Learner 1:**	Maybe the teacher will seize the phone.	
	Teacher:	I think the difference is ... when we saw the word *seize* (in a previous lesson), who did the seizing?	
	Learner 2:	police	
	Teacher:	Yes. What did they seize?	
	Learner 3:	phone, computer, passport …	
	Teacher:	From who?	
	Learner 3:	From maybe someone who do something bad.	
	Teacher:	Yeah, so they seize things from a criminal. Like what?	
f)	**Teacher:**	[Responding to a learner talking about the weekend] You can say *you are very tired* or another word …. [writing on WB] *really tired.* OK I feel very tired [class repeat] I feel *really tired* [class repeat]. Or another word for this [points to tired] *sleepy. So, I feel very sleepy* [class repeat] or I feel *really sleepy* [class repeat].	
g)	**Learner 1:**	[Talking about sharing photos online] *It violates their… violates their ...* [looks at teacher].	
	Teacher:	*privacy*	
	Learner 1:	… You say … what's the word?	
	Teacher:	*Privacy. It's the noun … of private … It violates my privacy.* It's not a public situation.	

➔

h)	**Teacher:**	[Pointing to examples on the whiteboard] I like this one. *If we didn't use our phones, we didn't die*. You're talking about the present, but there is an element of future, too, so I think you need to change this verb [points to *didn't*].	
	Learner:	*won't*	
	Teacher:	*Um, if we didn't use our phones we won't die?* I think that's OK. I'd go with *wouldn't*.	

Photocopiable task

Teacher training variation

If you are working with newer teachers or suspect your teachers are new to the concept of emergent language, you could take a flipped approach by instructing them to read **How to work with emergent language** (pages 53–74) before you meet.

Answer key

Task 6b: 1. f) 2. h) 3. a) 4. b) 5. j) 6. c) 7. d) 8. i) 9. e) 10. g)

Task 6b: a) clarification request, explicit reformulation, extension b) learner-initiated, explicit reformulation c) learner-initiated, recast d) interactional recast e) explicit reformulation, recall, elicitation f) explicit reformulation, extension g) learner-initiated, explicit reformulation, metalinguistic feedback h) sharing, explicit reformulation, metalinguistic feedback, elicitation.

Task 6a & 6b commentary

By becoming aware of the different types of intervention and the options available to them, teachers can develop confidence in responding to learners by being able to choose techniques that they feel comfortable with or that are suitable for their learners. Looking at transcripts in this way also shows how interventions do not necessarily close down communication but can actually keep it going.

You can see this in Dan's story. Dan was a teacher-in-training on a Trinity Dip TESOL course. After doing Tasks 6a and 6b, Dan could not only see the range of techniques he could use to work with emergent language, he was also prompted to re-evaluate his practices and beliefs, and to challenge things he had been taught on his initial training course.

Task 6 emergent language story: Dan

When Dan did this task, he was interested to see how many of the interventions overlapped, and to note that teachers didn't seem to use only one type at a time. He was also interested to see that teachers use correction techniques and explore emergent language during communicative stages. This conflicted with information he had been given on his initial training course, where he was taught that you should only correct learners after communicative tasks so as not to interrupt the communication. Doing Task 6 helped Dan see that the interruptions can in fact keep the conversation going or help with little 'roadblocks'.

Using lesson transcripts 3

Task 7: Identifying interventions in longer transcripts

Rationale

Task 6 was designed to help you develop your teacher knowledge by identifying the different intervention types that might be used in a lesson. This task enables you to further develop your understanding of these techniques as you identify ones used in a longer exchange. This task also encourages you to think about why the teacher uses different intervention techniques throughout the exchange, and demonstrates how everyone works together to help one of the learners tell their story. The transcript is taken from an adult ESOL class at a further education college in East London (thanks to Richard Gallen for the transcript and long-term inspiration).

Task 7: Identifying interventions in longer transcripts

A. Procedure

1. Look at the lesson transcript below. What is the learner describing? How successful are they in communicating their message by the end of the exchange?
2. Look at the underlined utterances 1–10 in B. Which intervention types can you identify? Note that an underlined utterance could constitute more than one intervention type, and you can use an intervention type more than once. Use the list of interventions (a–j) in Task 6 to help you. Answers on page 158. ➔

a) ____________________

b) ____________________

c) ____________________

d) ____________________

e) ____________________

f) ____________________

g) ____________________

h) ____________________

i) ____________________

j) ____________________

3. Look at the transcript again. How does the class work together to help the learner tell their story?
4. When you have completed the task, look at the commentary for Task 7 and compare your ideas.

B. Interventions in a longer class transcript

Learner 1:	When I go to market erm buy something, but specially my problem I think everybody, [1)]when I go something buy wrong colour, how to …?
Teacher:	Okay [2)]so it's when you go shopping in the market, and when you want to buy something?
Learner 1:	Yeah, sometime change.
Teacher:	[3)]When you say 'change', what do you mean 'change'?
Learner 1:	Sometime time I buy something and then when I go home for my children this is not ….
Teacher:	Ah okay.
Learner 2:	[Calling out] 'exchange'
Teacher:	'exchange' that's nice, L2. [4)]What did L2 say?
Learners chorus:	*exchange*
Teacher:	*exchange*, yeah, [5)]*exchange or return*.
Teacher:	[Writing on the board] [6)]'Can I exchange this?' 'Can I get a refund/my money back?'
Teacher:	[Reads out what is on the board] *Can I exCHANGE this?* Or *can I get a REfund?* [Learners repeat.]
Teacher:	[7)]So what's the difference between *can I exchange this* and *can I get a refund?*
Learner 3:	*Refund* is money back.
Teacher:	Yeah exactly. [8)]Refund is when you ask for….
Learner 3:	money change
Teacher:	Not money change, money BACK. ➔

Teacher:	[To Learner 1] So tell me again …
Learner 1:	When I go to market for change dress and when they say okay, I give you money or I give you change I am happy.
Teacher:	Okay.
Learner 1:	but when they say not refund your money, […] no change then I sad (pronounced **sed**) …
Teacher:	Then you said … what did you say then?
Learner 1:	Then I **sed**…
Teacher:	Okay, [9)]*I am SAD. Or I feel sad* (learners repeat 'I feel sad') *I get upset*.
Learner 4:	some shops
Teacher:	some shops?
Learner 4:	some shops don't …. Some shops not give the exchange and don't get the refund.
Teacher:	Ah so [laughing] [10)]you don't get an exchange OR a refund, oh OK.

Photocopiable task

Variation

Simplify the task by adding a jumbled list of the answers to the bottom of the task sheet and creating a matching task.

Teacher training variation

If you are working with newer teachers or suspect your teachers are new to the concept of emergent language, you could take a flipped approach by instructing them to read **How to work with emergent language** (pages 53–74) before you meet.

Answer key

Task 7: 1) learner-initiated 2) clarification request 3) clarification request 4) sharing 5) extension 6) extension 7) elicitation 8) elicitation 9) recast/extension 10) interactional recast

Task 7 commentary

Richard Gallen is an experienced ESOL teacher with a long-held interest in working with and researching emergent language in the ESOL classroom. A lot of his work can be found in the ESOL section of the Excellency Gateway website.

Task 7 emergent language story: Richard

Richard uses a variety of intervention types to work with emergent language. What is notable is that the primary purpose of his interventions is not to develop accuracy or focus on a specific form. Instead, his aim is to help the learners develop the story and keep the conversation going. At times, he is very involved, regularly asking for clarification or providing words or phrases for the learners. The reason he cites for this is that 'ESOL learners are speaking at the edge of their competence, so they need input, support, and guidance to help them'. In this way, he is helping the learners to maintain the conversation and say what they want to say, as well as supporting those that may not be following. He goes on to say that though you must be careful not to overdo it, the conversations can withstand the interventions, as long as you are stepping in 'without your grammar hat on'. He also says that he limits the amount of new language that he puts on the board. Though he does record some useful phrases, he suggests that this is something that you must think about carefully as many low-level ESOL learners will be distracted and slowed down by boarded correction.

As well as intervening to provide prompts or to check other learners' understanding, Richard also gives the learners the space to ask him for assistance and to help each other with new words. This stems from his belief that we learn through co-constructing meanings and stories. It is worth noting that the learners in this class come from what Richard terms a 'high-involvement culture', so this is what a conversation would look and feel like in the learners' L1 (in this case, Bengali). Much of the rationale underpinning Richard's work with emergent language is, therefore, not only down to his beliefs but also the teaching context he works in.

Using lesson transcripts 4

Task 8: Deciding when to intervene

Rationale

There is a body of literature and opinion that discourages teachers from intervening during communicative activities (for example, Hedge, 2000), with much of this thinking based on the belief that immediate intervention can divert the learners from the flow of speaking (for example, Scrivener, 2005). However, we have seen in previous chapters that there is a rationale for immediate intervention, especially if the intervention is designed to help the learners say what they want to say or get back on track after a communicative breakdown. This task is designed to help you to consider when it might be beneficial to intervene during student–student interaction, and to reflect on the rationale that underpins your choices.

Task 8: Deciding when to intervene

A. Procedure

1. Read the three lesson transcripts B1–3 below. Each transcript shows learners working in groups or pairs to complete a communicative task. As you read each transcript, answer the questions below.
   a) What language problem does each group encounter as they communicate?
   b) Do you need to intervene to help them with the problem or could you deal with it in a delayed feedback stage?
   c) What techniques might you use to work with the emergent language?
   d) What is your rationale for intervening or not?
2. Once you have competed the task, read the commentary for Task 8 and compare your ideas.

B. Three lesson transcripts

1. This extract is taken from an intermediate (B2) class. The students are part of a group of Brazilian teachers, who all share the same L1 (Portuguese), on a teacher and language development programme. In the task, they are discussing which influential English-speaking Brazilian could be used as a role model to motivate their learners. Once they have completed the task, each group presents their ideas to the rest of the class. It is worth noting here that the group requested corrective feedback at the start of the programme.

Learner 1:	Umm … I think we can use Marcos Pentos with the students as he had […] a difficult eh … *criação*
Learner 2:	*criação* is …?
Learner 3:	background?
Learner 2:	[Shrugs] It's possible.
Learner 3:	Yes.
Learner 1:	OK background … I think he's … good because he had a difficult background with no money and from a ... poor place … but he got apprenticeship.

➔

2. This extract is from a mid-intermediate (B1) class of adults who do not share the same L1. In this task, S1 (L1 Arabic) is telling S2 (L1 Japanese) how his life will be different in 10 years' time. The numbers in brackets represent the length of pauses, for instance, [4] refers to a four-second pause.

Learner 2:	How will life be different for you in ten years?
Learner 1:	I'll be, eh, quitting smoking […] no.
Learner 2:	no?
Learner 1:	no
Learner 2:	no what?
Learner 1:	not 'I'll be quitting smoking' [4] is ' will be…'
Learner 2:	Will be quit?
Learner 1:	will be quitted? [4]
Learner 2:	[Nodding] You will be quit. [4]
Learner 1:	You understand?
Learner 2:	Yeah, you will be quit.
Learner 1:	I will be quit. [3] [to self] Is not that.

3. This extract is taken from an intermediate (B2) class of adults who do not share the same L1. The learners have read a text about a 14-year-old boy who has committed a crime and are deciding on a suitable punishment.

Learner 1:	I think because this boy is age 14 so police put him … is not in jail … something to learn more and … put him to work for something for social or something like this.
Learner 2:	Yes, in my country has something like this. A social attendance that prevent he continue doing this.
Learner 1:	Yes, because he's still young so maybe can learn something good for him. And jail is not useful for this age.
Learner 3:	Jail is not the good solution. In my country we have this kind of school that will reform but it doesn't to work. I don't know in your countries.
Learner 4:	In our country there is a kind of prison for kids. Its conditions a bit nice … better than the prison and the kids are under 18 years old if they are arrest they go to …
Learner 2:	... This kind of prison. It's not a real prison. It's kind of to reform that kind of people. A reformer … Isn't it?

Photocopiable task

Teacher training variation

On a teacher education programme, this task could be used as an information exchange. Create groups and give a different extract to each group. The groups work together to discuss whether they would intervene in the situation or not. When they have finished, each group describes the situation to the other groups and presents their decision and rationale. Next, your teachers get together to create a rationale for when they might choose to intervene during communicative tasks and when they might not. For teachers working in the same institution, this task is a useful way to help a team agree on best practice for the context.

Task 8 commentary

In each of the extracts (B.1–3), each group has encountered a communicative barrier that may or may not require intervention by the teacher. These are outlined below:

B.1 In this exchange, the students understand the meaning of the word *criação*, but they do not know the English translation.

B.2 In this exchange, Learner 2 understands what Learner 1 is trying to convey. However, Learner 1 is not convinced that he is using the correct form (*will be quit*). This doubt has caused the conversation to stall as Learner 1 struggles to get past the issue.

B.3 In this exchange, the learners understand each other, and are taking turns effectively. However, they do not know the names of the punishments that they are suggesting. They therefore use circumlocution to get their meaning across.

The third part of this task asked you whether you would intervene in these situations or not and how you might work with the emergent language. Below are some options for the teacher. Are there any similarities to yours?

B.1 As the learners understand each other and have quickly moved on to discussing their rationale for choosing Marcos Pentos (the first Brazilian in space) as their role model, there does not seem to be an immediate need for the teacher to intervene during the task. However, as the learners do not know that the direct equivalent for *criação* is *upbringing*, it would be useful for the teacher to quickly provide this word to the group before they report back to the rest of the class. Once all the groups have shared their ideas, the teacher can then

share this interesting new word with the class by exploring typical collocations on the board:

a	*stable* *difficult* *privileged*	*upbringing*

B.2 In this task, the learners have stopped communicating ideas as they struggle to decide on the appropriate form. Their focus therefore has switched from meaning to form, which, as we saw in **How to work with emergent language** (pages 53–74), is quite a common occurrence in the language classroom. This presents a strong rationale for the teacher to step in and provide the appropriate form so that the learners can get back to focusing on meaning.

To do this, the teacher could briefly step in and directly give the two learners the correct form. However, it may also be worth using a **clarification request**, as it is unclear if the learner is planning to stop smoking in 10 years' time or will have given up before then. By using a clarification request, the teacher can quickly find out what S1 wants to say before providing the correct form. Once this is done, the learners can get back on-task.

As in the first extract (B.1), the teacher can also use the feedback stage to explore the different forms that the learners were struggling with. To start with, they could write the three forms on the board and **elicit** the difference in meaning, as you can see here:

In 10 years' time	*I will stop smoking* *I will have stopped smoking* *I will be stopping smoking*

To help convey the difference between the forms, the teacher can then use timelines or provide other examples using learners' ideas from the task.

B3. This scenario is perhaps the least clear cut as there is a rationale for either intervening or keeping your distance. As in the first extract (B.1), the learners involved in this task keep their conversation going by describing what they mean. This presents a rationale for the teacher to let the conversation flow and provide the unknown words (*community service/young offenders institute*) during feedback.

However, the words the learners want would be useful, and by having them provided at the point of need, the learners may be more likely to remember them in the future. In order not to disrupt the flow, perhaps the teacher could join in as a participant and use a combination of **interactional recast** and **confirmation request** to provide the language, as can be seen below. However, as it is possible that the learners merely acknowledge the intervention and move on with the discussion, the teacher can ask these learners to try to recall and share the new words in the feedback stage, thereby aiding memory and potential intake further.

Learner 1:	I think because this boy is age 14 so police put him … is not in jail … something to learn more and put him to work for something for social or something like this.
Learner 2:	Yes, in my country has something like this. A social attendance that prevent that it continue doing this.
Teacher:	You mean they could *do community service?* Why do you think that would be a good idea?

Observation task 1

Task 9: What did the learner say? What would I say?

Rationale

One of the chief concerns teachers have regarding emergent language is that it is difficult to know when to intervene and what language to pick up on. This concern has not only been expressed by novice teachers; it is also commonly mentioned by teachers on diploma- and master's-level courses, as well as experienced teachers. This task is a simple way to sensitise yourself to learner language before you try to work with it in classes.

This task involves recording learners doing a communicative activity and watching it back in your own time to tune into emergent language generated in the activity. Out of all the tasks we have used with teachers, this one has consistently been reported as useful in tuning in. First, it helps you to notice what the learners are saying and to think about what they are trying to say. It also gives you time to think about what emergent language you might focus on and how you might reformulate what was said.

When you feel more confident, you can use the photocopiable resource during a lesson as you monitor learners doing tasks in pairs or groups. The list of learner utterances you have noted down can readily be transferred to the board before you feed back on them. It's worth noting that as you become familiar with the contents of the document, you will gradually automatise the way that you deal with emergent language to the point that you may not need the document anymore. However, many teachers continue to use the resource, as they find it the most effective way of preparing to work with emergent language during feedback stages.

Task 9: What did the learner say? What would I say?

A. Procedure

1. Record part of a lesson (either one of your own or a colleague's) by video or audio. This must be a section where learners have a long turn.
2. Before you watch the recording, draw two columns on a piece of paper. Write 'What did the learner say?' at the top of column 1. Then write 'What would I say?' at the top of column 2 (see B below).
3. Listen to or watch your recording. As you listen, in the first column, note down word for word any learner utterances that you think would be useful to work with. It can be useful to number each example as you write it down and note the learner's name next to it.
4. Look at the utterances in column 1 and ask yourself: *What is the learner trying to say?*
5. Once you have decided, ask yourself: *What would I say in this situation?*
6. In column 2, write down how you would reformulate or extend each example. If you are not sure what the learner is trying to say, note down a clarification request you would use instead.
7. Look at the commentary for Task 9 to see an example of a completed document and a teacher's reflection.

B. What would I say?

1. Write down reformulations and alternatives to what the learner said. If you are unsure about what the learner means, write a clarification request.
2. When you are using this document in class, it is a good idea to note down the learner's name next to the utterance you record. This will allow you to prompt the learner to return to the point they were making in their discussion and help contextualise the reformulation that will follow. Another important element is to note when you ➔

are unsure what a learner means, as you want your reformulation to accurately reflect what the learner is trying to say. To do this, you can add a question mark next to the utterance or the potential reformulations. In feedback, this provides the opportunity to use a clarification request to find out what the learner wanted to say. You can then negotiate an alternative form that helps the learner get their meaning across clearly.

What did the learner say?	What would I say?
I don't do that if I were you. (Irina)	*Example: I wouldn't do that if I were you.*

Photocopiable task

Teacher training variation

This template can be used as an observation task on a training course, with teachers observing colleagues and filling in the table as they watch. They then bring their completed table to a training session to be used as a basis for discussion.

Task 9 commentary

As discussed in **What is emergent language?** (pages 7–12), feedback on emergent language does not need to focus only on learner errors. You can also look for examples of effective language use and explore ways of extending it, offering alternatives, giving more common ways to say the same thing, or making it more appropriate for the context or genre.

Figure 7.2 shows a completed task from a lesson in which intermediate (B2) adult learners were talking in groups about different personalities and keeping and telling secrets. The teacher has chosen to draw attention to idiomatic language as they felt that these items would suit the needs and interests of this specific group. The teacher's aim was to provide the learners with alternative ways of expressing their intended meanings, thereby extending their lexical range. This task therefore not only helps teachers work with errors, but also provides opportunities to explore useful collocations, formulaic chunks and patterns.

What did the learner say?	What would I say?
He's without feelings	He's hard-hearted
I won't tell your secret	I won't tell a soul your secret is safe with me
I don't like people tell your secret	I don't like it <u>when</u> people can't <u>keep</u> a <u>secret</u>

Figure 7.2: Result of Task 9 carried out by a teacher during a lesson

Task 9 emergent language story: Sam

Sam has been using this document for two years to develop his ability to monitor his feedback and develop a more focused approach to it. He has found that noting down learner language in this way has allowed him to examine more carefully what learners are saying as opposed to grasping at random bits of learner language to explore in feedback. He has also come to believe that his learners are less stimulated when the teacher 'decides what they should be saying'; by using the task, he believes he has been able to take a step back and consider how he can reflect what the learners *want* to say. His top recommendation for teachers when giving feedback is, 'Stay focused on what the learner is trying to say and avoid moving away from this.' By observing his learners, Sam has also been interested to see how his learners learn from other learners. This has helped him realise that the language in the lesson doesn't always have to come from the teacher, but that the learners' participation in the lesson can shape what is learnt.

Observation task 2

Task 10: Identifying your intervention practices

Rationale

Making audio and video recordings are two of the easiest ways of capturing spoken interaction in the classroom. Once you have recordings of your lessons, you can use them to explore and analyse the interactions you have with your learners and identify the extent to which your actions and techniques affect learning.

Observation tasks (sometimes known as observation instruments) and coding systems are some of the most reliable methods for helping teachers evaluate classroom interaction, enabling you to examine what is happening at different moments in your lessons (Walsh, 2011). The following observation task includes two typical observation techniques. These are box ticking, which helps you identify how frequently you use different intervention techniques, and note taking, which prompts you to record how your learners respond to the different intervention techniques you are using. Once you have examined your data, look at the reflective questions in Step 4. These will help you to think about the extent to which the techniques you are using impact on your learners, and to decide on best practice for future classes.

Task 10: Identifying your intervention practices

A. Procedure

1. Record all or part of a lesson in which you are interacting with your learners. To help you focus on your emergent language practices, this could be a stage in which you are discussing a topic or text, brainstorming ideas or doing feedback after a communicative task.
2. Watch the recording. Each time you identify a specific intervention type, put a tick in the appropriate box in column 2 of the table below. This will give you a tally of how often you use each technique.
3. In column 3, note down how the learners reacted in each instance. Did they self-correct or incorporate the new language in their speaking? Did they write down the new language in their notebooks? Or did they ignore the intervention and continue interacting? This will give you an insight into the impact of your interventions.
4. Rewatch the whole recording or certain interesting parts of the lesson and answer the following questions:
   a) What intervention types do I favour during interactional stages? Do I tend to use explicit or implicit techniques?
   b) What is my rationale for using each intervention type?
   c) What impact do my interventions have on the learners in terms of uptake?
   d) Are there any instances where my interventions could be more successful? How could I have done things differently?

Once you have done the task, look at the commentary for Task 10 on page 169.

➔

B. Observation task for identifying your emergent language practices

Type of intervention	Number of instances	Learner uptake (such as self-correction, incorporated into discourse, writing it down, ignoring it)
Explicit reformulation		
Recast		
Teacher clarification request		
Metalinguistic feedback		
Elicitation		
Extension		
Interactional recast		
Recalls		
Sharing		
Learner-initiated		

Photocopiable task

Teacher training variation

This template can be used as an observation task on a training course, with teachers observing colleagues and filling in the table as they watch. They then bring their completed table to a training session to be used as a basis for discussion.

Task 10 commentary

We, the authors, recorded ourselves teaching live classes as part of a research project run by Nick Andon at King's College London. This project generated a lot of interesting data about emergent language, and acted as the catalyst for this book. It also gave both of us the opportunity to observe our emergent language practices, and to take stock of the impact they have on our learners. Watching and analysing the recordings enabled us to think about the principles that underpin our approaches to teaching. Read Danny's reflections on the process below, which were drawn from a two-hour task-based lesson with a group of adult intermediate learners. When you have read the reflection, think about whether your findings are similar or different.

Task 10 emergent language story: Danny

The first thing that struck me was how often I intervened over the two hours. During feedback or open-class discussions, I regularly intervened to reformulate learner output, keep the conversation going and respond to content.

The other observation I made was that most of my interventions were explicit; I guess this comes from my belief that if learners notice (or are prompted to notice) a gap in their output and can close that gap, it is going to be memorable and lead to durable learning. In fact, I only used recasts four times, each time for pronunciation issues. I wasn't aware that that was something I did – it wasn't conscious. Most of the time, my learners responded to my interventions by using the new form or correcting themselves. This was true for the recasts, too.

One of the techniques I used most was elicitation, although equally, I often just gave the learners a new word or form, especially if they asked directly. I also used a lot of clarification requests. This is something I believe we should do more, as I think it's important to respond to output that causes miscomprehension as you would outside the classroom. If you could only use one type of intervention, I think this would be a good one to choose.

It's worth noting here that the students in this class are adult learners, so it is possible that teachers in this context might be more open to the idea of explicit forms of intervention. As we have seen in previous chapters, teachers working with teens or younger learners often feel differently about this.

Observation task 3

Task 11: Designing your own observation task

Rationale

As we saw in Task 10, one of the most useful ways of monitoring and tracking your development in a specific aspect of your teaching is to use observation tasks (sometimes known as observation instruments). These can either be found in training manuals and materials, or they can be created by teacher educators and given to teachers on training courses. Another option is for teachers to create their own observation tasks. There are three reasons for choosing this approach. First, it is not always possible to find an observation task that fully meets your needs or relates to your teaching context. Second, research has shown that teachers are more likely to benefit when they set their own research agenda and design their own data-gathering instruments (Walsh, 2011). Third, when observers are given observation tasks created by the teacher who is going to be observed, they are more likely to look for what the teacher wants to monitor as opposed to noting down general strengths and weaknesses (Howard, 2008).

This task prompts you to design an observation task for another teacher before you design your own.

Task 11: Designing your own observation task

A. Procedure

1. Look at the teacher trainee emergent language story below. What are the main interactional issues Amelia has identified in her teaching?
2. Design an observation task to help Amelia monitor her progress in this area and develop her emergent language skills. This could include ticking boxes to count how often something was seen or done during the lesson (as in Task 10), specific questions to answer (such as *Am I involving all the learners in the feedback stage?*), instructions to note down examples of teacher or learner actions (such as, *Note down examples of how I recorded reformulations on the board*) or statements for the observer to agree/disagree with (such as, *I give sufficient time for learners to respond to prompts: agree/disagree*).
3. Once you have done this, look at the commentary for Task 11 to see what Amelia did.
4. When you are ready, design an observation task to help you monitor your own work with emergent language.

B. A teacher trainee's emergent language story: Amelia

I was recently observed on a training course, and the tutor pointed out that as well as responding nicely to ideas and stories when chatting or doing feedback, I was also recasting a lot. I've learnt about recasting as an effective technique, and the tutor agreed that it is useful for keeping the communication going whilst also providing brief feedback on errors. However, the tutor also said that I echoed the learners a lot, which meant that they may not have noticed my recasts. This is because echoes and recasts can sound the same to learners, making the recasts less effective. The tutor also said that because I was recasting so much, the learners ➔

would often miss out on the opportunity to modify what they had said. The tutor therefore suggested I mix things up a bit. Another thing the tutor noticed was that I regularly say 'OK' or 'Good' when the learners speak. While it is nice to praise, this type of response often ends the speaker's turn, and it would be good if I responded with follow-up questions to encourage the learners to say more. I think I'd like to be a bit more explicit in my response to emergent language, and to make my recasts more noticeable by reducing echo. A colleague said I could continue to echo, but with a questioning intonation, as that shows the learner that there's an error. So I would like to try that. I would also like to encourage the learners to say more by asking more follow-up questions rather than just praising what they say.

Photocopiable task

Teacher training variation

Put your teachers into groups to do the task. Once each group has designed an observation task for Amelia, they present their ideas to the rest of the group. The course leader can then provide feedback on the potential effectiveness of each task. Once this is done, the teachers get into pairs to discuss what they would like to monitor in their own teaching. The pairs then work together to design observation tasks for each other.

Task 11 commentary

Look at the task Amelia created in Figure 7.3 on page 173. How does it compare with yours? Amelia has used the first column to find out how often she uses each response (as was done in Task 10). This should give her some basic data about which techniques she is favouring or potentially overusing. However, numbers don't tell the full story, so her second and third columns are useful as they will enable her to get a deeper insight into when she recasts or echoes, and how the learners respond to these moves. The requests for extra information in the bottom two rows are also useful as they will give her data and tips on how she can improve her practice. They also enable the observer to draw on their own experiences without dominating the agenda.

As she was on a training course, Amelia was able to hand this document to three fellow course participants. If you can get more than one observer to complete the table, the data is likely to be more reliable.

Type of response	Number of instances	What kind of language (e.g. grammar or lexis) was I responding to? (Please give examples.)	How did the learners respond? (For instance, did they modify their output, note down the correction, ignore the recast etc.? Please give examples.)
Recasting after learner errors			
Echo			
Praise/ Saying 'OK'			
Responding to message			
Please give other examples of ways I dealt with emergent language, e.g. eliciting.			
Please share any tips or ways that you work with emergent language.			

Figure 7.3: Amelia's observation task

Once you have compared Amelia's task to yours, read her story to see what she drew from the feedback.

Task 11 emergent language story: Amelia

The main thing Amelia got from this task was information about how learners responded to the recasts. The observers said that there were a handful of moments when learners self-corrected or used the reformulated version later, but there were more occasions when there was no evidence of uptake. This made Amelia think that she should use more explicit methods sometimes, but also that she needed to further reduce her echo, which was again quite high and could be the reason why the learners were not overtly noticing. ➔

She was pleased to see that all the teachers had noticed that she had tried out the technique of repeating some learner errors with a questioning intonation, and that this had led to more frequent instances of repair or learner reformulation. This, she felt, would encourage her to use this technique more often.

The feedback Amelia initially received from her tutor enabled her to make small changes to her practice. The observation task she then designed and gave her peers enabled her to recognise some progress in these areas, as well as highlighting points she would like to continue to work on. This is positive, and it is worth remembering that development often comes in small steps rather than large leaps.

Task planning 1

Task 12: Pre-empting learner language

Rationale

One reason teachers sometimes find it daunting to go straight into free tasks and work with what emerges is that they fear the unknown, and lack the confidence to deal with what comes up. It feels safer to plan and deliver lessons with preconceived language aims and answers. However, it is possible to both give learners extensive communicative practice and prepare yourself to deal with what emerges. This can be done by using what Ellis (2003) calls **focused tasks**.

A focused task is a free, communicative activity that is likely to generate specific language items when carried out by a proficient speaker. For example, when debating whether mobile phones should be banned in public places, a proficient speaker would be likely to use the modal verb *should* alongside phrases for presenting arguments and for agreeing and disagreeing. These might include 'sentence frames', such as *I see what you mean, but …* or *If we banned …, people would …*. Similarly, in a task in which someone talks about what they did during the school holidays, they will be expected to use past forms. As the language in a focused task can be pre-empted to some extent, you have more opportunities to prepare for what might come up when learners do the task. It can also help teachers to think about what aspects of language they might prioritise in a post-task feedback session.

The following task involves completing a planning template (see section C of Task 12 – thanks to Melissa Lamb for the inspiration) to help you pre-empt language forms that might come up during a focused task. When you are trying to predict what language is likely to come up, it can be useful to brainstorm ideas with a colleague. If this is not possible, you could record yourself or someone else acting out the communicative task that your learners are going on to do. The recording can then be used to help you notice what forms are typically used when performing the focused task and therefore which forms might emerge in the lesson. Note that it does not matter if pre-empted forms do not emerge in the lesson itself. They can either be explored in the post-task feedback stage as **extensions** or alternatives, or presented in a follow-up lesson.

The planning document is organised in layers, a bit like an onion, to encourage you to think about the different levels of language you might provide learners with, starting from the smallest relevant parts (words and collocations) to more overarching elements of language, in other words, the function. It can also help you to think about how each element fits together rather than looking at items separately. Putting it another way, it's possible to consider how a word like *legalise* could fit into a grammatical pattern (such as *We should legalise X*), and how this could be used with a sentence frame to create a functional phrase (I*n my opinion, we should legalise X*).

Task 12: Pre-empting learner language

A. Procedure

1. Look at the task outline for intermediate (B2) learners below. How would you set up this task for your learners?
2. Complete the planning document in section C below by adding in the language items you believe would be used to complete the task.
3. Now compare your ideas with those in the commentary for Task 12.

B. Task outline for intermediate (B2) learners

Student task outline

Work in a group. Think of three laws you would like to see implemented or abolished in your country or internationally. Give a reason for your ideas. You must all agree with your choices.

➔

C. Emergent language planning template

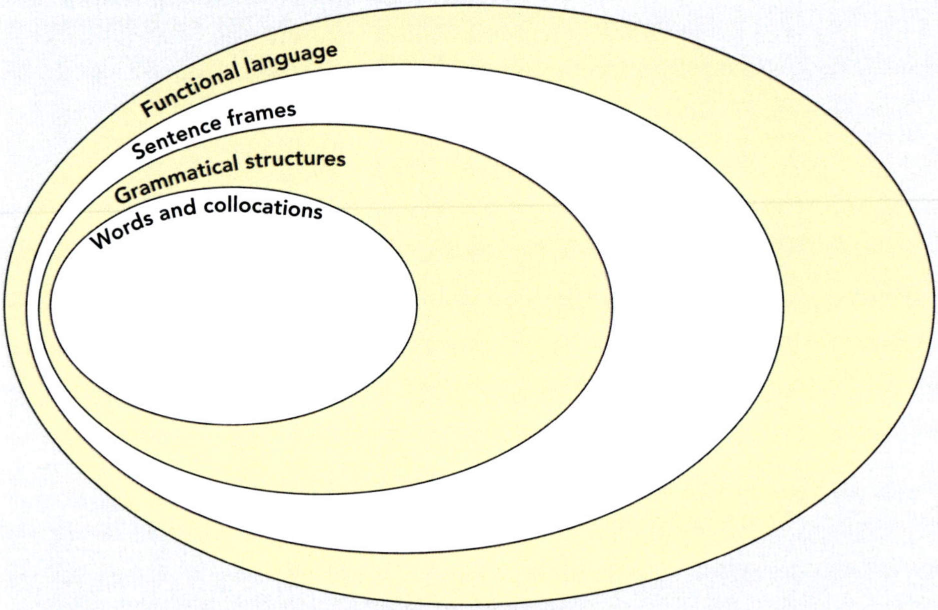

Photocopiable task

Teacher training variation

Make a recording of real learners performing the student task, where they think of laws to implement or abolish. In your development session, give the teachers-in-training time to complete the steps outlined above. This will give them practice pre-empting the language that might come up during the task. They can then listen to the recording of the learners doing the task to see if their ideas came up. This stage provides the teachers-in-training with further opportunities to develop their noticing or monitoring skills.

Task 12 commentary

The pre-empting document in Figure 7.4 below was created after the teacher interviewed colleagues and asked them which new laws they would implement or abolish. As mentioned above, this is a great way to help you pre-empt task-specific language, as it will show you what forms proficient speakers naturally use to do the task. However, we appreciate this may not be possible for some teachers to do on a regular basis.

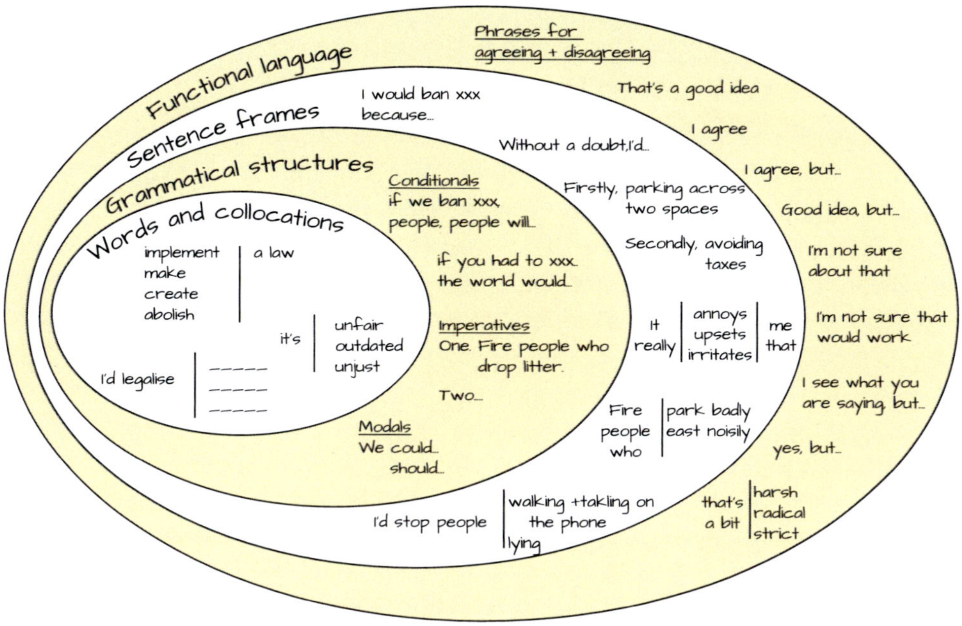

Figure 7.4: A completed planning document

Look at Figure 7.4 again. Is there anything there that you didn't think of? Is there anything you included that is not found above?

Unsurprisingly, there were a lot of examples of *would* being used to make suggestions or as part of conditional sentences. Another frequently occurring item was the use of the gerund at the start of sentences expressing ideas, for example, *Walking and texting should be a crime*. More surprising were the regular instances of imperatives. This was often done when the speaker listed each law numerically, for example, *One: ban people from ... Two: make ... illegal*. As you can see, pre-empting language by interviewing people or colleagues can be a useful way of showing a teacher which forms are most frequent, as this can then be discussed in the feedback.

Task planning 2

Task 13: Pre-empting learner language in your classes

Rationale

The planning task we saw in Task 12 is not only useful for helping you to pre-empt the forms that learners might use during a communicative task; it can also prime you to better notice the forms your learners use as they perform the task. This can, in turn, make you more confident when dealing with questions and emergent language in feedback.

This task is designed to develop your monitoring skills and your ability to notice the language that learners use during communicative stages. Doing this will not only develop your noticing skills; it will also enable you to assess your learners' skills and identify potential areas of language to explore in future lessons. Note that any recordings you make of you and colleagues doing tasks can be used as models for the learners to listen to.

Task 13: Pre-empting learner language in your classes

A. Procedure

1. **Before the lesson:** Prepare a focused task for your learners and follow the planning procedure for Task 12.
2. **During the lesson:** Listen to your learners performing the task. As you do so, tick off each item in the planning document that you hear them using.
3. **After the lesson:** Think about the following questions:
   - *How accurate were your predictions?*
   - *Which language forms were learners using effectively or consistently?*
   - *Which language forms did the learners need the most support with?*
   - *What were you able to deal with in feedback? What areas of language would you like to have worked with more?*

Photocopiable task

Teacher training variation

Make a recording of a group of learners performing the focused task. If this is not possible, you can make a recording with a colleague. In your development session, give your teachers-in-training time to complete Stage 1 of Task 13. This will give them practice pre-empting the language that might come up during the student task. They then listen to the recording ➔

of the learners doing the task to see if their ideas correspond to what learners actually said.

This stage provides the teachers with further opportunities to develop their noticing or monitoring skills.

Task 13 commentary

The completed planning document in Figure 7.4 (on page 177) was that of a teacher at the end of his CELTA course. During the course, he developed an interest in emergent language, and chose to use a focused task in his final lesson. This was done partly to challenge himself as he wanted to see if he could work with the language that came up and respond to learners at their point of need. The following reflection shows his planning document and his thoughts after the lesson. (Note that this was based on the same student task as the one described in Task 12.) As you look at the planning document, consider how closely Josh's thoughts match your own.

Task 13 emergent language story: Josh

Josh felt that it was useful to work with the pre-empting learner language planning document as it stopped him from feeling nervous or flustered when it came to working with emergent language. Breaking the language down into different categories also helped him to 'think like a learner about what I might say if I was doing the task'. This meant that at the start of the lesson, Josh felt more confident that he could work with what the learners produced. (See page 180 for Josh's completed planning document.)

At the end of the lesson, Josh felt happy that his predictions were relatively close to what came up in the lesson, especially with regard to the sentence frames and functional language. He also felt that it was easier to work with the language he had predicted when he was modifying or reformulating what the learners produced.

During his reflection, Josh felt that he should have thought about specific examples of grammar points that might come up in the lesson as well. This would have made him more confident about dealing with the grammatical issues and questions that emerged during the task. He also felt that some of the lexical items he chose as reformulations of learner output were graded a little too high for them. As such, he felt that he could have provided simpler or more common words or phrases in response to emergent language or learner's questions. This is a common issue for many teachers, however, and one that mostly disappears with practice and experience. ➔

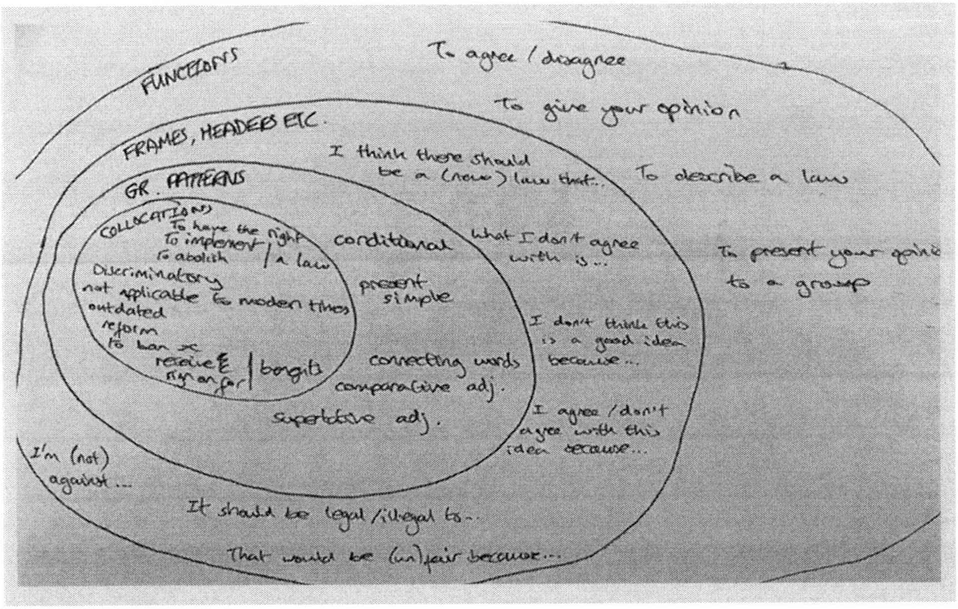

Tuning into learners

Task 14: Monitoring and giving feedback on content

Rationale

Teachers who want to gain confidence in working with emergent language must first think about how to encourage a focus on meaningful interaction in class. While the end goal is to be able to help their language development by providing them with useful reformulations, it is essential to start by tuning in to your learners, and focusing on their message *before* considering their language use. Developing your classroom interactional competence regarding how you monitor and provide feedback is key. Feedback on content requires you to record and remember who said what, and to decide whether there is anything interesting to share with the class. You must then manage the discourse in the feedback session by inviting learners to share what they have been talking about, responding naturally to the learners' contributions, and encouraging them to further take part in the conversation. This task prompts you to note down what learners are talking about and to think about how you will provide feedback on content.

Task 14: Monitoring and giving feedback on content

A. Procedure

1. In class, set the learners a meaning-focused speaking task where there is an exchange of ideas.
2. While the learners are busy speaking to each other, unobtrusively move around the group listening to what they are saying. Try to stay with each pair or group long enough to really tune into what they are saying to each other.
3. Make notes using the following prompts:
   a) Write down what the learners are saying in relation to the task you have set.
   b) When you hear an interesting comment about the topic, make a note of it with the learner's name next to it. You can use this as a prompt in feedback.
   c) Were the learners surprised or interested by something another learner said during the task? If yes, make a note of this.
   d) Before feedback, look at your notes and decide which comments you would like to share with the class. Avoid focusing on language at this stage as it will distract you from what the learners are trying to say to each other.
4. In feedback, invite learners to share their contributions. Use the following prompts: *Yoshuro said something very interesting about X. Can you tell us about this, Yoshuro? I was really interested in what you said, Miho. Can you tell us about …?*
5. Ask follow-up questions to encourage the learners to say more and extend their turns.
6. Once you have done this task, look at the commentary for Task 14.

Photocopiable task

Task 14 commentary

In feedback stages after a communicative task, it is common for new teachers to be preoccupied with providing the learners with language input. However, it is important to focus on meaning first. The more experienced you become as a teacher, the more space there is in your working memory to attend to form and meaning simultaneously. Rodrigo's story exemplifies the need to focus on meaning *before* dealing with form.

Task 14 emergent language story: Rodrigo

Rodrigo is a teacher from Colombia who wanted to extend his practice by doing a CELTA course. He was confident working with the target language, but the idea of emergent language was new to him. During an early teaching practice, he was focusing on developing the learners' speaking skills, and had set up a speaking fluency task where learners were doing a 'carousel', which is where the learners move in two concentric circles and talk to a different partner each time they move around. However, while monitoring the activity, Rodrigo was clearly concerned, remarking to his tutor, 'I can't hear any mistakes or gaps!'

Rodrigo's dilemma is not uncommon, and it calls for some basic guidelines for tuning in to learners before working on emergent language. As well as the difficulty in picking out language items to work on, there is also the danger of jumping straight in and clumsily grabbing at items of language. By following the steps in the task, you can spend time listening to learners and prepare for useful feedback on content as this is a prerequisite for working with emergent language.

By following Steps 1–3 in the task, Rodrigo was better able to notice what the learners were talking about, and he commented that it made him feel more relaxed that he was listening for a purpose. He was able to note down some interesting points that each pair in the group had been discussing. As a result, he conducted some useful feedback on content, which he facilitated with referential questions to explore what the learners had been talking about. He didn't pick up on any emergent language that arose, but this didn't matter as his goal was tuning in to the learner's message, and this is the first step towards working with their output.

Through Steps 4 and 5, Rodrigo felt he was becoming more confident in facilitating meaningful classroom interaction and making it more natural. Teachers need to be able to make feedback on content into a natural conversation with a relaxed environment for learners to take risks and receive feedback on emergent language. Rodrigo commented in subsequent lessons that as he felt more relaxed, and as the conversation was more natural, the learners' emergent language was easier to pick up on.

Improving your boardwork 1

Task 15: Learning how to effectively display new language

Rationale

Exploring emergent language in lessons (pages 75–102) looked at the choices teachers have when displaying emergent language on the board. We saw how clear and visual models help a teacher to clarify aspects of meaning, use, form and phonology. This task is designed to help you with this tricky area by prompting you to identify the different techniques available, and to think about why they are useful for learners.

Task 15: Pre-empting learner language in your classes

A. Procedure

Look at these five criteria for good boardwork (from **Exploring emergent language in lessons**, pages 75–102). Which of these features can you identify in the board below?

1. *Divide your board up into sections.*
2. *Elicit and provide extensions.*
3. *Go beyond single words by looking at lexical chunks.*
4. *Draw attention to patterns.*
5. *Mark, underline or use different colours or symbols to highlight key aspects of language, such as grammar or phonology.*

When you have finished, look at the Task 15 commentary on page 184 and compare your ideas.

B. Boardwork showing emergent language

The following boardwork was created during a lesson about films with a class of intermediate (B2) learners. First, the teacher gave the learners some discussion questions about their favourite films. After the learners had discussed the questions, the teacher used an extensive feedback stage to explore the emergent language. Note that in this extensive feedback stage, the teacher is adding to the board by displaying, reformulating and extending the language as they are interacting with the group. ➔

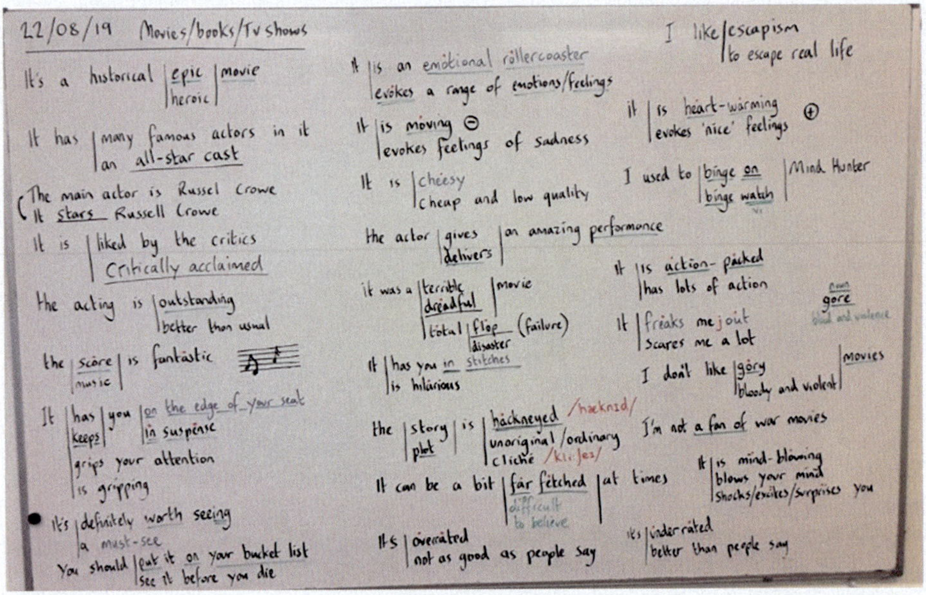

Photocopiable task

Task 15 commentary

This is a helpful board for learners as it draws their attention to a lot of the language they used and provides several suitable alternatives. The numbering below corresponds to the five criteria listed in the Task 15 procedure:

1. The board is divided into three neat columns.
2. The teacher has provided **extensions**. For example, the learners have said '*it has many famous actors in it*' and the teacher has provided them with the **extension** '*it has an all-star-cast*'. To do this, the teacher would write up the learner's utterance and then perhaps use **elicitation** to see if any of the learners know another way for saying the phrase. If they don't, the teacher can provide the **explicit reformulation**.
3. The teacher has gone beyond writing up single words, instead using vertical extensions and displaying everything as lexical chunks. For example, in *it has you on the edge of your seat*, *it keeps you in suspense* and *it grips your attention*, you can see the teacher focusing on fixed expressions and collocations.
4. The teacher has not always explicitly drawn attention to grammar patterns by, for example, highlighting or naming parts of speech. This is fine, as they

are mainly working with lexical chunks, which do not need to be formally analysed for form. However, the teacher could have used different colours to draw attention to parts of a chunk by, for example, highlighting the possessive adjective in *grip your attention*. This would allow the teacher to elicit other possessive adjectives that could go in the chunk. There is actually one example of the teacher drawing attention to a grammatical aspect of a chunk in *It's definitely worth seeing*. However, since the teacher has not highlighted grammatical features systematically, we might conclude that this was done in response to an error.

5. Although it can't be seen in the reproduction of this board, the teacher did use different colours to highlight aspects of form and phonology. They used some phonemic transcription to highlight features of connected speech within chunks, for example, it *freaks me* ***j*** *out*, and they highlighted prominent syllables with dots, in *emotional rollercoaster*, for example.

The teacher has been displaying, reformulating and extending the language as they are interacting with the group, and this has meant that they have boarded each item in the order that they occurred in the discussion. An alternative way to organise this board is to display each contribution under headings such as 'Phrases to describe the film' or 'Describing what you think of the film'. Note, though, that while this is an ideal way of organising the new language for the learners, grouping it in this way can be more challenging for the teacher, as it is hard to categorise new language as you go along.

Improving your boardwork 2

Task 16: Organising your board

Rationale

Once you are aware of the different techniques you can use to display language, a simple way to gather evidence of how effectively you are doing so is to take a photo of your board at the end of a lesson. You can then look back at it and think about how useful it might have been for your learners and how you might have done things differently. By doing this over a period, you will be able to see how your boardwork has developed from lesson to lesson. A good place to start is to see how effectively you are organising your board. This task provides you with practice in this area by looking at a teacher's photo of their board at the end of a lesson and thinking about how it can be improved.

The board in Task 16B was the result of a lesson for a B1 class in which the learners worked in groups to choose a suitable punishment for a 14-year-old boy who had been repeatedly caught stealing cars. Before they did the communicative task, the teacher brainstormed typical punishments for crimes. The learners then listened to a text describing the boy's background and his previous crimes and answered a series of comprehension questions. Before the communicative task, the teacher briefly elicited some useful phrases for agreeing and disagreeing (the target language of the lesson). As the learners performed the task, the teacher monitored and noted down emergent language to explore in feedback.

Task 16: Organising your board

A. Procedure

1. Look at the teacher's photo of their board below and answer the questions:
   a) How well has the teacher organised the language on the board? Does the order appear logical? Can you tell which stage of the lesson the items came from?
   b) How might you improve the way the teacher has dealt with the emergent language?
2. Take a blank piece of A4 paper and redesign the board so it is more effective. You can use ideas from Task 15 to help you.
3. Once you have completed the task, look at the commentary for Task 16 to compare your ideas.

B. A teacher's photo of their board at the end of the lesson

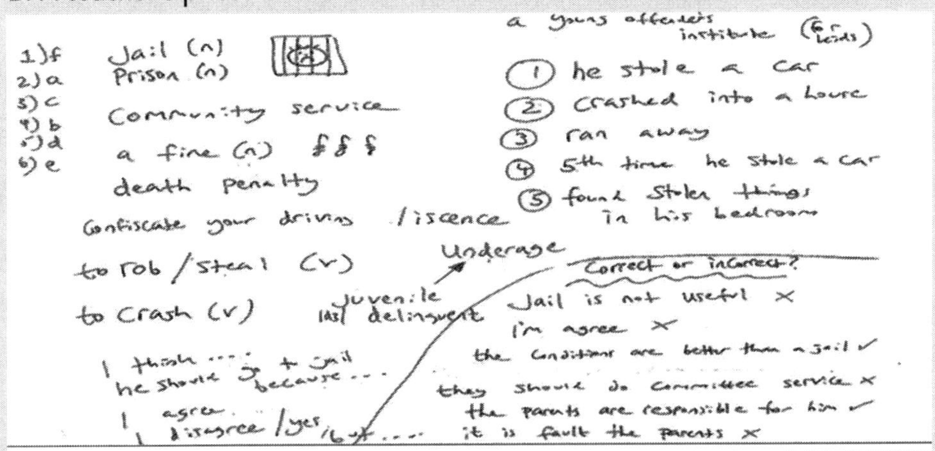

Photocopiable task

Task variation

This task can be done with a fellow teacher or teacher-in-training. To do this, each teacher takes a photo of their board. The teachers then work together to reconstruct their boards. At the end of the activity, the teachers note down any improvements they made. This can help you think about how you might organise your board in future lessons.

Task 16 commentary

There are several positive aspects to the way this board is laid out, especially considering the amount of material there was to fit in. The board writing is generally clear and there seems to be some organisation: ideas for the brainstorming task and useful agreeing/disagreeing phrases are on the left-hand side; the answers to the comprehension questions and language emerging from the task are on the right. Many teachers recommend displaying the relevant parts of speech, and the teacher has done this from time to time.

However, there are several ways in which the board could be improved. These are listed below, along with a board redesigned by a teacher after the lesson:

Figure 7.5: A redesigned board

1. **Organisation:** In the redesigned board, the teacher has used a line to separate the two sides of the board. The left-hand side has been used for displaying and analysing the target language. Beneath that, the teacher has displayed emergent language that they noted down as the learners did the communicative task; this will be explored during the post-task feedback stage, where the teacher will elicit reformulations for the incorrect utterances. The right-hand side has been used for emergent language that arose during the lead-in (for example, *rob* versus *steal*). The teacher has labelled each section.
2. **Presenting language in chunks:** As we saw in **Exploring emergent language in lessons** (pages 75–102), it is important to explore new lexis in chunks, rather than looking at words in isolation. This helps to show learners how the words are used, and adds to the meaning, as you can see with *rob* versus *steal*. By displaying the language in this way, the teacher also encourages the learners to record language in chunks in their lexical notebooks. (See Task 18 for ideas on setting up lexical notebooks.)
3. **Reformulating errors:** The errors that the learners have made have been clearly marked and reformulated. In real time, this helps learners notice the gap before they have a go at reformulating.
4. **Colour coding:** Though it cannot be seen in these images, some of the text on the second board is in different colours. The new language is in black, while aspects of grammatical form and phonology are marked in different colours. Colour-coding the content can be a useful way of helping learners to distinguish between different aspects of the input. Note that the teacher has occasionally marked the stress in a word using red, perhaps in response to misplaced stress during the lesson. This could have been done more consistently.

Task 16 emergent language story: Linda

Linda was a teacher-in-training on a diploma course. During the course, she chose to monitor her boardwork by taking a photo of it after each lesson she taught, and then reflecting on her progress. By taking photos of her boards, she was able to see a shift in the depth of her language analysis. For example, she observed that she had moved from recording only single words on the board to exploring collocations, chunks and patterns.

When she looked at her photos, Linda noticed that she hadn't been very systematic about how she organised her board, so she decided to experiment with ways of making her boardwork clearer. In subsequent lessons, she ➔

organised her board with a section on the right for emergent language. She also used different colours to draw attention to features of language: black for grammar, blue for lexis and red for phonology. By being systematic in her approach to boardwork, Linda felt that she was giving the learners a clearer record of what emerged in the lesson. It also allowed her to keep track of what language was dealt with in her classes.

Another thing Linda noticed was that sometimes her board was too full. She therefore started to take pictures before wiping sections off at different stages of the lesson. This meant she had a record to return to later in the same lesson. As a result, Linda developed the following criteria to help her order her board:

1) Be selective. Don't try to put too much up there.
2) Record language in chunks, not as single words.
3) Use gaps to draw learners' attention to features of emergent language.

Using your board

Task 17: Blanking the board

Rationale

One of the questions teachers most often ask about emergent language is what to do with it after they have dealt with it in class. This is an important question, as it is vital that the language that emerges in a lesson should not be viewed as incidental or as a less important add-on to the main aim. It is therefore important to encourage learners to note down emergent language as it is dealt with. It is also useful to recycle or review it at the end of a lesson or in future lessons. Making learners aware that this is something you regularly do will hopefully encourage them to review new language in their own time. As we saw in **Exploring emergent language in lessons** (pages 75–102), regularly reviewing and recycling new language increases the chance that learners will be able to use it or recall it in the future.

One effective way of recycling emergent language towards the end of a class is to erase or cover words, parts of phrases or collocations that you have written on the board previously. The learners then work out what has been deleted. After they have done this, they provide a definition of the new word or phrase and use it in a sentence. This activity can be done with learners in pairs or groups. It also works well as a competition with points awarded for correct answers, definitions and sentences.

The task below is designed to help you think about what you might erase from language items you have written on the board, and why. This board is the same as the one shown in Task 16 (in the lesson on films with a group of intermediate (B2) learners). Section B of the task shows the whiteboard at the end of the lesson.

Task 17: Blanking out the board

A. Procedure

1. Look at the whiteboard below. What different types of language have emerged during the lesson (for example, words, collocations, fixed expressions, functional phrases)?
2. Answer these questions:
   a) What words or parts of collocations/phrases could you erase to give learners practice recalling the new language?
   b) What is the rationale for your choices?
   c) What other techniques might you use to recycle or review this new language?

B. Whiteboard for erasing and recycling new lexis

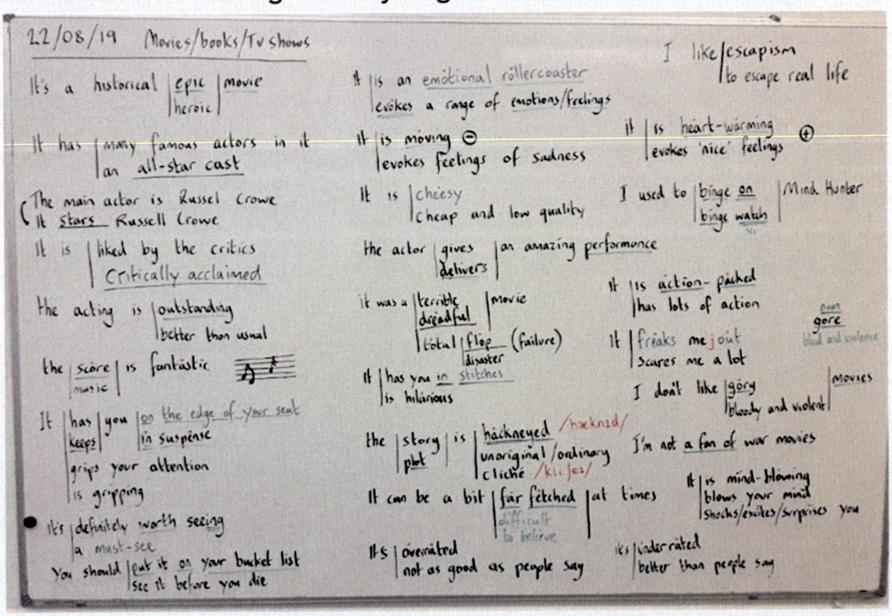

Photocopiable task

Teacher training variation

Encourage your teachers to take pictures of their boards at the end of their classes. The teachers then bring the photos to the session. In groups, they discuss what language might be useful to recycle and how it could be done.

Task 17 commentary

The teacher has used the board shown in Figure 7.6 as a revision activity at the start of another lesson. This revision activity took place a few days after the original lesson in order to provide some space between the first encounter with the language and the revision. To set this up, the teacher took a picture of the board at the end of the previous class and has then used a graphics editor (MS Paint) to blank out the words. The blanked board is then displayed on an interactive whiteboard in the follow-up lesson.

There is not one correct answer to the blanked-out items. However, it is important to note that the blanks have all been placed within the vertical extensions. That way, the teacher is encouraging the learners to recall some of the extensions that were generated in the class. It can also prompt the teacher to remind the learners about patterns.

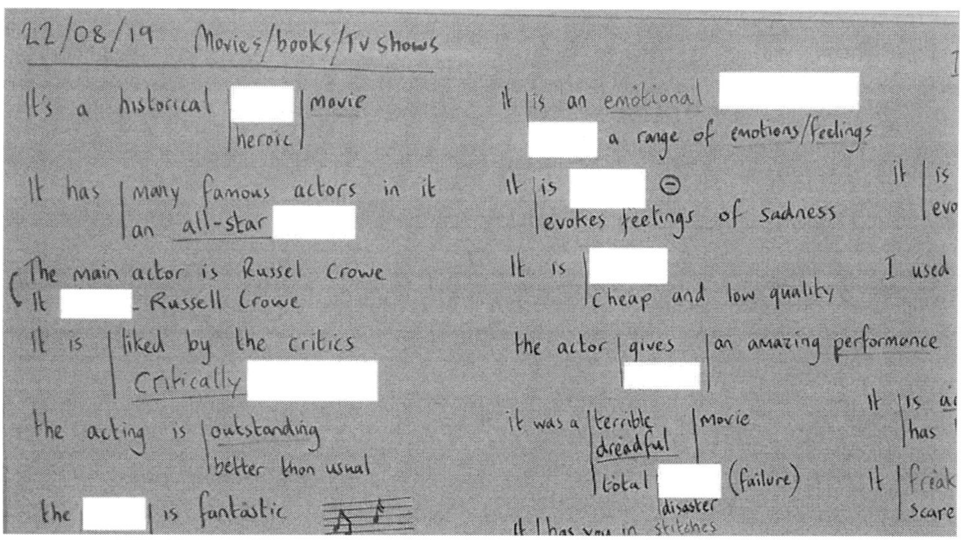

Figure 7.6: Blanked-out board for recycling learner language

As noted in **Exploring emergent language in lessons** (pages 75–102), recycling language is extremely important for memorisation. While it is advisable to leave some space between teaching and recycling new language, erasing parts of the board can also be done as a quick review at the end of a lesson or the beginning of another. By doing this, you are providing an opportunity for learners to encounter the new language again. This opportunity for noticing adds to the likelihood that the new language will be retained for future usage.

Learner training

Task 18: Creating a lexical notebook

Rationale

A key principle in the communicative approach to language learning is that learner autonomy should be encouraged (Mishan, 2005). As well as providing the learners with emergent language in class, the teacher can suggest effective study skills that encourage them to notice, record and review new language independently outside classroom time. Noticing, recording and reviewing are three key aspects of the **Lexical Approach** (Lewis, 1993), which Lewis saw as vital in turning input into intake. One simple way of putting Lewis's ideas into practice, as well as promoting learner autonomy and good study habits, is through training learners to record emergent language in a lexical notebook. This can be done in class, but they can also add language as they encounter it outside the classroom.

The following task allows you to examine two learners' lexical notebooks to notice strengths and then to formulate advice for them.

Task 18: Creating a lexical notebook

A. Procedure

1. Look at the two excerpts drawn from different learners' lexical notebooks below. Look at how they record language, then answer the questions below:
   a) How has each learner recorded the new lexis?
   b) What techniques have they used to organise the new language?
   c) What makes each example an effective lexical notebook entry?
   d) What advice would you give to improve the way each learner records new lexis?
2. When you have finished, look at the commentary for Task 18 and compare your ideas.

B. Excerpts from learners' lexical notebooks

Student A created their excerpt during a lesson on climate change, while Student B's is from a lesson on relationships. Though both excerpts may include a mixture of target language and emergent language, what is important here is how they record it.

Student A:

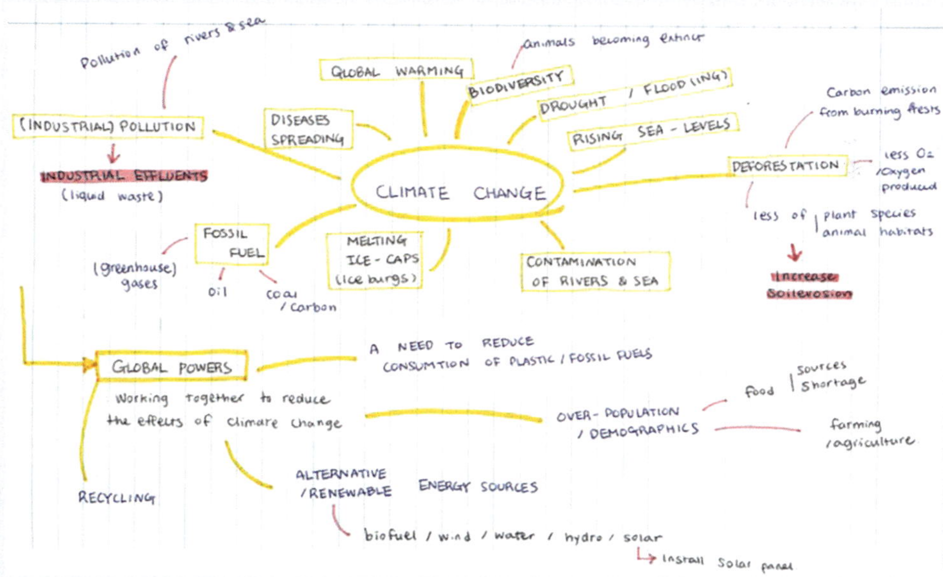

➔

Student B:

Vocabulary = Phrasal verbs (Relative relationships)

- go out with (sb)
  - * to have a romantic and usually sexual relationship with someone
  - ex = They went out with each other for five years befor getting married.
  - ex = How long have you been going out with him?
- fall for (sb)
  - * to suddenly have strong romantic feelings about someone
  - ex = She always falls for older men.
- split up with (sb) = break up
  - * If two people split up, they end their relationship or marriage
  - ex = She split up with her boyfriend last week.
- get on with (sb) = get along
  - * If two or more people get along, they like each other and are friendly to each other
  - ex: I don't really get on with my brother-in-law.
- fall out with (sb) = argue
  - * to argue with someone and stop being friendly with them
  - ex: He left home after falling out with his parents.
  - ex: She'd fallen out with her boyfriend over his ex-girfriend.

Photocopiable task

Task variation

This task can be used in class with learners to encourage them to notice features of a successful notebook. They can then be encouraged to create one for themselves or to improve the way they currently record new lexis.

Task 18 commentary

The following are positive points about the notebooks:

1. Both have organised the new lexis under clear topic headings, though they have used different techniques to do so. This is useful as it adds some order to the process of learning and recycling.
2. Both learners have looked at the new items in chunks rather than as individual words, for example, *she has split up with her boyfriend*, *reduce consumption of fossil fuels/plastics*.

3. Student A has used a mind map to organise the language around a particular topic. She may be using this strategy because she finds making links between the topic, the subtopics, and the words and phrases helps her to remember the language.
4. Student B has recorded a definition to accompany each item of lexis. They have done this in English, but could also do the same in their L1.
5. Student B has included example sentences. This shows them how the item is used in context.

The teacher can support the learners by encouraging them to notice what has been put on the board and to copy it down. In order to make their notebook even more useful, the learners could do the following:

1. Following the teacher's model on the board, they could include more vertical extensions to show how the items are used beyond the initial example. The teacher can support this by encouraging learners to copy down exactly what was recorded on the board. For example, writing *split up with smb* could be a little vague as it doesn't show who you would split up with and who you wouldn't, as in the example below:

split *break*	*up with*	*your husband* *your wife* *your partner* ~~*your friend*~~

protect *boost* *threaten*	*biodiversity*

2. They could mark the stress in each chunk or include features of connected speech if they can identify them, for example, *biodiVERSity*, *split up with‿someone*.
3. They could include a translation, although, as you can see in Andrea's story below, not all teachers would recommend this.

Task 18 emergent language story: Andrea

Andrea is a language teacher who regularly encourages and trains his learners to make lexical notebooks. Interestingly, Andrea draws on his own experience as a language learner and his belief that he was 'doing it all wrong'. He says, 'Nobody taught me how to do it, so I had one column of English words and one column of Italian translations. That's it. Just words and translations. In the end, I didn't know how to use words together.' Having learnt about lexical notebooks, Andrea now believes in the importance of recording language in chunks, writing example sentences and including alternative ways of saying the same thing. By doing this, he feels that translation isn't necessary.

Professional development

Questions for reflection

- Think back to the tasks you tried in this chapter. Which ones resonated best with you? When you used them, what did they make you think about regarding your teaching?

Things to try

- Look back at the tasks you found most useful. Is there anything you need to do or adapt to help you use them in future? Show them to colleagues and discuss how to incorporate them into best practice at your school. If you are teacher trainers, which tasks would be most useful to use with your teachers or on your training courses?

8. Emergent language in different teaching contexts

In this final chapter, we discuss the questions that teachers most often ask us with regard to working with emergent language. Typical questions include *How do you work with emergent language with lower levels / teens / younger learners? Is it difficult for teachers whose first language is not English to work with emergent language? Can you work with emergent language in exam classes or when following a syllabus? How can you work with emergent language when teaching online? How might the L1 be used when working with emergent language?* By answering these questions and more, we intend to dispel the common misconception that working with emergent language is difficult or inappropriate in certain contexts and situations. The following sections are based on our own experience in different contexts and those of teachers who work in these areas.

Why context matters

When choosing materials, approaches and techniques to use in the language classroom, it is important to consider the context that the learners are studying in. Key factors to consider are the age of the learners, the class size, the layout of the classroom, the goals or outcomes of the course, the length of lessons, the access to resources, and the backgrounds, needs, motivations and interests of the learners. We must also consider whether there are materials, approaches and techniques prescribed by institutes or educational requirements of the state.

Further aspects to consider are the principles and beliefs of teachers and how they view the language they are teaching in terms of norms or level of attainment. One of the criticisms levelled at the practice of working with emergent language is that as it involves the reformulation of learner output, it can be used to promote native-speaker norms or standards. The approach can therefore be seen to favour so called 'native-speaker teachers'. However, we believe that this is not, and should not be, the case. In fact, we would argue that language norms and standards are more likely to be imposed through teaching materials, where rules are explicitly stated and then adhered to in controlled practice exercises. In our view, there is more, not less, freedom of choice when working with emergent language.

As discussed in **Exploring emergent language in lessons** (pages 75–102), it is mainly down to the individual teacher to decide what emergent language to focus on. At times, the decision will be influenced by syllabus or assessment requirements, so there might be a greater focus on standard forms, errors and notions of correctness. However, depending on the context, teachers can be flexible with their approach and decide to work more freely with emergent language. This can include:

- focusing on emergent needs by helping learners say what they want to say at the time they want to say it. This can be related to classroom tasks, but it can also be related to the real-world needs of a learner or learner group.
- focusing on comprehensibility. This entails helping learners get their message across or dealing with issues that cause misunderstandings or communicative breakdowns.
- adding range and variety. This involves building on what learners can do by offering alternative ways of saying the same thing.
- exploring how ideas might be expressed differently depending on the specific genre.
- pushing learners to justify or expand on ideas, and to take more risks in their output.
- sharing words or phrases that might be interesting or useful to the learners.
- responding to learners' questions about language.
- exploring successful aspects of communication and intercultural communication. This includes looking at strategies learners use to communicate and maintain interaction, including the way they might use their own or other languages to do so.

It is worth noting, too, that emergent language through the co-construction of meaning will always be subject to the teacher's own idiolect (Seidlhofer, 2011). This means that, rather than basing reformulations on norms or standards, teachers often provide new language that they would use or that they think would work. As we saw in **How to work with emergent language** (pages 53–74), teachers often use phrases like 'I would say … ' or 'You could say … ' to introduce new forms. By doing so, they are sending a message that there is no one right way to say or do something.

Common questions

In this section, we look at how teachers in different contexts make space for emergent language opportunities. We will also reflect on how they respond to it and what kind of language they focus on.

Working with emergent language at low levels

It is perhaps at lower levels that there is the strongest rationale for regularly or predominantly working with emergent language, and this is simply down to the number of opportunities that are generated every time the learners attempt to communicate a genuine message. Nick Hamilton regularly works with elementary (A1) adult learners at a private language school in London. He explains that although these learners do not yet have the language to convey exactly what they want to say, it is important to remember that what they do bring to the classroom are their lives, experiences, feelings and opinions. It is these that need to be harnessed.

Nick believes that it is important to get lower-level learners communicating and improvising from the outset. This is done by getting them to talk about familiar topics such as food, family or leisure time. As they talk, the teacher feeds in the language that is needed to make the message clearer. As Nick says, the learners know what they mean. We just have to help them get that meaning across, and by doing so, we are introducing forms that don't need explaining as the meaning is already clear. This process naturally takes a lot of patience as the teacher actively listens and tries to work out what the learners need. It can be tiring, but what Nick often finds at the end of a lesson is a board full of useful lexis related to the learners' lives and experiences.

It is important to note here that new lexis is introduced in chunks rather than lists of single words. This is something Nick encourages the learners to notice from the start, getting them to count the number of words in a chunk to help make the point. In fact, a common phrase Nick uses in his teaching is 'four words, one meaning'. Nick also regularly provides the learners with useful functional expressions in response to their needs. For example, the first time a learner suggests that they don't understand, Nick will introduce the phrase *I don't understand*. The first time a learner makes a request, he will introduce *Can I ...?* These phrases are then built on through extensions, so learners can see the utility of a phrase through multiple examples, such as *Can I go to the bathroom/take this call/take a break? Can I ...?* – two words, one meaning.

This means that items like *can* are introduced as part of a functional lexical phrase rather than taught and analysed as a grammatical item. In other words, lexis comes first, grammar second. This is not simply based on principle. It is also a natural process in language learning. For example, Nick notes that you can regularly get learners talking about their past, and the more they do so, typical past forms will gradually emerge as you reformulate and display examples on the board. It is for this reason that Nick suggests you ignore the grammar discovery activities and exercises often found in lower-level coursebooks until the forms have emerged from interaction. The coursebook exercises can then be done to consolidate the learning generated through communication.

Nick also advocates exploiting the learners' L1. This is naturally easier to do in a context where the learners share the same L1, but learners also make use of their L1s in the multilingual classes that Nick currently works in. To do this, he asks the learners how they might say a new word or phrase in their language or if it is similar. For example, when a word like *coffee* comes up, he will ask learners if it is the same or similar in their language, which, for many, it is. This, he feels, enhances noticing, and potentially leads to better recall. For very low-level learners, knowing that some English words are the same as in their first language can also make the first steps in the learning process feel less daunting.

Work with emergent language when teaching teens

Vicky Saumell is a teacher and teacher educator working with secondary school students in Argentina. Her learners have only four hours of English classes a week, which is common in secondary schools, so she moved to incorporating **Project-Based Learning** (**PBL**) into the curriculum. She did this so she could cover more ground and respond to emerging needs while still meeting the syllabus requirements. PBL has much in common with TBLT, as there is a focus on the learners gaining knowledge and skills by working for an extended period to complete a task. In PBL, the learners typically research an authentic problem, question or challenge before delivering a product. For example, the learners might create a school magazine, design a healthy menu for the school cafe or plant and manage a small garden in the school or local area. In PBL, both the project and the product are done primarily in the L2.

To support emergent language during lessons, Vicky suggests choosing projects that are interesting, motivating and manageable for the learners. That way, the learners will be able to complete the task in the way that they wish, and emergent language work is done in response to their needs as they work together. In addition, she recommends that the teacher's confidence can be increased by using focused tasks which allow them to predict language that might be needed.

Aside from PBL, a common complaint for teachers in Vicky's context is that there isn't enough time to work with emergent language, as they need to fully exploit the coursebook. Vicky advocates supporting teachers in adapting coursebooks to create space for emergent language. Another difficulty teachers in her context face is that the classes have between 20 and 25 students and, as levels differ within the class, teachers struggle to pick up on language that will help all the learners. Vicky suggests differentiating the language input by providing individual feedback to learners as she monitors tasks. This way, she is able to help individuals and respond to varying needs in the class where necessary. She recommends then gathering examples that might be useful to share with all the learners in feedback.

Vicky also makes the point that the biggest myth about emergent language is that it is not compatible with using a coursebook and a PPP or forms-focused approach, all of which are often prescribed on teacher education courses. There are, in fact, many ways in which teachers can incorporate learner language into lessons by using projects and tasks or finding ways to adapt the coursebook to make room for it.

Alex Quinn taught English to teens in Colombia. She notes that one of the key factors for successful learning in this context is to build a positive relationship between the learner and the language. To do this, the learners have to 'see themselves' in the language, and this is done by creating space for them to talk about what they want to talk about, and to help them express the messages that they want to express. This involves creating space for interaction, choosing tasks that the learners are interested in (or letting them choose tasks) and focusing less on rules or standard forms. It also means responding to the learning opportunities created by the use of the L1, rather than shutting things down. Teens need to feel that they are active participants in their learning, and increasing engagement and agency are key to this. As the learners become more engaged and involved, more emergent language opportunities will arise.

Working with emergent language when teaching younger learners

Katy Kelly is a teacher and teacher educator who works with younger learners aged from four to twelve in Spain. Katy makes the point that in both private language academies and the state sector, there is often a preoccupation with classroom management and a focus on syllabus requirements to achieve the learning of discrete language items. In her opinion, this focus can be uninteresting for the learners and limits the possibility for communication. This leaves little scope to help learners say what they want or need to say, or to answer their questions about language.

Katy recommends that as well as meeting assessment and syllabus requirements, it is also important for teachers to work with emergent language. She feels strongly that teachers should support younger learners in expressing what they want to say, so she allows time at the beginning of lessons for discussions to develop, as well as creating more opportunities for conversation within classes. This enables her to listen to her learners and incorporate emergent language items into future lessons. She suggests that as well as managing the class efficiently and working towards the aims of lessons, teachers should look for opportunities to integrate emergent language into lessons. To do this, she believes that there needs to be a shift in the way teachers in her context are trained so that they feel more confident about interacting with younger learners and dealing with emergent language. They also need to feel that genuine interactions do not mean that they are losing control of the lesson, but are an opportunity to build rapport and motivation and to feed in relevant language in lessons. A further strategy that Katy suggests is for teachers to allow learners to use their first language (or any languages they know) when they need to, as this is a natural process in learning. Her advice for teachers is that there shouldn't be a rigid line between languages, and that teachers can make good use of mixing them to aid learning.

Working with emergent language in large classes

Yaye Binetou Mbaye, Mamadou Kally Diallo, Khassoum Diop and Mansour Sy Ndiaye are experienced teachers and teacher developers from Senegal who mostly work with large classes of teenagers. In the major cities, classes can comprise up to 50 students, but this number can rise to 70 or 80 in other areas. The key to generating emergent language opportunities in this context is to put students into groups. When doing this, Mansour recommends setting clear ground rules, one of which is that as long as the students are focusing on the task, noise is fine. All the teachers say that it is good to create groups of mixed proficiency and to appoint group leaders. This means that stronger students can help their less proficient peers to better understand the task and any aspect of language related to it. The teachers feel that this raises the groups' output and performance, and helps less proficient students to grow in confidence and talk more. For each group, they also nominate a learner who will report to the whole class after group work.

All four teachers advocate exploring any emergent language in delayed feedback after speaking tasks. This involves monitoring the learners as they work together and noting down examples of language to share with the rest of the class or explore for errors. The teachers also work with errors as they monitor, with Khassoum suggesting that he tends to elicit reformulations more frequently at this stage as the learners have more space to work things out. There is also the opportunity to work with emergent language when learners from each group report to the rest of the class, though Kally suggests he rarely intervenes at this point unless the learner is having trouble communicating their message, or he suspects that the others cannot hear them.

A final tip from Binetou and Kally is that in a larger class, when appointed learners are sharing what their group has discussed, it is important for their teacher to stand away from the speakers; this encourages the learner to address the whole class rather than just the teacher. This creates more cross-class interaction, which is difficult to maintain when there are a lot of learners. It also gives the teacher space to monitor the speaking and note down further examples of emergent language that are generated.

Working with emergent language in exam classes

There is a commonly held belief among teachers that there is not much scope to work with emergent language in exam preparation classes and courses. Perhaps this belief is based on experience of exam classes where the learners are regularly assessed using discrete-item tests. In this type of course, it is true that there will be fewer opportunities to work with emergent language as there is naturally a lot of language input, practice and revision of the items that are tested. However, this is not the case for learners taking the major English language tests offered today, such as IELTS or Cambridge examinations, such as CAE or FCE.

Steve Ferrara, who teaches IELTS and Cambridge exam classes, suggests that as the exams are very topic focused, lessons are often spent developing lexical range in the key topic areas, for example, the environment, technology or education. This can be done through giving learners typical exam questions to answer in groups, and seeing what language emerges as they discuss their ideas. Steve also comments that speaking and writing assessment criteria usually instructs examiners to look at fluency, coherence and lexical resources. He therefore uses time after speaking and writing tasks to explore how the learners' ideas and words have flowed together. While doing this, he reformulates learner language to provide a greater range of words and phrases for talking about the topic. For instance, when talking about crime, if a learner says that there are lots of 'small crimes' in their country, Steve suggests and explores extensions (for instance, he will give learners other ways of saying this, such as petty crimes and *misdemeanours*). Once a sufficient range of lexis has been reformulated, learners then switch partners and practise answering the same exam questions again while trying to use the new language.

Kezzie Moynihan, another experienced IELTS teacher, agrees with this, suggesting that she is perhaps more explicit in her feedback and reformulations in IELTS classes as she wants her input on their spoken and written performance to lead to greater success in the exam tasks. When providing feedback, she tends to ignore slips or errors of form and focuses instead on providing extensions. She will also give advice on how learners can convey their message more effectively, coherently, and with a greater range of lexical and functional phrases.

Working with emergent language in online classes

During the COVID-19 pandemic, many teachers, ourselves included, had to make the switch to working online, with most of our classes taking place synchronously on video conferencing platforms. Teaching online presented some challenges at first, as some aspects of the technology were new to us, and adapting face-to-face methodology to the online classroom took thought and experimentation. Much of our work with emergent language was the same, though. Having said that, we were able to gain several insights into how it can be focused on in online classes.

A common complaint from teachers is that it is hard to hear emergent language when everyone is talking. However, this issue is much less pronounced when learners are working in groups or pairs in breakout rooms, as teachers can monitor the learners without any background noise from other groups. This enables you to really focus on what the learners are saying. You can also monitor unobtrusively by switching off your camera. This is very useful as it allows you to make notes without the learners noticing and wondering what you are writing. You also have more space to prepare examples of language to display on a digital whiteboard as you are monitoring. This makes it easier to prepare for delayed feedback stages.

In terms of immediate intervention, some teachers found that the chat function has, in some ways, taken the place of recasts. We often see teachers using the chat function to provide a word learners need or to reformulate an unclear or unsuitable word as they are speaking. Like recasts, some of these are noticed by their learners and some are not. It is therefore a good idea to tell the learners to keep an eye open for chat notifications as they may contain a useful source of input. Because the reformulation is written, it also provides a record of the intervention for the learners. Another advantage of the chat function is that it enables the teacher to give discreet individual feedback on language use as they can send a message to the learner(s) directly. Finally, the learners can use the chat function to ask questions or seek support themselves.

Tim Matschak teaches German online to adults of different levels and of different language backgrounds. The tools he has found useful for working with emergent language are Jam board, a digital whiteboard that lets teachers and learners collaborate in real time, or a blank slide that he can write into synchronously. He mentions that in his context, it is important to train the learners to use the technology as some need support with tools like Jam board. When he wants to work on any emergent phonology issues, Tim says that he needs to modify his approach, so, rather than drilling language chorally, he encourages the learners to turn their microphones off and repeat after him without anyone else being able to hear. This enables the learners to experiment and try things out without being put on the spot.

Some platforms, such as Zoom, give you the option to save the video and the audio data. This allows teachers working with emergent language in online classes to make recordings of their learners speaking in open-class discussions or taking part in feedback stages. These can then be used by teachers to identify emergent issues or to pick useful words and phrases to explore in later lessons. The recordings can also be given to or played to the learners. As the learners watch, the teacher can set tasks to help them focus on how successfully they have performed the task or to pick out instances of their language use that they would like to talk about. As we discussed in **Teacher development and emergent language** (pages 105–128) and **Development tasks, ideas and commentaries** (pages 129–196), these recordings can also be used for teacher development.

Working with emergent language in challenging teaching contexts

There are many contexts around the world where resources for education are scarce. However, it is important to remember that when you are working with emergent language, it is the participants who are the resource for language development. One project that puts emergent language at the heart of what they do is the 'Hands Up Project', which supports remote English language learning in Palestine for younger learners and teens through storytelling and drama activities. Nick Bilbrough, who founded and runs the project, describes how, in a typical class, there is a teacher and learners in the physical space and a volunteer teacher present online in a different location. One learning activity they use involves giving the learners a topic to talk about with the teaching volunteer elsewhere in the world. Neither teacher can fully prepare for what the learners are going to say, so this paves the way for frequent emergent language opportunities. Nick makes the point that the role of the teacher in class is important as the learners use a mix of L1 and L2. For example, when the learners want to communicate something in English but don't know how to say it, they ask the teacher for help in Arabic. The teacher provides the language the learner needs and scaffolds the learner's contribution to their interaction with the volunteer online. Nick also points out that further opportunities to work with emergent language arise when the volunteer doesn't understand what the learner is saying.

Furthermore, the nature of online learning with the possibility of a weak internet connection provides a stronger need to negotiate meaning as it can cause misunderstandings. This can actually make the learner feel safer as it provides a non-face-threatening excuse for the volunteer to ask clarification questions. The teacher might also give learners the opportunity to reformulate their own utterances by making clarification requests.

Nick highlights the fact that there is an interesting and effective dynamic between the classroom teacher and the online volunteer. Because of the shared L1, the classroom teacher often understands the learners better than the volunteer does, and can feed in language through translation. The classroom teacher also knows the school curriculum and syllabus, and can see where emergent language can potentially be linked to it. On the other hand, the volunteer brings an intercultural element to the class. Because they don't know the culture very well, there is a natural information gap, which creates a need for emergent language as learners describe their lives and stories. It is interesting to see how this kind of interaction can create a need for communication and language, while also drawing on the scaffolding of the volunteer and the teacher. The internet makes this kind of class possible, but the main resource in these lessons is the learners, their life experiences and the stories they tell.

Working with emergent language in ESOL classes

In the UK, **English for Speakers of Other Languages** (**ESOL**) refers specifically to learners who have come to settle as migrant workers, asylum seekers or refugees. The focus of ESOL courses is on helping the participants develop their language skills in order to operate in society, find work or go on to further study. In ESOL classes, the lessons need to relate to the learners' daily lives; standard global coursebook topics are often not relevant or appropriate. Therefore, some teachers use a **dialogic** approach to help meet the real-world needs of the learners. This in turn fosters a community of practice for learning. Such an approach makes emergent language an important factor in this context, as it is key to helping learners to make their voices heard and to communicate their meanings. As learners' desire to get their message across is paramount, there is a real need for teachers to work with emergent language.

One ESOL organisation which has moved away from a set syllabus and prescribed course materials is English for Action. Melanie Cooke, a trustee of the organisation, states that emergent language is at the core of what they do. Using a range of techniques from drama to project work, they focus on enabling the learners to talk about what they want to talk about and helping them to use English in their everyday lives. At the start of the course, teachers take time to draw out what is important to the learners. This can be difficult to begin with, as the learners are not always forthcoming with their ideas, or are unsure about what they need. However, by interacting with the learners and using a range of activities, the teachers are able to create projects for the groups and generate discussion topics. English for Action also draws inspiration from approaches to education such as Critical Pedagogy; this approach is derived from the ideas of the Brazilian thinker Paolo Freire, who took an emancipatory approach to enabling people in deprived communities to be literate. Following this tradition, there is a political angle to their work, as they encourage the learners to engage with the society in which they live. For example, if housing is a major concern for a group, they might join a local campaign in order to find out about the issue and get involved in making a change. These projects and actions naturally create an emergent syllabus, and emergent language comes hand in hand with this.

Working with emergent language in one-to-one and ESP classes

Anne Timson is an **English for Specific Purposes (ESP)** teacher who has worked with learners from several different disciplines. She sees working with emergent language as essential in this kind of teaching as it facilitates a focus on real-world tasks the learner needs to perform in their job. She uses an output → feedback model, which concentrates on diagnosing what her clients are able to do already and responding when they need help. She sees the syllabus as an emergent concept from the outset as there is no coursebook that can meet the specific needs of her clients, regardless of level.

Anne stresses the importance of a detailed needs analysis at the start of the course. She often works with legal professionals, and makes the point that they are not interested in learning abstract grammar, but want to be able to carry out tasks in their job using another language. As such, she often uses a task–teach–task approach, selecting tasks that the learner needs to do their job, such as writing a report or making a presentation. Anne suggests not spending too much time planning target language, but notes that it is worth pre-empting what might come up in the task. Although there is an element of automatic prediction regarding the language, she says that, first and foremost, it is important to wait for what 'comes out' in the class rather than imposing language that you might have pre-empted.

Anne will often use transposition as a technique, for example, getting a learner to turn a written report into a spoken presentation. By doing this kind of transposition activity, affordances for reformulation arise. This is because the act of turning one genre into another opens up space for the teacher to look at genre-specific language. In this way, the teacher can explore the specific register of the learner's field and scaffold and support the learner as they work. One technique Anne recommends is to note down all of the emergent language and anything else that happened in the lesson on a handout for the learner(s). This is then presented to them at the end of the lesson as a record of work for each session and a point of reference for recycling the language.

Working with emergent language when focusing on intercultural communication

Chia Suan Chong is an expert in communication skills and intercultural communication, and has made this the focus of much of her work (see Chong, 2018). Chia makes the point that we need to look beyond lexis, grammar and phonology, and consider helping learners communicate effectively. With the groups she works with, she believes that teachers need to focus on whether the language that learners use is appropriate to the context, whether learners are using strategies to help them speak and be understood, whether learners are helping other people in their group be heard and whether they are shaping their message in a way that is cohesive and coherent.

Chia also makes the point that skills such as mediation need to be included as an aspect of emergent language. Mediation, which is now part of the CEFR, is a key facet of successful communication that occurs when we consider the needs of others and adjust what we are trying to say accordingly. Through mediation, we don't just think about what we want to say, but also how to say it.

Chia suggests that when we are training learners to communicate effectively, it can be useful to use activities that encourage mediation. For example, giving learners different texts or messages to summarise for others is a useful way of exploring how well learners can receive information and successfully pass it on to others, a necessary aspect of life. In feedback, teachers can use the time to explore how effectively the speaker might have simplified or adjusted the message for the audience, and how effectively their learners are using strategies like elaboration, explanation and exemplification to help their conversation partners understand. Depending on the focus of the lesson, Chia might also explore how a learner can help their group members form their ideas, express themselves and communicate their message. She might offer on-the-spot feedback or a delayed exploration on how a group has managed a conversation and how they have involved everyone, for example, by asking another group member for their input or ideas. She might also focus on how learners deal with culturally different views or conventions, or how they manage disagreements and conflict.

For the professional clients with whom Chia works, this kind of work is important because communication breakdowns are less often due to linguistic competency issues, and more a result of a lack of mutual understanding, and the necessary strategies to resolve these issues. In Chia's view, emergent language work should include a focus on communicative competence and conversation skills as a whole, and learners need to become aware of the fact that being fluent and competent in English means more than being good at grammar and vocabulary. Chia has found that including these skills in the lessons she has taught has helped her learners become more self-aware, more aware of their contexts and the people they speak to, and, subsequently, more successful when communicating in English.

Working with emergent language in EAP classes

Gemma Smith works on **English for Academic Purposes** (**EAP**) and pre-sessional courses at universities in the UK. Because these programmes are designed to help learners enter and prepare for university, much of the input is skills-based, with learners exploring strategies for doing research, understanding lectures and writing essays. A lot of work is also done analysing relevant genres by looking at essays, research articles and arguments.

Gemma says that it is in tutorials that the bulk of the emergent language work is done. The programmes she works on are designed to help the learners to understand the process a successful writer goes through, from researching and planning academic essays to submitting final drafts. She will therefore spend time in tutorials helping her learners with their drafts and developing their editing skill. To do this, Gemma will look at essays and ask her learners to explain things that they have not expressed clearly, so she will regularly use clarification requests and confirmation checks to find out what the learners want to say before helping them say it more clearly or simply. She also encourages learners to paraphrase when they could be more succinct or have filled their essays with quotes rather than using their own words. In fact, helping learners find their voice is a big part of these sessions. She will also encourage the learners to explore the impact and effect of their writing on a reader and how they can get their arguments and ideas across more effectively and appropriately. In a sense, this makes the teacher's role very similar to that of an editor as they help the learner with their writing before it reaches its final audience.

One tip Gemma has for helping learners in tutorials is to encourage them to record the sessions. That way, they can play back the recordings to listen to the reformulations they have suggested after prompting from the tutor. They can also note down the tutor's tips about organising essays and making them more coherent. By doing this, it can save time as the learner is not using the tutorial to rewrite sections. They also have their editor's voice to guide them as they redraft their essays.

Work with emergent language with monolingual groups

While working with emergent language in classes who share the same L1 is not in itself problematic, it is interesting to explore how teachers working in this context do so. Yiota Gkiaouri used to work with L1 Greek-speaking classes in Greece, teaching both younger learners and adults. As with many of the teachers whose ideas contributed to this chapter, a lot of her emergent language work was done as learners took part in tasks in pairs or small groups. However, one thing that she was able to do with her learners was switch between the L1 and the L2.

This would often be done as she monitored, and her learners would ask her how to say something or if they had the right word. Yiota therefore found that she could exploit the shared L1 to fill in lexical gaps and quickly and efficiently respond to questions about language. She points out, though, that not every learner feels comfortable switching back to their L1 as they feel reluctant to ask for help in this way. Teachers therefore need to be able to read the situation to judge when reformulations or explanations can be in the L1. Yiota also noticed that when her younger learners were enjoying a task and sharing life experiences, they would often switch to Greek. This is something that can be left to happen, as it is a shame to stop the learners sharing life experiences and engaging with the task and topic in order to impose how they do it. As with any task, the teacher can still make notes and explore useful words and expressions that learners might have used to talk about their experiences in the L2. Perhaps after feedback they can even then try to do the task again, but this time in the L2.

Another interesting way of exploiting the L1 with her adult learners would be to spend some time after speaking tasks exploring some of the differences between the languages. This was especially interesting when it came to looking at idiomatic expressions and whether they worked equally well in both languages or would need to be reformulated. Yiota gives the example of a learner saying, *I think this bike cost €100 in the water*, meaning *This bike must have cost €100, for sure*. Using the idiomatic expression 'in the water' to express certainty would be understood by a fellow Greek speaker as it is a direct translation from Greek. However, it would not make much sense to someone who didn't speak Greek. Yiota would therefore spend time in class looking at how a particular idiom or proverb would be said in Greek and how it would look different in English.

The extent to which a teacher can exploit the learners' L1 is often down to the school's policy. Yiota notes that some schools have a zero-tolerance policy, whereas others are more flexible. In reality, because teachers can be working with upwards of 30 learners of mixed ability, using the L1 is often the most efficient way of working with the emergent needs of different learners at different times.

Of course, teachers don't always speak the learners' L1. This can create a need for learners to collaborate to get their meaning across to their teacher. For example, a teacher working at a school in Hong Kong reported that when a learner has a problem saying what they want to say, they will often get help from other learners. This negotiation makes use of the L1 as the learners discuss what might be the most effective way for their classmate to get their point across. Because the teacher doesn't share an L1 with the learners, the learners are pushed to find ways of getting beyond communicative breakdowns. This is an important skill for the future when the learners might begin to communicate more in multilingual settings, for example, in the workplace.

Working work with emergent language when English is not your L1

It is interesting that we are often asked by teachers whose first language is not English whether they should expect it to be harder for them to work with emergent language. From our experience observing teachers on both pre-service and in-service courses, the answer to this question is no. Regardless of your L1, working with emergent language is a complex skill that takes time to develop, as we have suggested throughout the book. The key is to spend time tuning in to learners, monitoring the way you interact with them and working with what emerges. Over time, your confidence in this area will build and it will become a part of your practice. We have also seen that regardless of their L1, teachers who are new to working with emergent language seem to follow the same developmental path. First, they struggle to notice examples of emergent language, then, when they do, they are unsure of which items to deal with. We also regularly observe less experienced teachers reaching for easily noticeable errors that have not really caused a communicative issue, such as missing third person *-s*, plurals or articles. The same could be said for new teachers in other languages. For example, a newer Italian teacher might pick up on lack of adjective–noun agreement or issues with masculine and feminine word endings. It is only later that they start to pick up on language that has affected communication or caused misunderstanding.

Rather than focusing on the first language of the teacher, we believe that teachers who can speak the L1 of their learners have a significant advantage when it comes to working with emergent language. Sharing a language enables the teacher and their learners to use their mother tongue, which, as we have seen, is often an efficient way to negotiate meaning. As such, it is important for teachers to make an effort to learn the language of their learners if they do not already share an L1.

In fact, learning another language in general is extremely useful in developing your emergent language skills. For example, on training courses, teachers who do not have experience of learning a language in depth often choose quite complex or colloquial language in their reformulations, not recognising what constitutes suitable input for the level. Because teachers whose first language is not English have language learning experience by definition, they often have a better awareness of what is and isn't suitable at different levels.

An example of an inappropriate reformulation can be seen in the exchange between a teacher and a pre-intermediate (A2) learner in the following exchange:

Teacher:	Are you OK, Madee?
Learner:	*I sleep very bad last night**.
Teacher:	Oh, <u>you slept badly</u>. You could also say (writing on the board) *<u>I didn't sleep a wink last night</u>*, or *<u>I was tossing and turning all night</u>*.

In this example, it could be argued that the learner's initial utterance would more successfully communicate their message to the rest of the class than the two extensions that the teacher provides. The teacher has also not really responded to the learner's message or found out if they did in fact toss and turn all night.

Emergent language story 5: Anastasiia

Anastasiia Gavriushina took her CELTA in London, and was one of a number of course participants who did not have English as their first language. When the subject of emergent language came up in feedback, planning or input, Anastasiia would often say that she was at a disadvantage in this area as she did not have a 'feel' for the language. However, this did not come across in her assessed teaching practice, where she frequently took time in lessons to provide her learners with useful words and phrases or to reformulate their output. Let us look more closely at how she managed to do this so effectively.

The first factor was Anastasiia's belief that the only way she would develop her emergent language skills was to give it a go and see what happened. This is something she was happy to do having taught for some years in Russia with minimal guidance and support. This meant that she was used to experimentation, seeing how things worked, and adjusting as she went along. She also referred to her experience as a language learner. Before she started the CELTA course, Anastasiia joined a proficiency class, where she noticed that the teacher would regularly work with learner output through reformulation and extensions. This gave Anastasiia first-hand experience of the value of working with emergent language as it helped her pick up useful new phrases. ➔

She also benefited from the chance to observe the teacher and analyse their techniques. This experience prompted her to reflect on her previous language experience, so that when she worked with emergent language in class, she would ask herself what language she had found useful when she was at the same stage. This helped her make decisions about what language to share when helping her learners.

Most interestingly, Anastasiia also had a lot of practice in scaffolding and supporting learners in the house she shared during her course. Her housemates all spoke different languages, so English was the lingua franca. As the most proficient speaker in the group, Anastasiia would often help her housemates say what they wanted to say, or paraphrase when others didn't understand. Because they knew she was a teacher, her housemates would also regularly ask her how to say something or what word they could use. This meant she was working with emergent language all the time.

As we discussed in the introduction to this book, teacher learning is a social process, and teachers are made over time through interaction, experience, input, feedback and support. Coupled with her willingness to give things a go, Anastasiia developed her abilities to work with emergent language in exactly this way. This process is far more important than the language you speak.

Conclusion

The common factor linking all the contexts above is the teachers' belief that communication should be at the forefront of classes, and that learners need to be given greater agency in what they talk about and learn. Teachers should find time to move away from syllabus requirements and pre-set materials to give learners more opportunity to find their voice. This will not only be more engaging and motivating for learners, but it will also create classrooms that are rich in emergent language moments and learning opportunities. To ensure that this happens, there needs to be a shift in the way teachers are trained so that they build confidence in dealing with emergent language during their initial training, and/or are shown how to work with it in their contexts earlier in their careers. We hope that the content and tasks found in this book can help you gain more confidence and skills in working with emergent language, but we also hope that there is a greater emphasis on it in future training and materials.

Professional development

Questions for reflection

- Reflect on the emergent language stories you have seen in this chapter. Do any relate to your teaching experiences? What are your biggest takeaways that you could use in your own teaching?
- What changes will you be making to your teaching practice as a result of reading this chapter, or even the whole book? What steps will you have to put in place to make these changes happen?
- If you have tried out the activities in this book, what have you noticed about your learners' performance as a result? Are there any other changes in terms of their outlook or learning outcomes? If so, what are they? Why do you think they have occurred?

Things to try

- Look back at the emergent language stories in this chapter. Then create 2–3 of your own. Encourage a colleague to do the same. Then compare your stories and discuss what you can learn from them.
- Record your learners during a communicative task as you start off working with emergent language more in your teaching, and then repeat at the start of each week for 4–6 weeks (or over a semester). Then listen back to the recordings. What do you notice about your own behaviour and that of your learners?

Appendix

Glossary

action (also known as **goal-setting**) is where teachers decide on goals for classroom experimentation, based on their reflections on an issue to do with emergent language within their lesson which would have been discussed collegially in the stages of **exploration** and **discovery** as part of **cooperative development** (see below). During the final stage of the emergent language analysis discussion, the listener should come up with some practical ideas to target the issue (e.g. if echoing was a problem, they could decide consciously try to not to echo and instead prompt the learner to say more, or they could practise back-channelling unobtrusively, with active listening noises like 'Uh huh').

action research (Wallace, 1998 & Burns, 2009) is where teachers formulate a research question regarding classroom practice that they want to systematically investigate, and then subsequently carry out the research using real-time classes and recording the findings carefully and systematically.

affordance is an opportunity that arises in class for focusing on emergent language.

agency is the sense of control and feeling of ownership that a student has over their learning.

autonomy is related to independence and the learner's ability to make free decisions. It also describes how students take responsibility for their own learning, both in terms of what they learn and how they do so.

brainstorming is a whole-class or group activity that encourages learners to generate a free flow of ideas or words relating to the topic of the lesson, with the teacher listening and/or writing the contributions on the whiteboard. The teacher can decide whether to accept every idea or play a more evaluative role by rejecting ones that do not fit.

CAP is a teaching model, Context–Analysis–Practice, designed to help a teacher structure their lesson, which involves the context of the lesson being established, for example through a text; learners noticing the language in the text and exploring how it is used; and then moves on to practice, which can be either controlled or free, or both.

choral drilling is when the class repeats a chunk of language after you.

clarification requests (also referred to as **confirmation checks**) is when the speaker is questioned about what they have said to check meaning or understanding, indicating to the speaker that what they have said has been misunderstood by the listener(s). Clarification requests often include phrases such as *What do you mean? or I'm sorry, I don't understand*, which may be accompanied by the listener(s) indicating that they do not understand with their voice or facial expression. Such requests help the speaker notice that what they said has not been understood, thereby encouraging the speaker to say something in a different way (through **reformulation** or **repair**), or to provide more information so the listener(s) can understand them better so the communication gets back on track.

Classroom Interactional Competence (**CIC**) is 'teachers' and learners' ability to use interaction as a tool for mediating and assisting learning' (Walsh 2011:158). CIC puts interaction at the centre of learning, and understanding what CIC is helps teachers investigate and discover the extent to which they generate effective interaction in their classes.

Communicative Language Teaching (**CLT**) is a teaching approach which became popular in the 1970s. It recognised that the prime purpose of language is creating meaning, and therefore, that the teaching of language should focus on helping language learners understand and convey a genuine message.

comprehension questions can be divided into two categories: content questions, which prompt learners to demonstrate general understanding of what they read and listen to, and language questions, which focus learners' attention on a specific form. They are often closed questions (as in there is only one 'correct' answer), and can include short-answer questions, true or false, multiple choice, or 'yes or no' questions, and are frequently found in ELT coursebooks and materials, including examination papers.

confirmation request is similar to a **clarification request** (see above) and serves the same function; however, confirmation requests are different in that they indicate that an utterance has been partially understood or the listener is slightly unsure about what was said. In a confirmation request, you might use a signposting phrase such as *Are you saying that …?* or *So you mean …?*

consciousness raising is where learners are presented with examples of language in use in order to encourage them to notice features of meaning, use and form.

cooperative development is an approach to development where there is a listener and a speaker. The speaker talks about their lesson and the listener prompts to help the speaker explore an experience in class. Together they try to identify themes, reach conclusions and set goals for future classroom practice.

corrective feedback is the input learners receive on their performance: describing what has been produced and by offering/eliciting an alternative, asking what the learner could have done differently.

critical incident is an unplanned event in a lesson that teachers see as interesting or challenging. By noticing and formally reflecting on critical incidents, it may be possible for you to uncover new insights about your teaching or the learning process and come up with solutions to problems.

cross-class interaction allows learners the opportunity to communicate with each other as a whole class as they respond to each other's ideas and opinions across the classroom.

delayed feedback is when a teacher monitors their learners as they are interacting and notes down examples of errors and/or miscomprehension, without interrupting the flow. They then write the items on the board so they can be discussed during feedback.

dialogic reflection is a way of reflecting on your teaching. This can be intrapersonal, i.e. using a reflection instrument such as a checklist of classroom behaviour you want to examine, then thinking about what you can learn from it. It can also be interpersonal, where new understandings can be arrived at through discussion with others. By encouraging learners to share their thinking, teachers can diagnose needs, devise learning tasks, enhance understanding, assess progress, and guide their learners through the challenges they encounter.

dialogic teaching is collaborative and supportive teaching that uses communication to engage interest, stimulate thinking, advance understanding, expand ideas, and build and evaluate arguments, empowering students for lifelong learning and democratic engagement.

discovery (also known as **thematising**) occurs when a teacher/teacher trainer reflects on an issue to do with **emergent language** in their lesson and analyses it collegially during **cooperative development** (see above). During this middle stage of the emergent language analysis discussion, teachers can work together to summarise what has been discovered, e.g. *Although I was trying to encourage the learners by echoing what they said, the echoes were an interruption, and they ended the learner's turn.*

display questions are ones that the teacher already knows the answer to – so they are commonly used to elicit specific answers or reformulations, or to clarify understanding of language items – and are a key resource for helping teachers organise their lessons and manage learning, especially in feedback stages to comprehension tasks, discovery activities and controlled practice tasks.

Dogme ELT is a movement in language teaching which sought to remove a prescriptive syllabus of linguistic entities and replace it with interaction and a focus on emergent language. This approach sees learning as a social and dialogic process, where language 'emerges' rather than being 'input' in the traditional sense, i.e. it sees emergent language as language that arises in a lesson when learners are engaging meaningfully, with the teacher helping them by drawing their attention to language to aid the communication.

echo refers to instances when teachers repeat what learners have said to validate a response for the benefit of the class or share it with those that did not hear, and often ends the learner's communicative turn, as it is quite an unnatural response in real life. When used in response to stories, ideas or opinions told by the learners, it can create the impression that the teacher is not genuinely interested in what the learner has said, and overuse of the technique as a result can be detrimental to the flow of what learners are trying to communicate.

elicitation is a technique that teachers use to encourage the learners to reformulate their output themselves, as opposed to giving them an alternative form directly, enabling learners to notice the difference between their performance and the L2, whilst encouraging them to close that gap by repairing what they said.

emergence in language development sees the interplay between the physical (the body and the brain) and external sociocultural factors as integral to language development. Emergence sees the interaction of numerous complex systems as critical in the formulation and use of language. Van Lier sees emergence as happening 'when relatively simple elements combine together to form a higher-order system' (van Lier, 2004:5).

emergent grammar (first termed by Hopper, 1987) is based on the assumption that grammar is not a discrete set of rules that exist a priori, detached from the contexts of use, but rather, that grammar is provisional and that it emerges in discourse.

emergent language is unplanned language that is needed or produced by learners during meaning-focused interactions. This language is then explored through reformulation, clarification and support from the teacher.

emergent language moments (also known as **emergent language episodes**) can occur in moments of learner need, in occasions when learners seek support and in the language the learners notice around them (see **emergent language** above).

emergent lexicon (first termed by Bybee, 1988) is used to describe language development as the result of repeated experience of language use (like **emergent grammar**, see above).

engagement (also **learner engagement**) is meaningful and active participation in learning, which involves the learner's cognitive, affective and behavioural abilities.

English for Academic Purposes (**EAP**) is considered to be a subset of ESP (see below) and refers to the teaching of English to students in higher education and ones on pre-sessional university courses. These programmes are designed to help learners enter and prepare for university so much of the input is skills-based, with learners exploring strategies for doing research, understanding lectures, forming structured arguments and writing essays.

English for Speakers of Other Languages (**ESOL**) refers specifically in the UK to learners who have come to settle as migrant workers, asylum seekers or refugees. The focus of ESOL courses is on helping the participants develop their language skills in order to operate in society, find work or go on to further study.

English for Specific Purposes (**ESP**) refers to the teaching of English to people in work or on work-oriented courses, with reference to the particular vocabulary and skills they need. Working with emergent language is pertinent in this kind of teaching as it facilitates a focus on real-world tasks the learners need to perform in their job.

evaluative questions require considered responses to a text, and require some judgement or assessment, which calls for deeper cognitive processing than **personal response questions** (see below), and much deeper cognitive processing than closed **comprehension questions**.

Evidence-Based Reflective Practice (Mann & Walsh, 2017) is a data-led, evidence-based approach to reflective practice looking at the technical, practical and critical aspects of teaching

explicit intervention techniques are used to make it clear to the learner that their teacher is modifying, reformulating or responding to the learner's use of a specific language item or form. By using these techniques, the teacher is drawing the learner's attention to a language item and encouraging **noticing**, **uptake** and possibly **repair** (see below).

explicit reformulation refers to a moment in class in which the teacher provides a clear and overt alternative form in response to learner output, and usually comes immediately after the learner completes their turn during open-class interactions or during a feedback stage after learners have completed a communicative task in pairs or groups.

exploration (also known as **reflecting and focusing**) is the first stage of **cooperative development** (see above) when a teacher/teacher trainer reflects on an issue to do with emergent language in their lesson and explains it to the colleague. During this initial emergent language analysis discussion, the issue is pointed out (e.g. an observation task has revealed that the teacher uses lots of 'echo'), then it is analysed to establish why the issue is occurring. As the conversation progresses, the teacher is encouraged to focus on specific evidence from their lesson and to explore what happened (see **discovery** and **action** above).

exploratory action research (Smith & Paula Rebolledo 2018), which combines the ideas of action research and exploratory practice, and encourages teachers to share discoveries they have made with peers.

Exploratory Practice (Allwright & Hanks 2009) encourages teachers to investigate small areas of classroom practice that puzzle them

extensions are interventions where a teacher responds to a learner's use of a word or form by providing or eliciting alternative ways of saying the same thing, usually in response to a learner error.

false friends are words/phrases that look or sound the same as words in the learner's first language but in fact are unrelated, which can often be a source of misunderstanding during intercultural interactions, whether by changing the meaning of what the speaker is trying to say or by altering the connotation.

focus on form (**FonF**) is the incidental switch from meaning to provide learners with language they need to express their message, i.e. it's unplanned language input, provided when the learners need it.

focus on forms (**FonFs**) is the emphasis on specific items of pre-selected, discrete items of language.

focused task is a free, communicative activity that is likely to generate specific language items when carried out by a proficient speaker.

free decisions are unconscious or spontaneous acts, based on previously gained language knowledge.

grammaring (coined by Larsen-Freeman, 2003) sees the learning of grammar as a dynamic process whereby learners acquire grammars by experiencing and reflecting on language use. This view is in opposition to seeing grammar as a fixed body of knowledge and is part of the view of language as a complex adaptive system. This view of grammar sits within **emergent language** (see above).

grammaticisation is a classroom **grammaring** activity which encourages students to develop given lexical items into complete grammatical structures or full texts. Grammaticisation activities enable learners to explore the limits of their current linguistic knowledge which in turn provides opportunities for **emergent language** (see above).

horizontal extension, also known as **syntagmatic extension**, is a technique that teachers use to draw attention to the word order, grammatical features and patterns in an utterance. This is done by looking at a sentence from left to right and analysing what is possible in terms of word order and form.

implicit intervention techniques are used when the teacher decides not to interrupt the communication too much or feels that **recasting** is an efficient way of providing more input in a lesson as less time is taken up eliciting modifications or **repair** from learners (see below), whilst avoiding making learners feel like they have been put on the spot (as opposed to using **explicit intervention techniques**, see above).

individual drilling the learners repeat language individually or in pairs.

initiating a response is when a teacher asks a **display question** (or other) designed to get the learners to respond with an answer or idea.

intervention technique is any response to learner language that involves reformulation or emergent language input, such as **explicit reformulation**, **recast**, a **clarification request**, **elicitation**, **metalinguistic feedback** or **recall**.

interactional recast is a type of **recast** (see below), so it is implicit. In interactional recasts, the teacher provides an alternative form while maintaining communication and encouraging the learner to extend their speaking turn. In other words, rather than simply echoing what the learner has said, the teacher provides the reformulation at the same time as they respond to the message.

IRF exchange is a is a commonly noted form of classroom discourse that begins with the teacher **initiating a response** from the learners. The learner **responds** with an answer or idea, and the teacher **follows up** with an evaluation. An IRF exchange is the most common model of interaction in the language classroom and helps teachers to organise lessons and elicit and monitor learner responses. However, if they rely on it overtly, the opportunity for learners to take control of the interaction is limited, thereby diminishing their **sense of autonomy** (see below).

learner-initiated intervention is when a learner rather than the teacher triggers the emergent language episode by directly asking their teacher for help with a word or phrase for instance, using questions such as *How do you say …?* or *What is the word for…?* The learner may also indicate that they are unsure of how to complete their utterance by pausing and looking at the teacher or another learner for guidance.

learning opportunities are moments where language emerges in a lesson providing the teacher with items to work on through reformulations, extensions, etc.

Lexical Approach, the (identified by Lewis, 1993) is a methodology that sees the teaching and analysis of lexical phrases and chunks as key to acquiring a language.

lexical notebook is a notebook where learners record information about new language and display it in chunks to provide clear examples of meaning, use and language in context.

L1 refers to the learner's first language.

L2 refers to the language being learnt.

metalinguistic feedback is an explicit feedback technique where a teacher draws attention to the error, and then uses grammatical or linguistic terminology to provide information about it. By doing so, they signal to the learner the nature of the issue to help them come up with a more appropriate or comprehensible form.

monitoring is a technique that teachers use while students are working together in pairs or small groups. The teacher observes and assesses the learners as they work together, and gathers examples of emergent language.

noticing new language is a prerequisite for acquisition. By focusing on emergent language, an opportunity for new language to be noticed is created through teacher intervention, reformulation or discussion. The language comes from the learners' interaction, and emergent language work can help fill the gap in their current stage of language proficiency.

paradigmatic extensions (also known as **vertical extensions**, see below) is a technique that teachers use to draw attention to a sentence vertically in order to substitute, extend and explore other possibilities in terms of the meaning of an utterance.

paralinguistic prompt is when a teacher uses a facial expression or gesture to reinforce the intervention, which makes the intervention more explicit and as a result makes it more likely that the learner will notice what the teacher is doing and then modify their output.

paraphrasing is when 1.something that has already been stated (in either written or spoken form) is written or spoken in different words, often in a shorter and simpler form to make the meaning clearer; 2.someone else's thoughts or ideas are restated in a new speaker/writer's own words.

personal response questions encourage the learner to respond with an opinion or reaction to the content of a text.

PPP is a teaching model, Present–Practice–Production, designed to help a teacher structure their lesson, which involves the target language being presented; learners moving on to controlled practice exercises (such as gap-fills or those requiring them to reorder words to make a sentence); followed by opportunities for freer production.

post-lesson reflection occurs after class when a teacher might think about the effect of the technique they are using and whether they could be using it more frequently.

praise is an important way to develop and sustain the learners' use of the target language correctly or appropriately by building confidence and creating positive learning experiences, which is motivating. However, like **echoing** (see above), it can halt the flow of the speaker's speech as it can create the impression that the teacher is more interested in the learner's use of language than their ideas and opinions.

prediction task is often done before learners read or listen to a text, and involves them trying to work out what the text might be about, or what they might hear or read. The task is designed to engage the students in the topic of the text and gives them a reason to listen or read – namely, to confirm or reject their predictions.

Project-Based Learning is a method designed to help learners gain knowledge and skills through working to investigate and respond to an authentic, engaging and complex task, challenge or problem, over an extended period of time or number of lessons.

recall is another type of **elicitation** technique (see above). It refers to an instance in which the learners have misused or cannot recall a lexical item or grammatical form that the teacher believes they have been exposed to in previous lessons. As a prompt, the teacher uses phrases such as *Do you remember the word for ...? or What was the word we used for that?* to elicit from the learner or class.

recast is an **implicit reformulation** (see above) when the teacher reformulates all or part of a learner's utterance, most commonly on completion of their turn.

reflection-for-action (a term classified by Killion & Todnem, 1991) is a planning stage of mapping out a teacher's self-reflection to help them address issues in their teaching. During this planning stage the teacher decides how much **reflection-in-action** and **on-action** (see below) is necessary.

reflection-in-action (a term first coined by Schön, 1983) is when reflection for learning occurs in the moment in class and the teacher evaluates whether the technique they are using is working, and what they might need to do or adapt in future. By using this type of reflection, it helps teachers address any issues with their teaching.

reflection-on-action (a term classified by Schön, 1983) is when a teacher reflects on their teaching after class or after a **critical incident** (see above).

reflective practice is the process of exploring and reflecting on your teaching in order to make it more effective or better meet your learner's needs.

reformulation is an instance where the teacher (or another student) corrects, extends or modifies learner language, and where reformulations can be explicit (for example, the teacher makes it clear that they are reformulating) or implicit (the teacher reformulates without signalling that they are doing so).

repair is any move by a learner in which they modify, or self-correct, an error after an **intervention** (see above).

scaffolding mediates learning and is a process where a learner expresses a meaning, and the role of the teacher is to listen to the learner and help when needed, in other words, the teacher offers support during interaction with learners to support the communicative success of the speaker.

second language acquisition (**SLA**) is a general term to describe learning another language. It is also the traditional name for the theory of how languages are learned or picked up.

sense of autonomy is when learners are given a 'choice and voice' where possible, and can include 'big choices', such as letting them choose topics they want to discuss or tasks that they would like to do. Where this is not possible, teachers should ensure that learners are free to offer their own ideas and opinions in completing tasks. If learners feel that they have a voice, they are more likely to contribute during freer tasks, which in turn generates more emergent language opportunities.

sense of competence refers to learners feeling that they have the skills to manage the tasks their teacher gives them – they won't all achieve the same levels of proficiency in completing the task, but they should all feel that they can do it.

sense of relatedness refers to the quality and strength of relationships that learners have with both the teacher and their classmates, which can be encouraged through fostering positive relationships within the group, learning about the learners as individuals and finding out about their interests and beliefs. As a result, the teacher can select appropriate and relevant tasks that their learners will respond well to.

shadowing is when learners mouth the words alongside the teacher as the teacher says a chunk of language.

sharing refers to instances where a teacher has noticed examples of interesting or useful language that their learners have used in pairwork or a small group task. Because the rest of the class will not have heard the words or phrases, the teacher uses the feedback stage to share them. As we saw above, this stage is often known as **delayed feedback** (see above).

signposting language is used when a teacher clearly indicates that what the student has said was unclear or inaccurate (e.g. *'That's right, but you don't say [ ]'* or *'I wouldn't say [ ]. You could say [ ], but I think it's too strong. I think [...]'*) to make a **reformulation** (see above) explicit.

silent drilling is when the learners repeat language to themselves two or three times silently.

skills acquisition is the process of moving from conscious control of a skill to automaticity.

sociocultural theory (**SCT**), inspired by the work of Lev Vygotsky in the 1920s, describes people's cognitive development through engagement in social and cultural activities with other people, objects and events, e.g. **second language acquisition** (see above) arises from the process of meaning making in collaborative activity with other members of a given culture.

specific language aim outlines what the learners should be able to do by the end of a lesson, in any given language domain (e.g. using a specific grammar point) at a specific language proficiency.

special lesson syndrome is where teachers display specific techniques during an observation, rather than being natural and reacting in the way they normally would in an unobserved class.

syntagmatic relation highlights the linear relationship and explores the position between the words in a sentence (also known as **horizontal**

extensions or **syntagmatic extensions**, see above). The syntagmatic relation occurs on the horizontal axis, for instance, the combination of each word in *'When Zac was cooking paella'* forms a syntagmatic relationship. This sentence means (1) it is *paella* that Zac was cooking, not something else, and (2) It is *Zac* who was cooking the paella, not someone else.

target language refers to the pre-selected language points that are introduced and practised during a lesson. Target language is often included in lesson aims or learning outcomes. For example, *'by the end of the lesson the students will be able to use the present perfect simple to talk about life experiences'*. In this aim, the target language is *present perfect simple*.

Task-Based Language Teaching (**TBLT**) is an approach that became popular in the 1980s which embodies the belief that language is learnt through the creation of a need to communicate. In TBLT, learners perform tasks with communicative outcomes in which language is the vehicle for communication rather than being the destination, i.e. completing a task is the objective and language is supplied when required or in feedback.

task-specific language is the type of language needed to complete any given communicative task, e.g. if learners have been asked to debate a topic or negotiate an outcome, it would be useful for their teacher to provide feedback on the way they made suggestions, justified ideas, expressed agreement or disagreement, or held or relinquished their turns.

the apprenticeship of observation describes how, when we become teachers, we often subconsciously emulate and reject the teaching and learning roles that we have experienced ourselves.

to grammar is a dynamic process of meaning making that a focus on emergent language supports (see **grammaring** above).

translanguaging is where learners use their **L1** or other languages as a a resource for successful communication.

turn-taking describes how participants take, use or hand over turns in a conversation. Turns often overlap and **L2** learners often need to learn how to do take or hold turns effectively during a conversation or in discourse.

uptake is a process by which learners notice or react to teacher reformulations, and may involve learners acknowledging the intervention with a nod, using a new item or modifying their utterances.

vertical extension (also known as **paradigmatic extension**, see above) is a technique that teachers use to expand lexical range where they slot new or alternative words into the appropriate spaces in a sentence. This can also create opportunities for learners to notice patterns.

wait time is the amount of time the teacher leaves after asking a question. If the wait time is short, the communicative potential of the class is diminished. Research has shown that leaving a sufficient pause can increase learner participation.

zone of proximal development (**ZPD**) is the gap between what a learner can do without assistance and what they are capable of with guidance or collaboration with others. A more knowledgeable language user uses **scaffolding** to mediate learning in the ZPD.

Useful reading from Pavilion ELT

Barrett, B. & Sharma, P. (2018). *Best Practices for Blended Learning.*

Chong, C.S. (2018). *Successful International Communication.*

Dudley, E. (2018). *ETpedia Teenagers.*

Hadfield, J. & Clandfield, L. (2021). *Live Online Teaching.*

Hughes, J. (2016). *ETpedia Business English.*

Hughes, J., Rogers, L. & Reis Estevez, V. (2018). *ETpedia Exams.*

Kiourtzidis, N. (2015, reprinted 2020). *Become an Online English Teacher.*

Osbourne, P. (2019): *Teaching One to One 2nd Edition.*

Read, C. (2022). *Teaching and Learning English in the Early Years.*

Reis Estevez, V. (2016). *ETpedia Young Learners.*

Roland, R. (2018). *Understanding Teenagers in the ELT Classroom.*

Bibliography

Alexander, R. J. (2008). *Towards Dialogic Teaching: Rethinking classroom talk*. York: Dialogos.

Allwright, D. (2005). 'From teaching points to learning opportunities and beyond'. *TESOL Quarterly* **39** 1:9–31. Hoboken: John Wiley & Sons.

Allwright, D. & Hanks, J. (2009). *The Developing Language Learner: An introduction to exploratory practice*. Basingstoke: Palgrave Macmillan.

Anderson, J. (2017). 'Thinking CAP'. *English Teaching professional* **26** 3:13¬–15. Shoreham-by-Sea: Pavilion Publishing and Media.

Anderson, J. (2020). 'Reflection'. *ELT Journal* **74** 4:480–483. Oxford: Oxford Academic.

Anderson, J. R. (1982). 'Acquisition of cognitive skill'. *Psychological Review* **89** 4:369–406. Worcester, MA: American Psychological Association.

Andon, N. & Norrington-Davies, D. (2019, April). *How Do Experienced Teachers Work With Emergent Language?* Paper presented at the 53rd annual IATEFL Conference, Liverpool, UK.

Asari, Y. (2012). 'Types of recast and learners uptake'. *Dialogue* **10**:1–20.

Batstone, R. (2006). *Grammar*. Cambridge: Cambridge University Press.

Bilbrough, N. (2013). *Memory Activities for Language Learning*. Cambridge: Cambridge University Press.

Burns, A. (2009). *Doing Action Research in English Language Teaching: A guide for practitioners*. London: Routledge.

Bybee, J. (2010). *Language, Usage and Cognition*. Cambridge: Cambridge University Press.

Chinn, R. & Lamb, M. (2014, July). 'Giving feedback on language'. *IH London Blog*. London: IH London. Available from https://www.ihlondon.com/blog/posts/2014/giving-feedback-on-language/ (Last accessed 15 July 2019.)

Chinn, R. & Lamb, M. (2017, April). *Dialogues and Diagrams in Language Teacher Education*. Paper presented at the 51st annual IATEFL Conference, Glasgow, UK.

Chong, C. S. (2018). *Successful International Communication*. Shoreham-by-Sea: Pavilion Publishing and Media.

CoE. (2001). *Common European Framework of Reference for Languages: Learning, teaching, assessment*. Cambridge: Cambridge University Press. Available from https://www.coe.int/en/web/common-european-framework-reference-languages (Last accessed 8 March 2022.)

Cook, G. (2000). *Language Play, Language Learning*. Oxford: Oxford University Press.

Dewey, J. (1933). *How We Think: A restatement of the relation of reflective thinking to the educative process*. Boston: Houghton-Mifflin.

East, M. (2021). *Foundational Principles of Task-Based Language Teaching*. New York: Routledge.

Edge, J. (1992). 'Co-operative development'. *ELT Journal* **46** 1:62–70. Oxford: Oxford Academic.

Edge, J. (2002). *Continuing Cooperative Development: A discourse framework for individuals as colleagues*. Ann Arbor, MI: University of Michigan Press.

Egi, T. (2010). 'Uptake, modified output and learner perceptions of recasts: learner responses as language awareness'. *The Modern Language Journal* **94**:1–21.

Ellis, R. (1986). 'Activities and procedures for teacher training'. *ELT Journal* **40** 2:91–99. Oxford: Oxford Academic.

Ellis, R. (2000). 'Task-based research and language pedagogy'. *Language Teaching Research* **4** 3:193–220. Thousand Oaks: SAGE Journals.

Ellis, R. (2003). *Task-Based Language Learning and Teaching*. Oxford: Oxford University Press.

Ellis, R. (2009). 'Corrective feedback and teacher development'. *L2 Journal* **1** 1:3–18. Berkley, CA: UC Berkley.

Ellis, R. (2016). 'Focus on form: a critical review'. *Language Teaching Research* **20** 3:405–428. Thousand Oaks: SAGE Journals.

Ellis, R., Loewen, S. & Erlam, R. (2006). 'Implicit and explicit corrective feedback and the acquisition of L2 grammar'. *Studies in Second Language Acquisition* **28** 2:281–318. Cambridge: Cambridge University Press.

Farrell, T. (2022). *Reflective Practice in Language Teaching.* Cambridge: Cambridge University Press.

Farrell, T. S. (2008). 'Critical incidents in ELT initial teacher training'. *ELT Journal* **62** 1:3–10. Oxford: Oxford Academic.

Freeman, D. (2014). 'Reading comprehension questions: The distribution of different types in global EFL textbooks'. In Harwood, N. (Ed.) (2014). *English Language Teaching Textbooks: Content, consumption, production*. London: Palgrave McMillan.

Freeman, D. (2016). *Educating Second Language Teachers*. Oxford: Oxford University Press.

Gallen, R. (2021). 'Capturing and working with emergent language in the ESOL classroom'. *Excellent Gateway*. London: Education and Training Foundation. Available from: https://www.excellencegateway.org.uk/content/etf2675 (Last accessed 11 October 2022.)

Gibbs, G. (1988). *Learning by Doing: A guide to teaching and learning methods*. Birmingham: SCED.

Gil, G. (2002). 'Two complementary modes of foreign language classroom interaction'. ELT Journal 56 3:273–9. Oxford: Oxford Academic.

Gholami, L. & Gholami, J. (2018). 'Uptake in incidental focus-on-form episodes concerning formulaic language in advanced adult EFL classes'. *Language Teaching Research* **24** 2:1–31. Thousand Oaks: SAGE Journals.

Goh, C. & Burns, A. (2012). *Teaching Speaking: A holistic approach*. Cambridge: Cambridge University Press.

Harmer, J. (2009). *The Practice of English Language Teaching 3rd Edition*. Harlow: Pearson.

Heathfield, D. (2014). *Storytelling With Our Students*. Peaslake: DELTA Publishing.

Hedge, T. (2000). *Teaching and Learning in the Language Classroom*. Oxford: Oxford University Press.

Hobbs, V. (2007). 'Faking it or hating it: Can reflective practice be forced?' *Reflective Practice* **8** 3:405–417. London: Taylor & Francis Online.

Hoey, M. (2012). *Lexical Priming: A new theory of words and language.* London: Routledge.

Hopper, P. (1987). 'Emergent grammar'. In *Annual Meeting of the Berkeley Linguistics Society* **13**:139–157. Berkeley, CA: Berkeley Linguistics Society.

Howard, A. (2008). 'Teachers being observed: Coming to terms with classroom appraisal'. In Garton, S. & Richards, K. (Eds.) (2008). *Professional Encounters in TESOL* 87–104. London: Palgrave MacMillan.

Illés, E. & Akcan, S. (2017). 'Bringing real-life language use into EFL classrooms'. *ELT Journal* **71** 1:3–12. Oxford: Oxford Academic.

Killion, J. P. & Todnem, G. R. (1991). 'A process for personal theory building'. *Educational Leadership* **48** 6:14–16. Alexandria: ASCD.

Kolb, D. A. (1984). *Experiential Learning: Experience as the source of learning and development*. New Jersey: Prentice-Hall.

Lantolf, J. (2012). 'Sociocultural theory'. In Gass, S. & Mackey, A. (Eds.) (2012). *The Routledge Handbook of Second Language Acquisition* 57–71. London: Routledge.

Larsen-Freeman, D. (1996). 'Chaos/complexity science and second language acquisition'. *Applied Linguistics* **18** 2:141–165. Oxford: Oxford Academic.

Larsen-Freeman, D. (2003). *Teaching Language: From grammar to grammaring*. Boston: Heinle & Heinle Publishing.

Larsen-Freeman, D., Driver, P., Gao, X. & Mercer, S. (2021). 'Learner Agency: Maximizing learner potential'. *OUP Position Papers*. Oxford: Oxford University Press. Available from https://elt.oup.com/feature/global/expert/learner-agency?cc=gb&selLanguage=en (Last accessed 10 October 2022.)

Lee, E. (2013). 'Corrective feedback preferences and learner repair among advanced ESL students'. *System* **41** 2:217–230. Amsterdam: Science Direct.

Lee, Y.A. (2006). 'Respecifying display questions: Interactional resources for language teaching'. *TESOL Quarterly* **40** 4:691–713. Hoboken: John Wiley & Sons.

Lewis, M. (1993). *The Lexical Approach*. Hove: Language Teaching Publications.

Li, S. (2010). 'The effectiveness of corrective feedback: A meta-analysis'. Language Learning 60 2:309–365.

Li, S. (2017). 'Teacher and learner beliefs about corrective feedback'. In Nassaji, H. & Kartchava, E. (Eds.) (2017). *Corrective Feedback in Second Language Teaching and Learning*. Milton: Taylor & Francis.

Lightbown, P. & Spada, N. (2006). *How Languages Are Learned 3rd Edition*. Oxford: Oxford University Press.

Loewen, S. (2005). 'Incidental focus on form and second language learning'. *Studies in Second Language Acquisition* 27:361–386. Cambridge: Cambridge University Press.

Loewen, S. (2018). 'Focus on form versus focus on forms'. In Liontas, J. (Ed.) (2018). *The TESOL Encyclopaedia of English Language Teaching*. Hoboken, USA: John Wiley & Sons.

Long, M. (1991). 'Focus on form: A design feature in language teaching methodology'. In de Bot, K., Ginsberg, R. & Kramsch, C. (Eds.) (1991). *Foreign Language Research in Cross-Cultural Perspective* 39–52. Amsterdam: John Benjamins.

Long, M. (1996). 'The role of the linguistic environment in second language acquisition'. In Ritchie, W. & Bhatia, T. (Eds.) (1996). *Handbook of Second Language Acquisition* 413–468. San Diego: Academic Press.

Long, M. (2006). *Problems* in SLA. NJ: Erlbaum.

Long, M. (2014). *Second Language Acquisition and Task-Based Language Teaching*. Chichester: John Wiley & Sons.

Long, M. H. (1981). 'Input, interaction, and second-language acquisition'. *Annals of the New York Academy of Sciences* **379**:259–278. John Wiley & Sons Ltd. Available from https://doi.org/10.1111/j.1749-6632.1981.tb42014.x (Last accessed 10 October 2022.)

Lyster, R. (2004). 'Differential effects of prompts and recasts in form focused instruction'. *Studies in Second Language Acquisition* **26** 3:399–432. Cambridge: Cambridge University Press.

Lyster, R. & Mori, H. (2006). 'Interactional feedback and instructional counterbalance'. *Studies in Second Language Acquisition* **28** 2:269–300. Cambridge: Cambridge University Press.

Lyster, R. & Ranta, L. (1997). 'Corrective feedback and learner uptake: Negotiation of form in communicative classrooms'. *Studies in Second Language Acquisition* **19** 1:37–66. Cambridge: Cambridge University Press.

Lyster, R. & Saito, K. (2010). 'Oral feedback in classroom SLA: A meta-analysis'. *Studies in Second Language Acquisition* **32** 2:265–302. Cambridge: Cambridge University Press.

Malderez, A. & Weddell, M. (2007). *Teaching Teachers: Processes and practices*. London: Bloomsbury.

Mann, S. & Walsh, S. (2017). *Reflective Practice in English Language Teaching: Research-based principles and practices.* Abingdon: Routledge.

Mann, S., Davidson, A., Davis, M., Gakonga, J., Gamero, M., Harrison, T. & Mosavian, P. (2019). *Video in Language Teacher Education*. London: British Council.

McCarthy, M. (1990). *Vocabulary: Language teaching: A scheme for teacher education.* Oxford: Oxford University Press.

Meddings, L. & Thornbury, S. (2009). *Teaching Unplugged: Dogme in English language teaching.* Peaslake: Delta Publishing.

Mercer, N. (1995). *The Guided Construction of Knowledge: Talk amongst teachers and learners.* Clevedon: Multilingual Matters.

Mercer S. (2019). 'Language learner engagement: Setting the scene'. In Gao, X. (Ed.) (2019). *Second Handbook of English Language Teaching*, 643–660. Switzerland: Springer.

Mercer, S. & Dörnyei, Z. (2020). *Engaging Language Learners in Contemporary Classrooms.* Cambridge: Cambridge University Press.

Mishan, F. (2005). *Designing Authenticity into Language Learning Materials*. Bristol: Intellect Books.

Mishan, F. & Timmis, I. (2015). *Materials Development for TESOL*. Edinburgh: Edinburgh University Press.

Norrington-Davies, D. (2018). 'From rules to reasons and other tweaks'. In Bouckaert, M., Konings, M. & van Winkelhof, M. (Eds.) (2018). *Meaning-Focused Materials for Language Learning*, 19–36. Newcastle-Upon-Tyne: Cambridge Scholars Publishing.

Norrington-Davies, D. (2020). 'Emergent language'. *English Teaching professional* **128**: 4–6. Shoreham-by-Sea: Pavilion Publishing and Media.

Rahimi, M. & Zhang, L. (2015). 'Exploring non-native English speaking teachers' beliefs about corrective feedback in teaching oral English communication'. *System* **55**:111–122. Amsterdam: Science Direct.

Randall, M. & Thornton, B. (2001). *Advising and Supporting Teachers*. Cambridge: Cambridge University Press.

Richards, J. & Farrell, T. (2005). *Professional Development for Language Teachers: Strategies for teacher learning*. Cambridge: Cambridge University Press.

Roberts, R. (2014). 'Do something different with your coursebook'. *English Teaching professional* **90** 1:30–31. Shoreham-by-Sea: Pavilion Publishing and Media.

Rost, M. (1990). *Listening in Language Learning.* London: Longman.

Rutherford, W. E. (1987). *Second Language Grammar: Learning and teaching.* London: Longman.

Schmidt, R. (1990). 'The role of consciousness in second language learning'. *Applied Linguistics* **11** 2:129–158. Oxford: Oxford Academic. Available from https://doi.org/10.1093/applin/11.2.129 (Last accessed 11 October 2022.)

Schmidt, R. (2001). 'Attention'. In Robinson, P. (Ed.) (2001). *Cognition and Second Language Instruction*. Cambridge: Cambridge University Press.

Schön, D. A. (1983). *The Reflective Practitioner*. New York: Routledge.

Scrivener, J. (2005). *Learning Teaching.* Oxford: Macmillan.

Seidlhofer, B. (2011). *Understanding English as a Lingua Franca*. Oxford: Oxford University Press.

Sheen, Y. (2004). 'Corrective feedback and learner uptake in communicative classrooms across instructional settings'. *Language Teaching Research* **8** 3:263–300. Thousand Oaks: SAGE Journals.

Sheen, Y. (2006). 'Exploring the relationship between characteristics of recasts and learner uptake'. *Language Teaching Research* **10** 4:361–392. Thousand Oaks: SAGE Journals.

Sifakis, N., Lopriore, L., Dewey, M., Bayyurt, Y., Vettorel, P., Cavalheiro, L., Siqueira, D. & Kordia, S. (2018). 'ELF-awareness in ELT: Bringing together theory and practice'. *Journal of English as a Lingua Franca* **7** 1:155–209. Berlin: De Gruyter Mouton.

Sinclair, J. & Coulthard, M. (1975). *Towards an Analysis of Discourse*. Oxford: Oxford University Press.

Smith, R. & Rebolledo, P. (2018). *A Handbook for Exploratory Action Research*. London: British Council.

Swain, M. (1985). 'Communicative competence: Some roles of comprehensible input and comprehensible output in its development'. In Gass, S. & Madden, C. (Eds.) (1985). *Input in Second Language Acquisition* 235–256. New York: Newbury House.

Thornbury, S. (1996). 'Teachers research teacher talk'. *ELT Journal* **50** 4:279–289. Oxford: Oxford Academic.

Thornbury, S. (2005). 'Dogme: Dancing in the dark'. *Humanising Language Teaching* **7** 2. Oxford: Pilgrims.

Thornbury, S. (2017). *30 Language Teaching Methods*. Cambridge: Cambridge University Press.

Tomlinson, B. (Ed.) (2011). *Materials Development in Language Teaching 2nd Edition.* Cambridge: Cambridge University Press.

Ur, P. (1996). *A Course in Language Teaching*. Cambridge: Cambridge University Press.

Van Lier, L. (2000). 'From input to affordance: Social interactive learning from an ecological perspective'. In Lantolf, J. P. (Ed.) (2000). *Sociocultural Theory and Second Language Learning: Recent advances* 245–259. Oxford: Oxford University Press.

Van Lier, L. (2004). *The Ecology and Semiotics of Language Learning: A sociocultural perspective*. Boston: Kluwer Academic Publishers.

Van Patten, B. & Williams, J. (Eds.) (2015). *Theories in Second Language Acquisition. An introduction 2nd Edition*. New York: Taylor & Francis.

Vygotsky, L. (1978). 'Mind in society'. In Cole, M., John-Steiner, V., Scribner, S. & Souberman, E. (Eds.) (1980). *Mind in Society: The development of higher psychological processes.* Cambridge, MA: Harvard University Press.

Wallace, M. (1998). *Action Research for Language Teachers*. Cambridge: Cambridge University Press.

Walsh, S. (2002). 'Construction or obstruction: Teacher talk and learner involvement in the EFL classroom'. *Language Teaching Research* **6** 1:3–23. Thousand Oaks: SAGE Journals.

Walsh, S. (2011). *Exploring Classroom Discourse: Language in action*. Abingdon: Routledge.

Walsh, S. (2013). *Classroom Discourse and Teacher Development.* Edinburgh: Edinburgh University Press.

Walsh, S. & Mann, S. (2013). 'RP or "RIP"'. *Applied Linguistics Review* **4** 1:291–315. Berlin: De Gruyter Mouton.

Walsh, S. & Mann, S. (2017). *Reflective Practice in English Language Teaching: Research-based principles and practices*. London: Routledge.

Williams, J. (2001). 'The effectiveness of spontaneous attention to form'. *Systems* **29** 3:325–340. Amsterdam: Science Direct.

Willis, D. & Willis, J. (2007). *Doing Task-Based Teaching*. Oxford: Oxford University Press.

Willis, J. (1996). *A Framework for Task-Based Learning*. Harlow: Longman.

Woodward, T., Graves, K. & Freeman, D. (2018). *Teacher Development Over Time: Practical activities for language teachers*. London: Routledge.

Yatağanbaba, E. & Yıldırım, R. (2016). 'Teacher interruptions and limited wait time in EFL young learner classrooms'. *Procedia – Social and Behavioral Sciences* **232**:689–695. Amsterdam: Science Direct.

Yaylaci, Y. & Argynbayev, A. (2014). 'English–Russian false friends in ELT classes with intercultural communicative perspectives'. *Procedia – Social and Behavioral Sciences* **122**:58–64. Amsterdam: Science Direct.

Yoshida, R. (2008). 'Learners' perception of corrective feedback in pair work'. *Foreign Language Annals* **41** 3:525–541. Alexandria, Virginia: ACTL Language Connects.